PSYCHOLOGY
AND
THE EAST

from

The Collected Works of C. G. Jung

VOLUMES 10, 11, 13, and 18

BOLLINGEN SERIES XX

PSYCHOLOGY
AND
THE EAST

C. G. JUNG

TRANSLATED BY R. F. C. HULL

BOLLINGEN SERIES

PRINCETON UNIVERSITY PRESS

All the volumes comprising the Collected Works constitute number XX in Bollingen Series, under the editorship of Herbert Read, Michael Fordham, and Gerhard Adler; executive editor, William McGuire.

LIBRARY OF CONGRESS CATALOG CARD NUMBER: 77-92815
ISBN 0-691-01806-5
PRINTED IN THE UNITED STATES OF AMERICA

First Princeton / Bollingen Paperback Edition, 1978
Fifth printing, 1990

9 8 7

EDITORIAL NOTE

This selection includes the writings in Part Two of *Psychology and Religion: West and East* (Volume 11 of the Collected Works) and papers on the philosophy and culture of the East from other volumes of the edition. The predominant subject is religion, but Jung's definition of religion was a wide one. Religion, he stated, is "a careful and scrupulous observation of what Rudolf Otto aptly termed the *numinosum*"—that which we regard with awe. From that standpoint, Jung was struck by the contrasting methods of observation employed by religious men of the East and by those of the predominantly Christian West.

Jung's concern with Eastern religion and philosophy was evident in his first theoretical work, *Wandlungen und Symbole der Libido* (1912; revised 1952 as *Symbols of Transformation*), in which he employed symbolic material from the religious tradition of India and Iran as well as from Western sources. In *Psychological Types* (1921), the pages on the uniting symbol in Indian and Chinese philosophy are among the most fruitful of that rich and elaborate work. His first separate work in the genre was his commentary on *The Secret of the Golden Flower* (1929), which is not only a Taoist text concerned with Chinese yoga, but is also an alchemical treatise. It opens the present selection, and Jung's other writings on the religion and thought of Asia follow, in chronological order. The chief of these were written as forewords or commentaries to traditional texts: his psychological commentaries on *The Tibetan Book of the Dead* and *The Tibetan Book of the Great Liberation*; his famous foreword to the *I Ching*; an evaluation of a translation of the Discourses of the Buddha; and an essay, "The Holy Men of India," written to introduce Heinrich Zimmer's collection of the teachings of Shri Ramana Maharshi. Twice, Jung lent his efforts to introduce works on Eastern thought by contemporaries: D. T. Suzuki's *Introduction to Zen Buddhism* (1939) and Lily Abegg's study of the mind of East Asia (1949). "Yoga and the West" was written in 1936, before Jung's visit to India, for a journal published in Calcutta; "The Psychology of Eastern Meditation" originated as a lecture to the Swiss Society of Friends of East Asian Culture during the Second World War (1943). Two articles in a more popular vein, written after the journey to India in 1936, touch on religion and philosophy as well as art and the social scene.

It may be a matter for surprise that the foreword to the *I Ching* was included in the volume *Psychology and Religion*; it is a document that would scarcely be termed religious, in the common usage of that word. If, however, Jung's definition cited above be kept in mind, and it be remembered that the earlier interpretations of what is now known as synchronicity were essentially religious in Jung's sense and that the *I Ching* was studied by the most illustrious of the Eastern sages, the intention of the Editors of the Collected Works will be apparent.

Substantial comment on Eastern religion and philosophy is also to be found in Jung's letters (edited in two volumes by Gerhard Adler, in collaboration with Aniela Jaffé) and in his privately published Seminars.

TABLE OF CONTENTS

PSYCHOLOGY
AND
THE EAST

COMMENTARY ON
"THE SECRET OF THE GOLDEN FLOWER"

[In late 1929, in Munich, Jung and the sinologist Richard Wilhelm published *Das Geheimnis der goldenen Blüte: Ein chinesisches Lebensbuch*, consisting of Wilhelm's translation of an ancient Chinese text, *T'ai I Chin Hua Tsung Chih* (Secret of the Golden Flower), with his notes and discussion of the text, and a "European commentary" by Jung. Earlier the same year, the two authors had published in the *Europäische Revue* (Berlin), V: 2/8 (Nov.), 530–42, a much abbreviated version entitled "Tschang Scheng Schu; Die Kunst das menschliche Leben zu verlängern" (i.e., "Ch'ang Sheng Shu; The Art of Prolonging Life"), an alternative title of the "Golden Flower."

[In 1931, Jung's and Wilhelm's joint work appeared in English as *The Secret of the Golden Flower: A Chinese Book of Life*, translated by Cary F. Baynes (London and New York), containing as an appendix Jung's memorial address for Wilhelm, who had died in 1930. (For "In Memory of Richard Wilhelm," see Vol. 15 of the *Collected Works*.)

[A second, revised edition of the German original was published in 1938 (Zurich), with a special foreword by Jung and his Wilhelm memorial address. Two more (essentially unaltered) editions followed, and in 1957 appeared a fifth, entirely reset edition (Zurich), which added a related text, the *Hui Ming Ching*, and a new foreword by Salome Wilhelm, the translator's widow.

[Mrs. Baynes prepared a revision of her translation, and this appeared in 1962 (New York and London), including Jung's foreword and the additional Wilhelm material. (Her revised translation of Jung's commentary alone had appeared in an anthology, *Psyche and Symbol*, edited by Violet S. de Laszlo, Anchor Books, New York, 1958.)

[The following translation of Jung's commentary and his foreword is based closely on Mrs. Baynes' version, from which some of the editorial

3

notes have also been taken over. Four pictures of the stages of meditation, from the *Hui Ming Ching,* which accompanied the "Golden Flower" text, have been reproduced because of their pertinence to Jung's commentary; the examples of European mandalas have not been retained, since most of them were published, in a different context, in "Concerning Mandala Symbolism," Vol. 9, part i, of the *Collected Works,* and in the paperback *Mandala Symbolism.*

—Editors.]

FOREWORD TO THE SECOND GERMAN EDITION

My deceased friend, Richard Wilhelm, co-author of this book, sent me the text of *The Secret of the Golden Flower* at a time that was crucial for my own work. This was in 1928. I had been investigating the processes of the collective unconscious since the year 1913, and had obtained results that seemed to me questionable in more than one respect. They not only lay far beyond everything known to "academic" psychology, but they also overstepped the bounds of any medical, purely personal, psychology. They confronted me with an extensive phenomenology to which hitherto known categories and methods could no longer be applied. My results, based on fifteen years of effort, seemed inconclusive, because no possibility of comparison offered itself. I knew of no realm of human experience with which I might have backed up my findings with some degree of assurance. The only analogies—and these, I must say, were far removed in time —I found scattered among the reports of the heresiologists. This connection did not in any way ease my task; on the contrary, it made it more difficult, because the Gnostic systems consist only in small part of immediate psychic experiences, the greater part being speculative and systematizing recensions. Since we possess only very few complete texts, and since most of what is known comes from the reports of Christian opponents, we have, to say the least, an inadequate knowledge of the history as well as the content of this strange and confused literature, which is so difficult to evaluate. Moreover, considering the fact that a period of not less than seventeen to eighteen hundred years separates us from that age, support from that quarter seemed to me extraordinarily risky. Again, the connections were for the most part of a subsidiary nature and left gaps at just the most important points, so that I found it impossible to make use of the Gnostic material.

5

The text that Wilhelm sent me helped me out of this difficulty. It contained exactly those items I had long sought for in vain among the Gnostics. Thus the text afforded me a welcome opportunity to publish, at least in provisional form, some of the essential results of my investigations.

At that time it seemed to me a matter of no importance that *The Secret of the Golden Flower* is not only a Taoist text concerned with Chinese yoga, but is also an alchemical treatise. A deeper study of the Latin treatises has taught me better and has shown me that the alchemical character of the text is of prime significance, though I shall not go into this point more closely here. I would only like to emphasize that it was the text of the *Golden Flower* that first put me on the right track. For in medieval alchemy we have the long-sought connecting link between Gnosis and the processes of the collective unconscious that can be observed in modern man.[1]

I would like to take this opportunity to draw attention to certain misunderstandings to which even well-informed readers of this book have succumbed. Not infrequently people thought that my purpose in publishing it was to put into the hands of the public a recipe for achieving happiness. In total misapprehension of all that I say in my commentary, these readers tried to imitate the "method" described in the Chinese text. Let us hope these representatives of spiritual profundity were few in number!

Another misunderstanding gave rise to the opinion that, in my commentary, I was to some extent describing my own therapeutic method, which, it was said, consisted in my instilling Eastern ideas into my patients for therapeutic purposes. I do not believe there is anything in my commentary that lends itself to that sort of superstition. In any case such an opinion is altogether erroneous, and is based on the widespread view that psychology was invented for a specific purpose and is not an empirical science. To this category belongs the superficial as well as unintelligent opinion that the idea of the collective unconscious is "metaphysical." On the contrary, it is an *empirical* concept to

[1] The reader will find more about this in two essays published by me in the *Eranos Jahrbuch 1936* and *1937*. [This material is now contained in *Psychology and Alchemy*, Parts II and III.—EDITORS.]

be put alongside the concept of instinct, as is obvious to anyone who will read with some attention.

C. G. J.

Küsnacht/Zurich, 1938

1. DIFFICULTIES ENCOUNTERED BY A EUROPEAN IN TRYING TO UNDERSTAND THE EAST

1   A thorough Westerner in feeling, I cannot but be profoundly impressed by the strangeness of this Chinese text. It is true that some knowledge of Eastern religions and philosophies helps my intellect and my intuition to understand these things up to a point, just as I can understand the paradoxes of primitive beliefs in terms of "ethnology" or "comparative religion." This is of course the Western way of hiding one's heart under the cloak of so-called scientific understanding. We do it partly because the *misérable vanité des savants* fears and rejects with horror any sign of living sympathy, and partly because sympathetic understanding might transform contact with an alien spirit into an experience that has to be taken seriously. Our so-called scientific objectivity would have reserved this text for the philological acumen of sinologists, and would have guarded it jealously from any other interpretation. But Richard Wilhelm penetrated too deeply into the secret and mysterious vitality of Chinese wisdom to allow such a pearl of intuitive insight to disappear into the pigeon-holes of specialists. I am greatly honoured that his choice of a psychological commentator has fallen upon me.

2   This, however, involves the risk that this precious example of more-than-specialist insight will be swallowed by still another specialism. Nevertheless, anyone who belittles the merits of Western science is undermining the foundations of the Western mind. Science is not indeed a perfect instrument, but it is a superb and invaluable tool that works harm only when it is taken as an end in itself. Science must serve; it errs when it usurps the throne. It must be ready to serve all its branches, for each, because of its insufficiency, has need of support from the others. Science is the tool of the Western mind, and with it one can open more doors than with bare hands. It is part and parcel of

our understanding, and it obscures our insight only when it claims that the understanding it conveys is the only kind there is. The East teaches us another, broader, more profound, and higher understanding—understanding through life. We know this only by hearsay, as a shadowy sentiment expressing a vague religiosity, and we are fond of putting "Oriental wisdom" in quotation marks and banishing it to the dim region of faith and superstition. But that is wholly to misunderstand the realism of the East. Texts of this kind do not consist of the sentimental, overwrought mystical intuitions of pathological cranks and recluses, but are based on the practical insights of highly evolved Chinese minds, which we have not the slightest justification for undervaluing.

3   This assertion may seem bold, perhaps, and is likely to cause a good deal of head-shaking. Nor is that surprising, considering how little people know about the material. Its strangeness is indeed so arresting that our puzzlement as to how and where the Chinese world of thought might be joined to ours is quite understandable. The usual mistake of Western man when faced with this problem of grasping the ideas of the East is like that of the student in *Faust*. Misled by the devil, he contemptuously turns his back on science and, carried away by Eastern occultism, takes over yoga practices word for word and becomes a pitiable imitator. (Theosophy is our best example of this.) Thus he abandons the one sure foundation of the Western mind and loses himself in a mist of words and ideas that could never have originated in European brains and can never be profitably grafted upon them.

4   An ancient adept has said: "If the wrong man uses the right means, the right means work in the wrong way." [1] This Chinese saying, unfortunately only too true, stands in sharp contrast to our belief in the "right" method irrespective of the man who applies it. In reality, everything depends on the man and little or nothing on the method. The method is merely the path, the direction taken by a man; the way he acts is the true expression of his nature. If it ceases to be this, the method is nothing more than an affectation, something artificially pieced on, rootless and sapless, serving only the illegitimate goal of self-deception. It becomes a means of fooling oneself and of evading what may

1 [*The Secret of the Golden Flower* (1962 edn.), p. 63.]

9

perhaps be the implacable law of one's being. This is far removed from the earthiness and self-reliance of Chinese thought. It is a denial of one's own nature, a self-betrayal to strange and unclean gods, a cowardly trick for the purpose of feigning mental superiority, everything in fact that is profoundly contrary to the spirit of the Chinese "method." For these insights spring from a way of life that is complete, genuine, and true to itself; from that ancient, cultural life of China which grew logically and organically from the deepest instincts, and which, for us, is forever inaccessible and impossible to imitate.

5   Western imitation is a tragic misunderstanding of the psychology of the East, every bit as sterile as the modern escapades to New Mexico, the blissful South Sea islands, and central Africa, where "the primitive life" is played at in deadly earnest while Western man secretly evades his menacing duties, his *Hic Rhodus hic salta*. It is not for us to imitate what is foreign to our organism or to play the missionary; our task is to build up our Western civilization, which sickens with a thousand ills. This has to be done on the spot, and by the European just as he is, with all his Western ordinariness, his marriage problems, his neuroses, his social and political delusions, and his whole philosophical disorientation.

6   We should do well to confess at once that, fundamentally, we do not understand the utter unworldliness of a text like this—that actually we do not want to understand it. Have we, perhaps, a dim suspicion that a mental attitude which can direct the glance inward to that extent is detached from the world only because these people have so completely fulfilled the instinctive demands of their natures that there is nothing to prevent them from glimpsing the invisible essence of things? Can it be that the precondition for such a vision is liberation from the ambitions and passions that bind us to the visible world, and does not this liberation come from the sensible fulfilment of instinctive demands rather than from the premature and fear-ridden repression of them? Are our eyes opened to the spirit only when the laws of the earth are obeyed? Anyone who knows the history of Chinese culture and has carefully studied the *I Ching*, that book of wisdom which for thousands of years has permeated all Chinese thought, will not lightly wave these doubts aside. He will be aware that the views set forth in our text are nothing extraor-

dinary to the Chinese, but are actually inescapable psychological conclusions.

7   For a long time the spirit, and the sufferings of the spirit, were positive values and the things most worth striving for in our peculiar Christian culture. Only in the course of the nineteenth century, when spirit began to degenerate into intellect, did a reaction set in against the unbearable dominance of intellectualism, and this led to the unpardonable mistake of confusing intellect with spirit and blaming the latter for the misdeeds of the former. The intellect does indeed do harm to the soul when it dares to possess itself of the heritage of the spirit. It is in no way fitted to do this, for spirit is something higher than intellect since it embraces the latter and includes the feelings as well. It is a guiding principle of life that strives towards superhuman, shining heights. Opposed to this *yang* principle is the dark, feminine, earthbound *yin*, whose emotionality and instinctuality reach back into the depths of time and down into the labyrinth of the physiological continuum. No doubt these are purely intuitive ideas, but one can hardly dispense with them if one is trying to understand the nature of the human psyche. The Chinese could not do without them because, as the history of Chinese philosophy shows, they never strayed so far from the central psychic facts as to lose themselves in a one-sided over-development and over-valuation of a single psychic function. They never failed to acknowledge the paradoxicality and polarity of all life. The opposites always balanced one another—a sign of high culture. One-sidedness, though it lends momentum, is a mark of barbarism. The reaction that is now beginning in the West against the intellect in favour of feeling, or in favour of intuition, seems to me a sign of cultural advance, a widening of consciousness beyond the narrow confines of a tyrannical intellect.

8   I have no wish to depreciate the tremendous differentiation of the Western intellect; compared with it the Eastern intellect must be described as childish. (Naturally this has nothing to do with intelligence.) If we should succeed in elevating another, and possibly even a third psychic function to the dignified position accorded to the intellect, then the West might expect to surpass the East by a very great margin. Therefore it is sad indeed when the European departs from his own nature and

imitates the East or "affects" it in any way. The possibilities open to him would be so much greater if he would remain true to himself and evolve out of his own nature all that the East has brought forth in the course of the millennia.

9   In general, and looked at from the incurably externalistic standpoint of the intellect, it would seem as if the things the East values so highly were not worth striving for. Certainly the intellect alone cannot comprehend the practical importance Eastern ideas might have for us, and that is why it can classify them as philosophical and ethnological curiosities and nothing more. The lack of comprehension goes so far that even learned sinologists have not understood the practical use of the *I Ching*, and consider the book to be no more than a collection of abstruse magic spells.

2. MODERN PSYCHOLOGY OFFERS A POSSIBILITY OF UNDERSTANDING

10   Observations made in my practical work have opened out to
me a quite new and unexpected approach to Eastern wisdom. In
saying this I should like to emphasize that I did not have any
knowledge, however inadequate, of Chinese philosophy as a
starting point. On the contrary, when I began my career as a
psychiatrist and psychotherapist, I was completely ignorant of
Chinese philosophy, and only later did my professional experience show me that in my technique I had been unconsciously
following that secret way which for centuries had been the preoccupation of the best minds of the East. This could be taken for
a subjective fancy—which was one reason for my previous reluc-
tance to publish anything on the subject—but Richard Wilhelm,
that great interpreter of the soul of China, enthusiastically confirmed the parallel and thus gave me the courage to write about
a Chinese text that belongs entirely to the mysterious shadow-
land of the Eastern mind. At the same time—and this is the extraordinary thing—its content forms a living parallel to what
takes place in the psychic development of my patients, none of
whom is Chinese.

11   In order to make this strange fact more intelligible to the
reader, it must be pointed out that just as the human body
shows a common anatomy over and above all racial differences,
so, too, the human psyche possesses a common substratum transcending all differences in culture and consciousness. I have
called this substratum the collective unconscious. This unconscious psyche, common to all mankind, does not consist merely
of contents capable of becoming conscious, but of latent predis-
positions towards identical reactions. The collective unconscious
is simply the psychic expression of the identity of brain structure
irrespective of all racial differences. This explains the analogy,
sometimes even identity, between the various myth motifs and

13

symbols, and the possibility of human communication in general. The various lines of psychic development start from one common stock whose roots reach back into the most distant past. This also accounts for the psychological parallelisms with animals.

12   In purely psychological terms this means that mankind has common instincts of ideation and action. All conscious ideation and action have developed on the basis of these unconscious archetypal patterns and always remain dependent on them. This is especially the case when consciousness has not attained any high degree of clarity, when in all its functions it is more dependent on the instincts than on the conscious will, more governed by affect than by rational judgment. This ensures a primitive state of psychic health, but it immediately becomes lack of adaptation when circumstances arise that call for a higher moral effort. Instincts suffice only for a nature that remains more or less constant. An individual who is guided more by the unconscious than by conscious choice therefore tends towards marked psychic conservatism. This is the reason why the primitive does not change in the course of thousands of years, and also why he fears anything strange and unusual. It might easily lead to maladaptation, and thus to the greatest psychic dangers—to a kind of neurosis, in fact. A higher and wider consciousness resulting from the assimilation of the unfamiliar tends, on the other hand, towards autonomy, and rebels against the old gods who are nothing other than those mighty, primordial images that hitherto have held our consciousness in thrall.

13   The stronger and more independent our consciousness becomes, and with it the conscious will, the more the unconscious is thrust into the background, and the easier it is for the evolving consciousness to emancipate itself from the unconscious, archetypal pattern. Gaining in freedom, it bursts the bonds of mere instinctuality and finally reaches a condition of instinctual atrophy. This uprooted consciousness can no longer appeal to the authority of the primordial images; it has Promethean freedom, but it also suffers from godless hybris. It soars above the earth and above mankind, but the danger of its sudden collapse is there, not of course in the case of every individual, but for the weaker members of the community, who then, again like Prometheus, are chained to the Caucasus of the unconscious. The

wise Chinese would say in the words of the *I Ching:* When *yang* has reached its greatest strength, the dark power of *yin* is born within its depths, for night begins at midday when *yang* breaks up and begins to change into *yin.*

14   The doctor is in a position to see this cycle of changes translated literally into life. He sees, for instance, a successful businessman attaining all his desires regardless of death and the devil, and then, having retired at the height of his success, speedily falling into a neurosis, which turns him into a querulous old woman, fastens him to his bed, and finally destroys him. The picture is complete even to the change from masculine to feminine. An exact parallel to this is the story of Nebuchadnezzar in the Book of Daniel, and Caesarean madness in general. Similar cases of one-sided exaggeration of the conscious standpoint, and the resultant *yin*-reaction from the unconscious, form no small part of the psychiatrist's clientele in our time, which so overvalues the conscious will as to believe that "where there's a will there's a way." Not that I wish to detract in the least from the high moral value of the will. Consciousness and the will may well continue to be considered the highest cultural achievements of humanity. But of what use is a morality that destroys the man? To bring the will and the capacity to achieve it into harmony seems to me to require more than morality. Morality *à tout prix* can be a sign of barbarism—more often wisdom is better. But perhaps I look at this with the eyes of a physician who has to mend the ills following in the wake of one-sided cultural achievements.

15   Be that as it may, the fact remains that a consciousness heightened by an inevitable one-sidedness gets so far out of touch with the primordial images that a breakdown ensues. Long before the actual catastrophe, the signs of error announce themselves in atrophy of instinct, nervousness, disorientation, entanglement in impossible situations and problems. Medical investigation then discovers an unconscious that is in full revolt against the conscious values, and that therefore cannot possibly be assimilated to consciousness, while the reverse is altogether out of the question. We are confronted with an apparently irreconcilable conflict before which human reason stands helpless, with nothing to offer except sham solutions or dubious compromises. If these evasions are rejected, we are faced with the

question as to what has become of the much needed unity of the personality, and with the necessity of seeking it. At this point begins the path travelled by the East since the beginning of things. Quite obviously, the Chinese were able to follow this path because they never succeeded in forcing the opposites in man's nature so far apart that all conscious connection between them was lost. The Chinese owe this all-inclusive consciousness to the fact that, as in the case of the primitive mentality, the yea and the nay have remained in their original proximity. Nonetheless, it was impossible not to feel the clash of opposites, so they sought a way of life in which they would be what the Indians call *nirdvandva,* free of opposites.

16   Our text is concerned with this way, and the same problem comes up with my patients also. There could be no greater mistake than for a Westerner to take up the direct practice of Chinese yoga, for that would merely strengthen his will and consciousness against the unconscious and bring about the very effect to be avoided. The neurosis would then simply be intensified. It cannot be emphasized enough that we are not Orientals, and that we have an entirely different point of departure in these matters. It would also be a great mistake to suppose that this is the path every neurotic must travel, or that it is the solution at every stage of the neurotic problem. It is appropriate only in those cases where consciousness has reached an abnormal degree of development and has diverged too far from the unconscious. This is the *sine qua non* of the process. Nothing would be more wrong than to open this way to neurotics who are ill on account of an excessive predominance of the unconscious. For the same reason, this way of development has scarcely any meaning before the middle of life (normally between the ages of thirty-five and forty), and if entered upon too soon can be decidedly injurious.

17   As I have said, the essential reason which prompted me to look for a new way was the fact that the fundamental problem of the patient seemed to me insoluble unless violence was done to one or the other side of his nature. I had always worked with the temperamental conviction that at bottom there are no insoluble problems, and experience justified me in so far as I have often seen patients simply outgrow a problem that had destroyed others. This "outgrowing," as I formerly called it, proved on

further investigation to be a new level of consciousness. Some higher or wider interest appeared on the patient's horizon, and through this broadening of his outlook the insoluble problem lost its urgency. It was not solved logically in its own terms, but faded out when confronted with a new and stronger life urge. It was not repressed and made unconscious, but merely appeared in a different light, and so really did become different. What, on a lower level, had led to the wildest conflicts and to panicky outbursts of emotion, from the higher level of personality now looked like a storm in the valley seen from the mountain top. This does not mean that the storm is robbed of its reality, but instead of being in it one is above it. But since, in a psychic sense, we are both valley and mountain, it might seem a vain illusion to deem oneself beyond what is human. One certainly does feel the affect and is shaken and tormented by it, yet at the same time one is aware of a higher consciousness looking on which prevents one from becoming identical with the affect, a consciousness which regards the affect as an object, and can say, "I *know* that I suffer." What our text says of indolence, "Indolence of which a man is conscious, and indolence of which he is unconscious, are a thousand miles apart," [1] holds true in the highest degree of affect.

18   Now and then it happened in my practice that a patient grew beyond himself because of unknown potentialities, and this became an experience of prime importance to me. In the meantime, I had learned that all the greatest and most important problems of life are fundamentally insoluble. They must be so, for they express the necessary polarity inherent in every self-regulating system. They can never be solved, but only outgrown. I therefore asked myself whether this outgrowing, this possibility of further psychic development, was not the normal thing, and whether getting stuck in a conflict was pathological. Everyone must possess that higher level, at least in embryonic form, and must under favourable circumstances be able to develop this potentiality. When I examined the course of development in patients who quietly, and as if unconsciously, outgrew themselves, I saw that their fates had something in common. The new thing came to them from obscure possibilities either outside or inside themselves; they accepted it and grew with its

1 [*The Golden Flower* (1962 edn.), p. 42.]

help. It seemed to me typical that some took the new thing from outside themselves, others from inside; or rather, that it grew into some persons from without, and into others from within. But the new thing never came exclusively either from within or from without. If it came from outside, it became a profound inner experience; if it came from inside, it became an outer happening. In no case was it conjured into existence intentionally or by conscious willing, but rather seemed to be borne along on the stream of time.

19   We are so greatly tempted to turn everything into a purpose and a method that I deliberately express myself in very abstract terms in order to avoid prejudicing the reader in one way or the other. The new thing must not be pigeon-holed under any heading, for then it becomes a recipe to be used mechanically, and it would again be a case of the "right means in the hands of the wrong man." I have been deeply impressed by the fact that the new thing prepared by fate seldom or never comes up to conscious expectations. And still more remarkable, though the new thing goes against deeply rooted instincts as we have known them, it is a strangely appropriate expression of the total personality, an expression which one could not imagine in a more complete form.

20   What did these people do in order to bring about the development that set them free? As far as I could see they did nothing (*wu wei*[2]) but let things happen. As Master Lü-tsu teaches in our text, the light circulates according to its own law if one does not give up one's ordinary occupation. The art of letting things happen, action through non-action, letting go of oneself as taught by Meister Eckhart, became for me the key that opens the door to the way. We must be able to let things happen in the psyche. For us, this is an art of which most people know nothing. Consciousness is forever interfering, helping, correcting, and negating, never leaving the psychic processes to grow in peace. It would be simple enough, if only simplicity were not the most difficult of all things. To begin with, the task consists solely in observing objectively how a fragment of fantasy develops. Nothing could be simpler, and yet right here the difficulties begin. Apparently one has no fantasy fragments—or yes, there's one, but it is too stupid! Dozens of good reasons are brought against

2 [The Taoist idea of action through non-action.—C.F.B.]

it. One cannot concentrate on it—it is too boring—what would come of it anyway—it is "nothing but" this or that, and so on. The conscious mind raises innumerable objections, in fact it often seems bent on blotting out the spontaneous fantasy activity in spite of real insight and in spite of the firm determination to allow the psychic process to go forward without interference. Occasionally there is a veritable cramp of consciousness.

21   If one is successful in overcoming the initial difficulties, criticism is still likely to start in afterwards in the attempt to interpret the fantasy, to classify it, to aestheticize it, or to devalue it. The temptation to do this is almost irresistible. After it has been faithfully observed, free rein can be given to the impatience of the conscious mind; in fact it must be given, or obstructive resistances will develop. But each time the fantasy material is to be produced, the activity of consciousness must be switched off again.

22   In most cases the results of these efforts are not very encouraging at first. Usually they consist of tenuous webs of fantasy that give no clear indication of their origin or their goal. Also, the way of getting at the fantasies varies with individuals. For many people, it is easiest to write them down; others visualize them, and others again draw or paint them with or without visualization. If there is a high degree of conscious cramp, often only the hands are capable of fantasy; they model or draw figures that are sometimes quite foreign to the conscious mind.

23   These exercises must be continued until the cramp in the conscious mind is relaxed, in other words, until one can let things happen, which is the next goal of the exercise. In this way a new attitude is created, an attitude that accepts the irrational and the incomprehensible simply because it is happening. This attitude would be poison for a person who is already overwhelmed by the things that happen to him, but it is of the greatest value for one who selects, from among the things that happen, only those that are acceptable to his conscious judgment, and is gradually drawn out of the stream of life into a stagnant backwater.

24   At this point, the way travelled by the two types mentioned earlier seems to divide. Both have learned to accept what comes to them. (As Master Lü-tsu teaches: "When occupations come to us, we must accept them; when things come to us, we must un-

derstand them from the ground up." [3]) One man will now take chiefly what comes to him from outside, and the other what comes from inside. Moreover, the law of life demands that what they take from outside and inside will be the very things that were always excluded before. This reversal of one's nature brings an enlargement, a heightening and enrichment of the personality, if the previous values are retained alongside the change—provided that these values are not mere illusions. If they are not held fast, the individual will swing too far to the other side, slipping from fitness into unfitness, from adaptedness into unadaptedness, and even from rationality into insanity. The way is not without danger. Everything good is costly, and the development of personality is one of the most costly of all things. It is a matter of saying yea to oneself, of taking oneself as the most serious of tasks, of being conscious of everything one does, and keeping it constantly before one's eyes in all its dubious aspects—truly a task that taxes us to the utmost.

25   A Chinese can always fall back on the authority of his whole civilization. If he starts on the long way, he is doing what is recognized as being the best thing he could possibly do. But the Westerner who wishes to set out on this way, if he is really serious about it, has all authority against him—intellectual, moral, and religious. That is why it is infinitely easier for him to imitate the Chinese way and leave the troublesome European behind him, or else to seek the way back to the medievalism of the Christian Church and barricade himself behind the wall separating true Christians from the poor heathen and other ethnographic curiosities encamped outside. Aesthetic or intellectual flirtations with life and fate come to an abrupt halt here: the step to higher consciousness leaves us without a rearguard and without shelter. The individual must devote himself to the way with all his energy, for it is only by means of his integrity that he can go further, and his integrity alone can guarantee that his way will not turn out to be an absurd misadventure.

26   Whether his fate comes to him from without or from within, the experiences and happenings on the way remain the same. Therefore I need say nothing about the manifold outer and inner events, the endless variety of which I could never exhaust in any case. Nor would this be relevant to the text under discus-

3 [*The Golden Flower* (1962 edn.), p. 51.]

sion. On the other hand, there is much to be said about the psychic states that accompany the process of development. These states are expressed symbolically in our text, and in the very same symbols that for many years have been familiar to me from my practice.

3. THE FUNDAMENTAL CONCEPTS

A. TAO

27   The great difficulty in interpreting this and similar texts[1] for the European is that the author always starts from the central point, from the point we would call the goal, the highest and ultimate insight he has attained. Thus our Chinese author begins with ideas that demand such a comprehensive understanding that a person of discriminating mind has the feeling he would be guilty of ridiculous pretension, or even of talking utter nonsense, if he should embark on an intellectual discourse on the subtle psychic experiences of the greatest minds of the East. Our text, for example, begins: "That which exists through itself is called the Way." The *Hui Ming Ching* begins with the words: "The subtlest secret of the Tao is human nature and life."

28   It is characteristic of the Western mind that it has no word for Tao. The Chinese character is made up of the sign for "head" and the sign for "going." Wilhelm translates Tao by *Sinn* (Meaning). Others translate it as "way," "providence," or even as "God," as the Jesuits do. This illustrates our difficulty. "Head" can be taken as consciousness,[2] and "going" as travelling a way, and the idea would then be: to go consciously, or the conscious way. This is borne out by the fact that the "light of heaven" which "dwells between the eyes" as the "heart of heaven" is used synonymously with Tao. Human nature and life are contained in the "light of heaven" and, according to the *Hui Ming Ching,* are the most important secrets of the Tao. "Light" is the symbolical equivalent of consciousness, and the nature of consciousness is expressed by analogies with light. The *Hui Ming Ching* is introduced with the verses:

[1] Cf. the *Hui Ming Ching* (Book of Consciousness and Life) in *The Secret of the Golden Flower* (1962 edn.), pp. 69ff.

[2] The head is also the "seat of heavenly light."

If thou wouldst complete the diamond body with no outflowing,
Diligently heat the roots of consciousness[3] and life.
Kindle light in the blessed country ever close at hand,
And there hidden, let thy true self always dwell.

29   These verses contain a sort of alchemical instruction as to the
method or way of producing the "diamond body," which is also
mentioned in our text. "Heating" is necessary; that is, there
must be an intensification of consciousness in order that light
may be kindled in the dwelling place of the true self. Not only
consciousness, but life itself must be intensified: the union of
these two produces conscious life. According to the *Hui Ming
Ching*, the ancient sages knew how to bridge the gap between
consciousness and life because they cultivated both. In this way
the *sheli*, the immortal body, is "melted out" and the "great
Tao is completed." [4]

30   If we take the Tao to be the method or conscious way by
which to unite what is separated, we have probably come close
to the psychological meaning of the concept. At all events, the
separation of consciousness and life cannot very well be understood as anything else than what I described earlier as an aberra-
tion or uprooting of consciousness. There can be no doubt,
either, that the realization of the opposite hidden in the unconscious—the process of "reversal"—signifies reunion with the unconscious laws of our being, and the purpose of this reunion is
the attainment of conscious life or, expressed in Chinese terms,
the realization of the Tao.

B. THE CIRCULAR MOVEMENT AND THE CENTRE

31   As I have pointed out, the union of opposites[5] on a higher
level of consciousness is not a rational thing, nor is it a matter of
will; it is a process of psychic development that expresses itself in
symbols. Historically, this process has always been represented
in symbols, and today the development of personality is still depicted in symbolic form. I discovered this fact in the following way. The spontaneous fantasy products I discussed earlier

3 In the *Hui Ming Ching*, "human nature" (*hsing*) and "consciousness" (*hui*) are
used interchangeably.
4 *The Golden Flower* (1962 edn.), p. 70.
5 Cf. *Psychological Types*, ch. V.

become more profound and gradually concentrate into abstract structures that apparently represent "principles" in the sense of Gnostic *archai*. When the fantasies take the form chiefly of thoughts, intuitive formulations of dimly felt laws or principles emerge, which at first tend to be dramatized or personified. (We shall come back to these again later.) If the fantasies are drawn, symbols appear that are chiefly of the *mandala*[6] type. *Mandala* means "circle," more especially a magic circle. Mandalas are found not only throughout the East but also among us. The early Middle Ages are especially rich in Christian mandalas; most of them show Christ in the centre, with the four evangelists, or their symbols, at the cardinal points. This conception must be a very ancient one, because Horus and his four sons were represented in the same way by the Egyptians.[7] It is known that Horus with his four sons has close connections with Christ and the four evangelists. An unmistakable and very interesting mandala can be found in Jakob Böhme's book *XL Questions concerning the Soule*.[8] It is clear that this mandala represents a psychocosmic system strongly coloured by Christian ideas. Böhme calls it the "Philosophical Eye" [9] or the "Mirror of Wisdom," by which is obviously meant a *summa* of secret knowledge. Most mandalas take the form of a flower, cross, or wheel, and show a distinct tendency towards a quaternary structure reminiscent of the Pythagorean *tetraktys,* the basic number. Mandalas of this sort also occur as sand paintings in the religious ceremonies of the Pueblo and Navaho Indians.[10] But the most beautiful mandalas are, of course, those of the East, especially the ones found in Tibetan Buddhism, which also contain the symbols mentioned in our text. Mandala drawings are often produced by the mentally ill, among them persons who certainly

---

[6] [For a fuller discussion of the *mandala,* see "A Study in the Process of Individuation" and "Concerning Mandala Symbolism" in *The Archetypes and the Collective Unconscious.* For examples of European mandalas, see the latter work and the paperback *Mandala Symbolism.*—EDITORS.]

[7] Cf. Wallis Budge, *The Gods of the Egyptians.*

[8] [The mandala is reproduced in "A Study in the Process of Individuation," p. 297.]

[9] Cf. the Chinese concept of the heavenly light between the eyes.

[10] Matthews, "The Mountain Chant: A Navajo Ceremony" (1887), and Stevenson, "Ceremonial of Hasjelti Dailjis" (1891).

did not have the least idea of any of the connections we have discussed.[11]

32   Among my patients I have come across cases of women who did not draw mandalas but danced them instead. In India there is a special name for this: *mandala nrithya*, the mandala dance. The dance figures express the same meanings as the drawings. My patients can say very little about the meaning of the symbols but are fascinated by them and find that they somehow express and have an effect on their subjective psychic state.

33   Our text promises to "reveal the secret of the Golden Flower of the great *One*." The golden flower is the light, and the light of heaven is the Tao. The golden flower is a mandala symbol I have often met with in the material brought me by my patients. It is drawn either seen from above as a regular geometric pattern, or in profile as a blossom growing from a plant. The plant is frequently a structure in brilliant fiery colours growing out of a bed of darkness, and carrying the blossom of light at the top, a symbol recalling the Christmas tree. Such drawings also suggest the origin of the golden flower, for according to the *Hui Ming Ching* the "germinal vesicle" is the "dragon castle at the bottom of the sea." [12] Other synonyms are the "yellow castle," the "heavenly heart," the "terrace of living," the "square inch field of the square foot house," the "purple hall of the city of jade," the "dark pass," the "space of former heaven." [13] It is also called the "boundary region of the snow mountains," the "primordial pass," the "kingdom of greatest joy," the "boundless country," the "altar upon which consciousness and life are made." "If a dying man does not know this germinal vesicle," says the *Hui Ming Ching*, "he will not find the unity of consciousness and life in a thousand births, nor in ten thousand aeons." [14]

34   The beginning, where everything is still one, and which therefore appears as the highest goal, lies at the bottom of the sea, in the darkness of the unconscious. In the germinal vesicle, consciousness and life (or human nature and life, *hsing-ming*) are still a "unity, inseparably mixed like the sparks in the

11 The mandala of a somnambulist is reproduced in *Psychiatric Studies*, p. 40.
12 *The Golden Flower* (1962 edn.), p. 70.
13 [Ibid., p. 22.]
14 [Ibid., p. 70.]

refining furnace." "Within the germinal vesicle is the fire of the ruler." "All the sages began their work at the germinal vesicle." [15] Note the fire analogies. I know a series of European mandala drawings in which something like a plant seed surrounded by membranes is shown floating in the water. Then, from the depths below, fire penetrates the seed and makes it grow, causing a great golden flower to unfold from the germinal vesicle.

35   This symbolism refers to a quasi-alchemical process of refining and ennobling. Darkness gives birth to light; out of the "lead of the water region" grows the noble gold; what is unconscious becomes conscious in the form of a living process of growth. (Indian Kundalini yoga offers a perfect analogy.[16]) In this way the union of consciousness and life takes place.

36   When my patients produce these mandala pictures, it is naturally not the result of suggestion; similar pictures were being made long before I knew their meaning or their connection with the practices of the East, which, at that time, were wholly unknown to me. The pictures arise quite spontaneously, and from two sources. One source is the unconscious, which spontaneously produces fantasies of this kind; the other is life, which, if lived with utter devotion, brings an intuition of the self, of one's own individual being. When the self finds expression in such drawings, the unconscious reacts by enforcing an attitude of devotion to life. For in complete agreement with the Eastern view, the mandala is not only a means of expression but also produces an effect. It reacts upon its maker. Age-old magical effects lie hidden in this symbol, for it is derived from the "protective circle" or "charmed circle," whose magic has been preserved in countless folk customs.[17] It has the obvious purpose of drawing a *sulcus primigenius*, a magical furrow around the centre, the temple or *temenos* (sacred precinct), of the innermost personality, in order to prevent an "outflowing" or to guard by apotropaic means against distracting influences from outside. Magical practices are nothing but projections of psychic events, which then exert a counter-influence on the psyche and put a

---

[15] [Ibid., p. 71.]
[16] Cf. Avalon, *The Serpent Power.*
[17] Cf. the excellent collection in Knuchel, *Die Umwandlung in Kult, Magie und Rechtsbrauch.*

kind of spell upon the personality. Through the ritual action, attention and interest are led back to the inner, sacred precinct, which is the source and goal of the psyche and contains the unity of life and consciousness. The unity once possessed has been lost, and must now be found again.

37   The unity of the two, life and consciousness, is the Tao, whose symbol would be the central white light, also mentioned in the *Bardo Thödol*.[18] This light dwells in the "square inch" or in the "face," that is, between the eyes. It is a visualization of the "creative point," of that which has intensity without extension, in conjunction with the "field of the square inch," the symbol for that which has extension. The two together make the Tao. Human nature (*hsing*) and consciousness (*hui*) are expressed in light symbolism, and therefore have the quality of intensity, while life (*ming*) would coincide with extensity. The one is *yang*-like, the other *yin*-like. The afore-mentioned mandala of a somnambulist girl, aged fifteen and a half, whom I had under observation some thirty years ago, shows in its centre a spring of "Primary Force," or life energy without extension, whose emanations clash with a contrary spatial principle—in complete analogy with the basic idea of our Chinese text.

38   The "enclosure," or *circumambulatio,* is expressed in our text by the idea of "circulation." The circulation is not merely movement in a circle, but means, on the one hand, the marking off of the sacred precinct and, on the other, fixation and concentration. The sun-wheel begins to turn; the sun is activated and begins its course—in other words, the Tao begins to work and takes the lead. Action is reversed into non-action; everything peripheral is subordinated to the command of the centre. Therefore it is said: "Movement is only another name for mastery." Psychologically, this circulation would be the "movement in a circle around oneself," so that all sides of the personality become involved. "The poles of light and darkness are made to rotate," that is, there is an alternation of day and night.

39   The circular movement thus has the moral significance of activating the light and dark forces of human nature, and together with them all psychological opposites of whatever kind they may be. It is nothing less than self-knowledge by means of self-

18 Evans-Wentz, *The Tibetan Book of the Dead.*

brooding (Sanskrit *tapas*). A similar archetypal concept of a perfect being is that of the Platonic man, round on all sides and uniting within himself the two sexes.

40   One of the best modern parallels is the description which Edward Maitland, the biographer of Anna Kingsford,[19] gave of his central experience. He had discovered that when reflecting on an idea, related ideas became visible, so to speak, in a long series apparently reaching back to their source, which to him was the divine spirit. By concentrating on this series, he tried to penetrate to their origin. He writes:

> I was absolutely without knowledge or expectation when I yielded to the impulse to make the attempt. I simply experimented on a faculty . . . being seated at my writing-table the while in order to record the results as they came, and resolved to retain my hold on my outer and circumferential consciousness, no matter how far towards my inner and central consciousness I might go. For I knew not whether I should be able to regain the former if I once quitted my hold of it, or to recollect the facts of the experience. At length I achieved my object, though only by a strong effort, the tension occasioned by the endeavour to keep both extremes of the consciousness in view at once being very great.
>
> Once well started on my quest, I found myself traversing a succession of spheres or belts . . . the impression produced being that of mounting a vast ladder stretching from the circumference towards the centre of a system, which was at once my own system, the solar system, the universal system, the three systems being at once diverse and identical. . . . Presently, by a supreme, and what I felt must be a final effort . . . I succeeded in polarizing the whole of the convergent rays of my consciousness into the desired focus. And at the same instant, as if through the sudden ignition of the rays thus fused into a unity, I found myself confronted with a glory of unspeakable whiteness and brightness, and of a lustre so intense as well-nigh to beat me back. . . . But though feeling that I had to explore further, I resolved to make assurance doubly sure by piercing if I could the almost blinding lustre, and seeing what it enshrined. With a great effort I succeeded, and the glance revealed to me that which I had felt must be there. . . . It was the dual form of the Son . . . the unmanifest made manifest, the unformulate formulate, the unindividuate individuate, God as the Lord, proving through His duality that God is Substance as well as Force, Love

[19] *Anna Kingsford, Her Life, Letters, Diary, and Work*, pp. 129f. I am indebted for this reference to my colleague, Dr. Beatrice Hinkle, New York.

as well as Will, Feminine as well as Masculine, Mother as well as Father.

41   He found that God is two in one, like man. Besides this he noticed something that our text also emphasizes, namely "suspension of breathing." He says ordinary breathing stopped and was replaced by an internal respiration, "as if by breathing of a distinct personality within and other than the physical organism." He took this being to be the "entelechy" of Aristotle and the "inner Christ" of the apostle Paul, the "spiritual and substantial individuality engendered within the physical and phenomenal personality, and representing, therefore, the rebirth of man on a plane transcending the material."

42   This genuine[20] experience contains all the essential symbols of our text. The phenomenon itself, the vision of light, is an experience common to many mystics, and one that is undoubtedly of the greatest significance, because at all times and places it proves to be something unconditioned and absolute, a combination of supreme power and profound meaning. Hildegard of Bingen, an outstanding personality quite apart from her mysticism, writes in much the same way about her central vision:

> Since my childhood I have always seen a light in my soul, but not with the outer eyes, nor through the thoughts of my heart; neither do the five outer senses take part in this vision. . . . The light I perceive is not of a local kind, but is much brighter than the cloud which supports the sun. I cannot distinguish height, breadth, or length in it. . . . What I see or learn in such a vision stays long in my memory. I see, hear, and know in the same moment. . . . I cannot recognize any sort of form in this light, although I sometimes see in it another light that is known to me as the living light. . . . While I am enjoying the spectacle of this light, all sadness and sorrow vanish from my memory.[21]

43   I myself know a few individuals who have had personal experience of this phenomenon. So far as I have been able to understand it, it seems to have to do with an acute state of consciousness, as intense as it is abstract, a "detached" consciousness

20 Such experiences are genuine, but their genuineness does not prove that all the conclusions or convictions forming their content are necessarily sound. Even in cases of lunacy one comes across perfectly valid psychic experiences. [Author's note added in the first (1931) English edition.]
21 [*Acta S. Hildegardis*, in Migne, *P.L.*, vol. 197, col. 18.]

(see infra, pars. 64ff.), which, as Hildegard implies, brings into awareness areas of psychic happenings ordinarily covered in darkness. The fact that the general bodily sensations disappear during the experience suggests that their specific energy has been withdrawn and has apparently gone towards heightening the clarity of consciousness. As a rule, the phenomenon is spontaneous, coming and going on its own initiative. Its effect is astonishing in that it almost always brings about a solution of psychic complications and frees the inner personality from emotional and intellectual entanglements, thus creating a unity of being which is universally felt as "liberation."

44   Such a symbolic unity cannot be attained by the conscious will because consciousness is always partisan. Its opponent is the collective unconscious, which does not understand the language of the conscious mind. Therefore it is necessary to have the magic of the symbol which contains those primitive analogies that speak to the unconscious. The unconscious can be reached and expressed only by symbols, and for this reason the process of individuation can never do without the symbol. The symbol is the primitive exponent of the unconscious, but at the same time an idea that corresponds to the highest intuitions of the conscious mind.

45   The oldest mandala drawing known to me is a palaeolithic "sun-wheel," recently discovered in Rhodesia. It, too, is based on the quaternary principle. Things reaching so far back into human history naturally touch upon the deepest layers of the unconscious, and can have a powerful effect on it even when our conscious language proves itself to be quite impotent. Such things cannot be thought up but must grow again from the forgotten depths if they are to express the supreme insights of consciousness and the loftiest intuitions of the spirit, and in this way fuse the uniqueness of present-day consciousness with the age-old past of life.

4. PHENOMENA OF THE WAY

A. THE DISINTEGRATION OF CONSCIOUSNESS

46   The meeting between the narrowly delimited, but intensely clear, individual consciousness and the vast expanse of the collective unconscious is dangerous, because the unconscious has a decidedly disintegrating effect on consciousness. According to the *Hui Ming Ching*, this effect belongs to the peculiar phenomena of Chinese yoga. It says: "Every separate thought takes shape and becomes visible in colour and form. The total spiritual power unfolds its traces. . . ." [1] The relevant illustration in the text [stage 4] shows a sage sunk in contemplation, his head surrounded by tongues of fire, out of which five human figures emerge; these five again split up into twenty-five smaller figures.[2] This would be a schizophrenic process if it were to become a permanent state. Therefore the *Hui Ming Ching*, as though warning the adept, continues: "The shapes formed by the spirit-fire are only empty colours and forms. The light of human nature (*hsing*) shines back on the primordial, the true."

47   So we can understand why the figure of the protecting circle was seized upon. It is intended to prevent the "outflowing" and to protect the unity of consciousness from being burst asunder by the unconscious. The text seeks to mitigate the disintegrating effect of the unconscious by describing the thought-figures as "empty colours and forms," thus depotentiating them as much as possible. This idea runs through the whole of Buddhism (especially the Mahayana form) and, in the instructions to the dead in *The Tibetan Book of the Dead*, it is even pushed to the point of explaining the favourable as well as the unfavourable gods as illusions still to be overcome. It is certainly not within the com-

---

1 *The Golden Flower* (1962 edn.), pp. 76f. [For elucidation of the four pictures from the *Hui Ming Ching* reproduced here, see ibid., pp. 75-77.—EDITORS.]

2 These are recollections of earlier incarnations that arise during contemplation.

坐禪圖

此是修真要訣學者可以養神
若活七十年便是百四十
無事此靜坐一日如兩日
靜坐少思寡欲實心養氣存神

坐久忽所知忽覺月在地
冷泠天風來蹇然到胛肺
俯視一泓水澄湛無物澈
中有戢鱗逐默黙自相笑

帝二乙癸巳
太乙之觀已
礼二十九甲
藥一之足正

Stage 1: Gathering the light

Pages 30–33:
Four stages of meditation,
with inspirational texts,
from the *Hui Ming Ching*

嬰兒現形圖

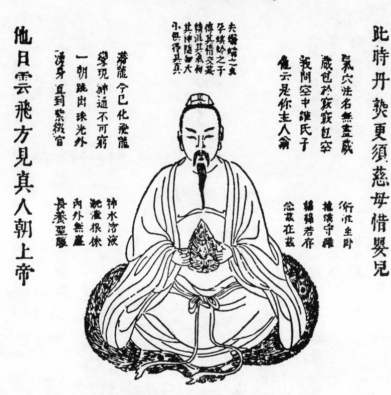

此時丹熟更須慈母惜嬰兒

他日雲飛方見真人朝上帝

氣穴法名無盡藏
藏色於寂寂包空
我聞空中誰氏子
佛云是你主人翁

衍法坐臥
地液守雞
綿綿若存
念茲在茲

夫嬰兒之氣
孕媄於之干
傅其佛交媄
持兆其氣桐
其神陸加大
小供得其真

游龍今已化飛龍
變現神通不可窮
一朝跳出珠光外
湧身直到紫微宮

神水溶液
沉灌根株
內外無塵
長養聖胎

Stage 2: Origin of a new being in the place of power

33

端拱冥心圖

Stage 3: Separation of the spirit-body for independent existence

Stage 4: The centre in the midst of conditions

petence of the psychologist to establish the metaphysical truth or untruth of this idea; he must be content to determine so far as possible its psychic effect. He need not bother himself whether the shape in question is a transcendental illusion or not, since faith, not science, has to decide this point. In any case we are moving on ground that for a long time has seemed to be outside the domain of science and was looked upon as wholly illusory. But there is no scientific justification for such an assumption; the substantiality of these things is not a scientific problem since it lies beyond the range of human perception and judgment and thus beyond any possibility of proof. The psychologist is concerned not with the substantiality of these complexes but with psychic experience. Without a doubt they are psychic contents that can be experienced, and their autonomy is equally indubitable. They are fragmentary psychic systems that either appear spontaneously in ecstatic states and evoke powerful impressions and effects, or else, in mental disturbances, become fixed in the form of delusions and hallucinations and consequently destroy the unity of the personality.

48   Psychiatrists are always ready to believe in toxins and the like, and even to explain schizophrenia in these terms, putting next to no emphasis on the psychic contents as such. On the other hand, in psychogenic disturbances (hysteria, obsessional neurosis, etc.), where toxic effects and cell degeneration are out of the question, split-off complexes are to be found similar to those occurring in somnambulistic states. Freud would like to explain these spontaneous split-offs as due to unconscious repression of sexuality, but this explanation is by no means valid in all cases, because contents that the conscious mind cannot assimilate can emerge just as spontaneously out of the unconscious, and in these cases the repression theory is inadequate. Moreover, their autonomy can be observed in daily life, in affects that obstinately obtrude themselves against our will and, in spite of the most strenuous efforts to repress them, overwhelm the ego and force it under their control. No wonder the primitive sees in these moods a state of possession or sets them down to a loss of soul. Our colloquial speech reflects the same thing when we say: "I don't know what has got into him today," "he is possessed of the devil," "he is beside himself," etc. Even legal practice recognizes a degree of diminished responsibility in a state of affect.

Autonomous psychic contents are thus quite common experiences for us. Such contents have a disintegrating effect upon consciousness.

49 But besides the ordinary, familiar affects there are subtler, more complex emotional states that can no longer be described as affects pure and simple but are fragmentary psychic systems. The more complicated they are, the more they have the character of personalities. As constituents of the psychic personality, they necessarily have the character of "persons." Such fragmentary systems are to be found especially in mental diseases, in cases of psychogenic splitting of the personality (double personality), and of course in mediumistic phenomena. They are also encountered in the phenomenology of religion. Many of the earlier gods developed from "persons" into personified ideas, and finally into abstract ideas. Activated unconscious contents always appear at first as projections upon the outside world, but in the course of mental development they are gradually assimilated by consciousness and reshaped into conscious ideas that then forfeit their originally autonomous and personal character. As we know, some of the old gods have become, via astrology, nothing more than descriptive attributes (martial, jovial, saturnine, erotic, logical, lunatic, and so on).

50 The instructions of *The Tibetan Book of the Dead* in particular help us to see how great is the danger that consciousness will be disintegrated by these figures. Again and again the dead are instructed not to take these shapes for truth, not to confuse their murky appearance with the pure white light of *Dharmakaya* (the divine body of truth). That is to say, they are not to project the *one* light of highest consciousness into concretized figures and dissolve it into a plurality of autonomous fragmentary systems. If there were no danger of this, and if these systems did not represent menacingly autonomous and disintegrative tendencies, such urgent instructions would not be necessary. Allowing for the simpler, polytheistic attitude of the Eastern mind, these instructions would be almost the equivalent of warning a Christian not to let himself be blinded by the illusion of a personal God, let alone by the Trinity and the host of angels and saints.

51 If tendencies towards dissociation were not inherent in the human psyche, fragmentary psychic systems would never have

37

been split off; in other words, neither spirits nor gods would ever have come into existence. That is also the reason why our time has become so utterly godless and profane: we lack all knowledge of the unconscious psyche and pursue the cult of consciousness to the exclusion of all else. Our true religion is a monotheism of consciousness, a possession by it, coupled with a fanatical denial of the existence of fragmentary autonomous systems. But we differ from the Buddhist yoga doctrines in that we even deny that these systems are experienceable. This entails a great psychic danger, because the autonomous systems then behave like any other repressed contents: they necessarily induce wrong attitudes since the repressed material reappears in consciousness in a spurious form. This is strikingly evident in every case of neurosis and also holds true for the collective psychic phenomena. Our time has committed a fatal error; we believe we can criticize the facts of religion intellectually. Like Laplace, we think God is a hypothesis that can be subjected to intellectual treatment, to be affirmed or denied. We completely forget that the reason mankind believes in the "daemon" has nothing whatever to do with external factors, but is simply due to a naïve awareness of the tremendous inner effect of autonomous fragmentary systems. This effect is not abolished by criticizing it—or rather, the name we have given it—or by describing the name as false. The effect is collectively present all the time; the autonomous systems are always at work, for the fundamental structure of the unconscious is not affected by the deviations of our ephemeral consciousness.

52   If we deny the existence of the autonomous systems, imagining that we have got rid of them by a mere critique of the name, then the effect which they still continue to exert can no longer be understood, nor can they be assimilated to consciousness. They become an inexplicable source of disturbance which we finally assume must exist somewhere outside ourselves. The resultant projection creates a dangerous situation in that the disturbing effects are now attributed to a wicked will outside ourselves, which is naturally not to be found anywhere but with our neighbour *de l'autre côté de la rivière*. This leads to collective delusions, "incidents," revolutions, war—in a word, to destructive mass psychoses.

53   Insanity is possession by an unconscious content that, as

such, is not assimilated to consciousness, nor can it be assimilated since the very existence of such contents is denied. This attitude is equivalent to saying: "We no longer have any fear of God and believe that everything is to be judged by human standards." This hybris or narrowness of consciousness is always the shortest way to the insane asylum. I recommend the excellent account of this problem in H. G. Wells's novel *Christina Alberta's Father,* and Schreber's *Memoirs of My Nervous Illness.*

54   It must stir a sympathetic chord in the enlightened European when it is said in the *Hui Ming Ching* that the "shapes formed by the spirit-fire are only empty colours and forms." That sounds thoroughly European and seems to suit our reason to a T. We think we can congratulate ourselves on having already reached such a pinnacle of clarity, imagining that we have left all these phantasmal gods far behind. But what we have left behind are only verbal spectres, not the psychic facts that were responsible for the birth of the gods. We are still as much possessed by autonomous psychic contents as if they were Olympians. Today they are called phobias, obsessions, and so forth; in a word, neurotic symptoms. The gods have become diseases; Zeus no longer rules Olympus but rather the solar plexus, and produces curious specimens for the doctor's consulting room, or disorders the brains of politicians and journalists who unwittingly let loose psychic epidemics on the world.

55   So it is better for Western man if he does not know too much about the secret insights of the Oriental sages to begin with, for, as I have said, it would be a case of the "right means in the hands of the wrong man." Instead of allowing himself to be convinced once more that the daemon is an illusion, he ought to experience once more the reality of this illusion. He should learn to acknowledge these psychic forces anew, and not wait until his moods, nervous states, and delusions make it clear in the most painful way that he is not the only master in his house. His dissociative tendencies are actual psychic personalities possessing a differential reality. They are "real" when they are not recognized as real and consequently projected; they are relatively real when they are brought into relationship with consciousness (in religious terms, when a cult exists); but they are unreal to the extent that consciousness detaches itself from its contents. This last stage, however, is reached only when life has been lived so

exhaustively and with such devotion that no obligations remain unfulfilled, when no desires that cannot safely be sacrificed stand in the way of inner detachment from the world. It is futile to lie to ourselves about this. Wherever we are still attached, we are still possessed; and when we are possessed, there is one stronger than us who possesses us. ("Verily I say unto thee, thou shalt by no means come out thence, until thou hast paid the uttermost farthing.") It is not a matter of indifference whether one calls something a "mania" or a "god." To serve a mania is detestable and undignified, but to serve a god is full of meaning and promise because it is an act of submission to a higher, invisible, and spiritual being. The personification enables us to see the relative reality of the autonomous system, and not only makes its assimilation possible but also depotentiates the daemonic forces of life. When the god is not acknowledged, egomania develops, and out of this mania comes sickness.

56　　Yoga takes acknowledgment of the gods as something self-evident. Its secret instruction is intended only for those whose consciousness is struggling to disentangle itself from the daemonic forces of life in order to enter into the ultimate undivided unity, the "centre of emptiness," where "dwells the god of utmost emptiness and life," as our text says.[3] "To hear such a teaching is difficult to attain in thousands of aeons." Evidently the veil of Maya cannot be lifted by a merely rational resolve; it requires a most thoroughgoing and persevering preparation consisting in the full payment of all debts to life. For as long as unconditional attachment through *cupiditas* exists, the veil is not lifted and the heights of a consciousness free of contents and free of illusion are not attained; nor can any trick nor any deceit bring this about. It is an ideal that can ultimately be realized only in death. Until then there are the real and relatively real figures of the unconscious.

B. ANIMUS AND ANIMA

57　　According to our text, among the figures of the unconscious there are not only the gods but also the animus and anima. The word *hun* is translated by Wilhelm as animus. And indeed, the term "animus" seems appropriate for *hun,* the character for

[3] [*The Golden Flower,* p. 22.]

which is made up of the sign for "clouds" and that for "demon."
Thus *hun* means "cloud-demon," a higher breath-soul belonging to the *yang* principle and therefore masculine. After death,
hun rises upward and becomes *shen,* the "expanding and self-
revealing" spirit or god. "Anima," called *p'o,* and written with
the characters for "white" and "demon," that is, "white ghost,"
belongs to the lower, earthbound, bodily soul, the *yin* principle,
and is therefore feminine. After death, it sinks downward and
becomes *kuei* (demon), often explained as "the one who returns" (i.e., to earth), a revenant, a ghost. The fact that the
animus and anima part after death and go their ways independ-
ently shows that, for the Chinese consciousness, they are distin-
guishable psychic factors; originally they were united in "the
one effective, true human nature," but in the "house of the Creative" they are two. "The animus is in the heavenly heart." "By
day it lives in the eyes [i.e., in consciousness]; at night it houses
in the liver." It is "that which we have received from the great
emptiness, that which is identical in form with the primal beginning." The anima, on the other hand, is the "energy of the
heavy and the turbid"; it clings to the bodily, fleshly heart. Its
effects are "sensuous desires and impulses to anger." "Whoever
is sombre and moody on waking . . . is fettered to the anima." [4]

58   Many years ago, before Wilhelm acquainted me with this
text, I used the term "anima" [5] in a way quite analogous to the
Chinese definition of *p'o,* and of course entirely apart from any
metaphysical premise. To the psychologist, the anima is not a
transcendental being but something quite within the range of
experience, as the Chinese definition makes clear: affective states
are immediate experiences. Why, then, speak of the anima and
not simply of moods? The reason is that affects have an autonomous character, and therefore most people are under their
power. But affects are delimitable contents of consciousness,
parts of the personality. As such, they partake of its character
and can easily be personified—a process that still continues today, as I have shown. The personification is not an idle invention, since a person roused by affect does not show a neutral
character but a quite distinct one, entirely different from his
ordinary character. Careful investigation has shown that the

4 [*The Golden Flower,* pp. 26 and 28.]
5 Cf. *Two Essays on Analytical Psychology,* pars. 296ff.

affective character of a man has feminine traits. From this psychological fact derives the Chinese doctrine of the *p'o* soul as well as my own concept of the anima. Deeper introspection or ecstatic experience reveals the existence of a feminine figure in the unconscious, hence the feminine name: anima, psyche, *Seele*. The anima can be defined as the image or archetype or deposit of all the experiences of man with woman. As we know, the poets have often sung the anima's praises.[6] The connection of anima with ghost in the Chinese concept is of interest to parapsychologists inasmuch as mediumistic "controls" are very often of the opposite sex.

59   Although Wilhelm's translation of *hun* as "animus" seems justified to me, nonetheless I had important reasons for choosing the term "Logos" for a man's "spirit," for his clarity of consciousness and his rationality, rather than the otherwise appropriate expression "animus." Chinese philosophers are spared certain difficulties that aggravate the task of the Western psychologist. Like all mental and spiritual activity in ancient times, Chinese philosophy was exclusively a component of the masculine world. Its concepts were never understood psychologically, and therefore were never examined as to how far they also apply to the feminine psyche. But the psychologist cannot possibly ignore the existence of woman and her special psychology. For these reasons I would prefer to translate *hun* as it appears in man by "Logos." Wilhelm in his translation uses Logos for *hsing*, which can also be translated as "essence of human nature" or "creative consciousness." After death, *hun* becomes *shen*, "spirit," which is very close, in the philosophical sense, to *hsing*. Since the Chinese concepts are not logical in our sense of the word, but are intuitive ideas, their meanings can only be elicited from the ways in which they are used and from the constitution of the written characters, or from such relationships as obtain between *hun* and *shen*. *Hun,* then, would be the light of consciousness and reason in man, originally coming from the *logos spermatikos* of *hsing,* and returning after death through *shen* to the Tao. Used in this sense the expression "Logos" would be especially appropriate, since it includes the idea of a universal being, and thus covers the fact that man's clarity of consciousness and rationality are something universal rather than indi-

6 Cf. *Psychological Types,* ch. V.

vidually unique. The Logos principle is nothing personal, but is in the deepest sense impersonal, and thus in sharp contrast to the anima, which is a personal demon expressing itself in thoroughly personal moods ("animosity"!).

60 In view of these psychological facts, I have reserved the term "animus" strictly for women, because, to answer a famous question, *mulier non habet animam, sed animum*. Feminine psychology exhibits an element that is the counterpart of a man's anima. Primarily, it is not of an affective nature but is a quasi-intellectual factor best described by the word "prejudice." The conscious side of woman corresponds to the emotional side of man, not to his "mind." Mind makes up the "soul," or better, the "animus" of woman, and just as the anima of a man consists of inferior relatedness, full of affect, so the animus of woman consists of inferior judgments, or better, opinions. As it is made up of a plurality of preconceived opinions, the animus is far less susceptible of personification by a single figure, but appears more often as a group or crowd. (A good example of this from parapsychology is the "Imperator" group in the case of Mrs. Piper.[7]) On a low level the animus is an inferior Logos, a caricature of the differentiated masculine mind, just as on a low level the anima is a caricature of the feminine Eros. To pursue the parallel further, we could say that just as *hun* corresponds to *hsing*, translated by Wilhelm as Logos, so the Eros of woman corresponds to *ming*, "fate" or "destiny," interpreted by Wilhelm as Eros. Eros is an interweaving; Logos is differentiating knowledge, clarifying light. Eros is relatedness, Logos is discrimination and detachment. Hence the inferior Logos of woman's animus appears as something quite unrelated, as an inaccessible prejudice, or as an opinion which, irritatingly enough, has nothing to do with the essential nature of the object.

61 I have often been accused of personifying the anima and animus as mythology does, but this accusation would be justified only if it could be proved that I concretize these concepts in a mythological manner for psychological use. I must declare once and for all that the personification is not an invention of mine,

---

7 Cf. Hyslop, *Science and a Future Life,* pp. 113ff. [Mrs. Leonora Piper, an American psychic medium active about 1890–1910 in the U.S. and England, was studied by William James, Mrs. Henry Sidgwick, Hyslop, and others. A group of five of her psychic controls had the collective name "Imperator."—EDITORS.]

but is inherent in the nature of the phenomena. It would be unscientific to overlook the fact that the anima is a psychic, and therefore a personal, autonomous system. None of the people who make the charge against me would hesitate for a second to say, "I dreamed of Mr. X," whereas, strictly speaking, he dreamed only of a representation of Mr. X. The anima is nothing but a representation of the personal nature of the autonomous system in question. What the nature of this system is in a transcendental sense, that is, beyond the bounds of experience, we cannot know.

62   I have defined the anima as a personification of the unconscious in general, and have taken it as a bridge to the unconscious, in other words, as a function of relationship to the unconscious. There is an interesting point in our text in this connection. The text says that consciousness (that is, the personal consciousness) comes from the anima. Since the Western mind is based wholly on the standpoint of consciousness, it must define the anima in the way I have done. But the East, based as it is on the standpoint of the unconscious, sees consciousness as an effect of the anima. And there can be no doubt that consciousness does originate in the unconscious. This is something we are apt to forget, and therefore we are always attempting to identify the psyche with consciousness, or at least to represent the unconscious as a derivative or an effect of consciousness (as in the Freudian repression theory). But, for the reasons given above, it is essential that we do not detract from the reality of the unconscious, and that the figures of the unconscious be understood as real and effective factors. The person who has understood what is meant by psychic reality need have no fear that he has fallen back into primitive demonology. If the unconscious figures are not acknowledged as spontaneous agents, we become victims of a one-sided belief in the power of consciousness, leading finally to acute tension. A catastrophe is then bound to happen because, for all our consciousness, the dark powers of the psyche have been overlooked. It is not we who personify them; they have a personal nature from the very beginning. Only when this is thoroughly recognized can we think of depersonalizing them, of "subjugating the anima," as our text expresses it.

63   Here again we find an enormous difference between Buddhism and the Western attitude of mind, and again there is a

dangerous semblance of agreement. Yoga teaching rejects all fantasy products and we do the same, but the East does so for entirely different reasons. In the East there is an abundance of conceptions and teachings that give full expression to the creative fantasy; in fact, protection is needed against an excess of it. We, on the other hand, regard fantasy as worthless subjective day-dreaming. Naturally the figures of the unconscious do not appear in the form of abstractions stripped of all imaginative trappings; on the contrary, they are embedded in a web of fantasies of extraordinary variety and bewildering profusion. The East can reject these fantasies because it has long since extracted their essence and condensed it in profound teachings. But we have never even experienced these fantasies, much less extracted their quintessence. We still have a large stretch of experience to catch up with, and only when we have found the sense in apparent nonsense can we separate the valuable from the worthless. We can be sure that the essence we extract from our experience will be quite different from what the East offers us today. The East came to its knowledge of inner things in childlike ignorance of the external world. We, on the other hand, shall explore the psyche and its depths supported by an immense knowledge of history and science. At present our knowledge of the external world is the greatest obstacle to introspection, but the psychological need will overcome all obstructions. We are already building up a psychology, a science that gives us the key to the very things that the East discovered—and discovered only through abnormal psychic states.

5. THE DETACHMENT OF CONSCIOUSNESS FROM THE OBJECT

64   By understanding the unconscious we free ourselves from its
domination. That is really also the purpose of the instructions
in our text. The pupil is taught to concentrate on the light of
the innermost region and, at the same time, to free himself from
all outer and inner entanglements. His vital impulses are guided
towards a consciousness void of content, which nevertheless permits all contents to exist. The *Hui Ming Ching*[1] says of this
detachment:

A halo of light surrounds the world of the law.
We forget one another, quiet and pure, all-powerful and empty.
The emptiness is irradiated by the light of the heart of heaven.
The water of the sea is smooth and mirrors the moon in its surface.
The clouds disappear in blue space; the mountains shine clear.
Consciousness reverts to contemplation; the moon-disk rests alone.

65   This description of fulfilment depicts a psychic state that
can best be characterized as a detachment of consciousness from
the world and a withdrawal to a point outside it, so to speak.
Thus consciousness is at the same time empty and not empty. It
is no longer preoccupied with the images of things but merely
contains them. The fullness of the world which hitherto pressed
upon it has lost none of its richness and beauty, but it no longer
dominates. The magical claim of things has ceased because the
interweaving of consciousness with world has come to an end.
The unconscious is not projected any more, and so the primordial *participation mystique* with things is abolished. Consciousness is no longer preoccupied with compulsive plans but dissolves in contemplative vision.

66   How did this effect come about? (We assume, of course, that
the Chinese author was first of all not a liar; secondly, that he
was of sound mind; and thirdly, that he was an unusually intel-

[1] [*The Golden Flower* (1962 edn.), pp. 77f.]

ligent man.) To understand and explain this detachment, we must proceed by a roundabout way. It is an effect that cannot be simulated; nothing would be more childish than to make such a psychic state an object of aesthetic experiment. I know this effect very well from my practice; it is the therapeutic effect *par excellence*, for which I labour with my students and patients, and it consists in the dissolution of *participation mystique*. By a stroke of genius, Lévy-Bruhl singled out what he called *participation mystique* as being the hallmark of the primitive mentality.[2] What he meant by it is simply the indefinitely large remnant of non-differentiation between subject and object, which is still so great among primitives that it cannot fail to strike our European consciousness very forcibly. When there is no consciousness of the difference between subject and object, an unconscious identity prevails. The unconscious is then projected into the object, and the object is introjected into the subject, becoming part of his psychology. Then plants and animals behave like human beings, human beings are at the same time animals, and everything is alive with ghosts and gods. Civilized man naturally thinks he is miles above these things. Instead of that, he is often identified with his parents throughout his life, or with his affects and prejudices, and shamelessly accuses others of the things he will not see in himself. He too has a remnant of primitive unconsciousness, of non-differentiation between subject and object. Because of this, he is magically affected by all manner of people, things, and circumstances, he is beset by disturbing influences nearly as much as the primitive and therefore needs just as many apotropaic charms. He no longer works magic with medicine bags, amulets, and animal sacrifices, but with tranquillizers, neuroses, rationalism, cult of the will, etc.

67 But if the unconscious can be recognized as a co-determining factor along with consciousness, and if we can live in such a way that conscious and unconscious demands are taken into account as far as possible, then the centre of gravity of the total personality shifts its position. It is then no longer in the ego, which is merely the centre of consciousness, but in the hypothetical point between conscious and unconscious. This new centre might be called the self. If the transposition is successful, it does away with the *participation mystique* and results in a personality that

2 Lévy-Bruhl, *Primitive Mentality*.

suffers only in the lower storeys, as it were, but in its upper storeys is singularly detached from painful as well as from joyful happenings.

68   The production and birth of this superior personality is what is meant when our text speaks of the "holy fruit," the "diamond body," or any other kind of incorruptible body. Psychologically, these expressions symbolize an attitude that is beyond the reach of emotional entanglements and violent shocks—a consciousness detached from the world. I have reasons for believing that this attitude sets in after middle life and is a natural preparation for death. Death is psychologically as important as birth and, like it, is an integral part of life. What happens to the detached consciousness in the end is a question the psychologist cannot be expected to answer. Whatever his theoretical position he would hopelessly overstep the bounds of his scientific competence. He can only point out that the views of our text in regard to the timelessness of the detached consciousness are in harmony with the religious thought of all ages and with that of the overwhelming majority of mankind. Anyone who thought differently would be standing outside the human order and would, therefore, be suffering from a disturbed psychic equilibrium. As a doctor, I make every effort to strengthen the belief in immortality, especially with older patients when such questions come threateningly close. For, seen in correct psychological perspective, death is not an end but a goal, and life's inclination towards death begins as soon as the meridian is passed.

69   Chinese yoga philosophy is based upon this instinctive preparation for death as a goal. In analogy with the goal of the first half of life—procreation and reproduction, the means of perpetuating one's physical existence—it takes as the goal of spiritual existence the symbolic begetting and birth of a "spirit-body," or "breath-body," which ensures the continuity of detached consciousness. It is the birth of the pneumatic man, known to the European from antiquity, but which he seeks to produce by quite other symbols and magical practices, by faith and a Christian way of life. Here again we stand on a foundation quite different from that of the East. Again the text sounds as though it were not so very far from Christian ascetic morality, but nothing could be more mistaken than to assume that it actually means the same thing. Behind our text is a civilization thou-

sands of years old, one which is built up organically on primitive instincts and knows nothing of that brutal morality so suited to us as recently civilized Teutonic barbarians. For this reason the Chinese are without the impulse towards violent repression of the instincts that poisons our spirituality and makes it hysterically exaggerated. The man who lives with his instincts can also detach from them, and in just as natural a way as he lived with them. Any idea of heroic self-conquest would be entirely foreign to the spirit of our text, but that is what it would infallibly amount to if we followed the instructions literally.

70   We must never forget our historical antecedents. Only a little more than a thousand years ago we stumbled out of the crudest beginnings of polytheism into a highly developed Oriental religion which lifted the imaginative minds of half-savages to a height that in no way corresponded to their spiritual development. In order to keep to this height in some fashion or other, it was inevitable that the instinctual sphere should be largely repressed. Thus religious practice and morality took on a decidedly brutal, almost malignant, character. The repressed elements naturally did not develop, but went on vegetating in the unconscious, in their original barbarism. We would like to scale the heights of a philosophical religion, but in fact are incapable of it. To grow up to it is the most we can hope for. The Amfortas wound and the Faustian split in the Germanic man are still not healed; his unconscious is still loaded with contents that must first be made conscious before he can be free of them. Recently I received a letter from a former patient which describes the necessary transformation in simple but trenchant words. She writes:

Out of evil, much good has come to me. By keeping quiet, repressing nothing, remaining attentive, and by accepting reality—taking things as they are, and not as I wanted them to be—by doing all this, unusual knowledge has come to me, and unusual powers as well, such as I could never have imagined before. I always thought that when we accepted things they overpowered us in some way or other. This turns out not to be true at all, and it is only by accepting them that one can assume an attitude towards them.[3] So now I intend to play the game of life, being receptive to whatever comes to me, good and bad, sun and shadow forever alternating, and, in

3 Dissolution of *participation mystique.*

this way, also accepting my own nature with its positive and nega-
tive sides. Thus everything becomes more alive to me. What a fool
I was! How I tried to force everything to go according to the way
I thought it ought to!

71   Only on the basis of such an attitude, which renounces none
of the Christian values won in the course of Christian development, but which, on the contrary, tries with Christian charity and
forbearance to accept even the humblest things in one's own nature, will a higher level of consciousness and culture become
possible. This attitude is religious in the truest sense, and therefore therapeutic, for all religions are therapies for the sorrows
and disorders of the soul. The development of the Western intellect and will has given us an almost fiendish capacity for aping
such an attitude, with apparent success, despite the protests of
the unconscious. But it is only a matter of time before the
counterposition asserts itself all the more harshly. Aping an attitude always produces an unstable situation that can be over-
thrown by the unconscious at any time. A safe foundation is
found only when the instinctive premises of the unconscious
win the same respect as the views of the conscious mind. No one
should blind himself to the fact that this necessity of giving due
consideration to the unconscious runs violently counter to our
Western, and in particular the Protestant, cult of consciousness.
Yet, though the new always seems to be the enemy of the old,
anyone with a more than superficial desire to understand cannot
fail to discover that without the most serious application of the
Christian values we have acquired, the new integration can
never take place.

6. THE FULFILMENT

72   A growing familiarity with the spirit of the East should be taken merely as a sign that we are beginning to relate to the alien elements within ourselves. Denial of our historical foundations would be sheer folly and would be the best way to bring about another uprooting of consciousness. Only by standing firmly on our own soil can we assimilate the spirit of the East.

73   Speaking of those who do not know where the true springs of secret power lie, an ancient adept says, "Worldly people lose their roots and cling to the treetops." The spirit of the East has grown out of the yellow earth, and our spirit can, and should, grow only out of our own earth. That is why I approach these problems in a way that has often been charged with "psychologism." If "psychology" were meant, I should indeed be flattered, for my aim as a psychologist is to dismiss without mercy the metaphysical claims of all esoteric teachings. The unavowed purpose of gaining power through words, inherent in all secret doctrines, ill accords with our profound ignorance, which we should have the modesty to admit. I quite deliberately bring everything that purports to be metaphysical into the daylight of psychological understanding, and do my best to prevent people from believing in nebulous power-words. Let the convinced Christian believe, by all means, for that is the duty he has taken upon himself; but whoever is not a Christian has forfeited the charisma of faith. (Perhaps he was cursed from birth with not being able to believe, but merely to know.) Therefore, he has no right to put his faith elsewhere. One cannot grasp anything metaphysically, one only can do so psychologically. Therefore I strip things of their metaphysical wrappings in order to make them objects of psychology. In that way I can at least extract something understandable from them and avail myself of it, and I also discover psychological facts and processes that before were veiled in symbols and beyond my comprehension. In doing so I

51

may perhaps be following in the footsteps of the faithful, and may possibly have similar experiences; and if in the end there should be something ineffably metaphysical behind it all, it would then have the best opportunity of showing itself.

74   My admiration for the great philosophers of the East is as genuine as my attitude towards their metaphysics is irreverent.[1] I suspect them of being symbolical psychologists, to whom no greater wrong could be done than to take them literally. If it were really metaphysics that they mean, it would be useless to try to understand them. But if it is psychology, we can not only understand them but can profit greatly by them, for then the so-called "metaphysical" comes within the range of experience. If I assume that God is absolute and beyond all human experience, he leaves me cold. I do not affect him, nor does he affect me. But if I know that he is a powerful impulse of my soul, at once I must concern myself with him, for then he can become important, even unpleasantly so, and can affect me in practical ways— which sounds horribly banal, like everything else that is real.

75   The epithet "psychologism" applies only to a fool who thinks he has his soul in his pocket. There are certainly more than enough such fools, for although we know how to talk big about the "soul," the depreciation of everything psychic is a typically Western prejudice. If I make use of the concept "autonomous psychic complex," my reader immediately comes up with the ready-made prejudice that it is "nothing but a psychic complex." How can we be so sure that the soul is "nothing but"? It is as if we did not know, or else continually forgot, that everything of which we are conscious is an image, and that image *is* psyche. The same people who think that God is depreciated if he is understood as something moved in the psyche, as well as the moving force of the psyche—i.e., as an autonomous complex —can be so plagued by uncontrollable affects and neurotic states that their wills and their whole philosophy of life fail them miserably. Is that a proof of the impotence of the psyche? Should Meister Eckhart be accused of "psychologism" when he says, "God must be born in the soul again and again"? I think the accusation of "psychologism" can be levelled only at an intellect

[1] The Chinese philosophers—in contrast to the dogmatists of the West—are only grateful for such an attitude, because they also are masters of their gods. [Note by Richard Wilhelm in original edn.]

that denies the genuine nature of the autonomous complex and seeks to explain it rationalistically as the consequence of known causes, i.e., as something secondary and unreal. This is just as arrogant as the metaphysical assertion that seeks to make a God outside the range of our experience responsible for our psychic states. Psychologism is simply the counterpart of this metaphysical presumption, and is just as childish. Therefore it seems to me far more reasonable to accord the psyche the same validity as the empirical world, and to admit that the former has just as much "reality" as the latter. As I see it, the psyche is a world in which the ego is contained. Maybe there are fishes who believe that they contain the sea. We must rid ourselves of this habitual illusion of ours if we wish to consider metaphysical assertions from the standpoint of psychology.

76   A metaphysical assertion of this kind is the idea of the "diamond body," the incorruptible breath-body which grows in the golden flower or in the "field of the square inch." [2] This body is

2 Our text is somewhat unclear as to whether by "continuation of life" a survival after death or a prolongation of physical existence is meant. Expressions such as "elixir of life" and the like are exceedingly ambiguous. In the later additions to the text it is evident that the yoga instructions were also understood in a purely physical sense. To a primitive mind, there is nothing disturbing in this odd mixture of the physical and the spiritual, because life and death are by no means the complete opposites they are for us. (Particularly interesting in this connection, apart from the ethnological material, are the communications of the English "rescue circles" with their thoroughly archaic ideas.) The same ambiguity with regard to survival after death is found in early Christianity, where immortality depends on very similar assumptions, i.e., on the idea of a breath-body as the carrier of life. (Geley's paraphysiological theory would be the latest incarnation of this ancient idea.) But since in our text there are warnings about the superstitious use of it—warnings, for example, against the making of gold—we can safely insist on the spiritual purport of the instructions without contradicting their meaning. In the states which the instructions seek to induce the physical body plays an increasingly unimportant part anyway, since it is replaced by the breath-body (hence the importance of breath control in all yoga exercises). The breath-body is not something "spiritual" in our sense of the word. It is characteristic of Western man that he has split apart the physical and the spiritual for epistemological purposes. But these opposites exist together in the psyche and psychology must recognize this fact. "Psychic" means physical *and* spiritual. The ideas in our text all deal with this "intermediate" world which seems unclear and confused because the concept of psychic reality is not yet current among us, although it expresses life as it actually is. Without soul, spirit is as dead as matter, because both are artificial abstractions; whereas man originally regarded spirit as a volatile body, and matter as not lacking in soul.

a symbol for a remarkable psychological fact which, precisely because it is objective, first appears in forms dictated by the experience of biological life—that is, as fruit, embryo, child, living body, and so on. This fact could be best expressed by the words "It is not I who live, it lives me." The illusion of the supremacy ·of consciousness makes us say, "I live." Once this illusion is shattered by a recognition of the unconscious, the unconscious will appear as something objective in which the ego is included. The attitude towards the unconscious is then analogous to the feeling of the primitive to whom the existence of a son guarantees continuation of life—a feeling that can assume grotesque forms, as when the old Negro, angered at his son's disobedience, cried out, "There he stands with my body, but does not even obey me!"

77   It is, in fact, a change of feeling similar to that experienced by a father to whom a son has been born, a change known to us from the testimony of St. Paul: "Yet not I, but Christ liveth in me." The symbol "Christ" as "son of man" is an analogous psychic experience of a higher spiritual being who is invisibly born in the individual, a pneumatic body which is to serve us as a future dwelling, a body which, as Paul says, is put on like a garment ("For as many of you as have been baptized into Christ have put on Christ"). It is always a difficult thing to express, in intellectual terms, subtle feelings that are nevertheless infinitely important for the individual's life and well-being. It is, in a sense, the feeling that we have been "replaced," but without the connotation of having been "deposed." It is as if the guidance of life had passed over to an invisible centre. Nietzsche's metaphor, "in most loving bondage, free," would be appropriate here. Religious language is full of imagery depicting this feeling of free dependence, of calm acceptance.

78   This remarkable experience seems to me a consequence of the detachment of consciousness, thanks to which the subjective "I live" becomes the objective "It lives me." This state is felt to be higher than the previous one; it is really like a sort of release from the compulsion and impossible responsibility that are the inevitable results of *participation mystique*. This feeling of liberation fills Paul completely; the consciousness of being a child of God delivers one from the bondage of the blood. It is also a feeling of reconciliation with all that happens, for which

54

reason, according to the *Hui Ming Ching,* the gaze of one who has attained fulfilment turns back to the beauty of nature.

79   In the Pauline Christ symbol the supreme religious experiences of West and East confront one another: Christ the sorrow-laden hero, and the Golden Flower that blooms in the purple hall of the city of jade. What a contrast, what an unfathomable difference, what an abyss of history! A problem fit for the crowning work of a future psychologist!

80   Among the great religious problems of the present is one which has received scant attention, but which is in fact the main problem of our day: the evolution of the religious spirit. If we are to discuss it, we must emphasize the difference between East and West in their treatment of the "jewel," the central symbol. The West lays stress on the human incarnation, and even on the personality and historicity of Christ, whereas the East says: "Without beginning, without end, without past, without future." [3] The Christian subordinates himself to the superior divine person in expectation of his grace; but the Oriental knows that redemption depends on the work he does on himself. The Tao grows out of the individual. The *imitatio Christi* has this disadvantage: in the long run we worship as a divine example a man who embodied the deepest meaning of life, and then, out of sheer imitation, we forget to make real our own deepest meaning—self-realization. As a matter of fact, it is not altogether inconvenient to renounce one's own meaning. Had Jesus done so, he would probably have become a respectable carpenter and not a religious rebel to whom the same thing would naturally happen today as happened then.

81   The imitation of Christ might well be understood in a deeper sense. It could be taken as the duty to realize one's deepest conviction with the same courage and the same self-sacrifice shown by Jesus. Happily not everyone has the task of being a leader of humanity, or a great rebel; and so, after all, it might be possible for each to realize himself in his own way. This honesty might even become an ideal. Since great innovations always begin in the most unlikely places, the fact that people today are not nearly as ashamed of their nakedness as they used to be might be the beginning of a recognition of themselves as they really are. Hard upon this will follow an increasing recognition

[3] *The Golden Flower* (1962 edn.), p. 77.

of many things that formerly were strictly taboo, for the reality of the earth will not forever remain veiled like the *virgines velandae* of Tertullian. Moral unmasking is but a step further in the same direction, and behold, there stands man as he is, and admits to himself that he is as he is. If he does this in a meaningless way he is just a muddled fool; but if he knows the significance of what he is doing he could belong to a higher order of man who makes real the Christ symbol, regardless of the suffering involved. It has often been observed that purely concrete taboos or magical rites in an early stage of a religion become in the next stage something psychic, or even purely spiritual symbols. An outward law becomes in the course of time an inward conviction. Thus it might easily happen to contemporary man, especially Protestants, that the person Jesus, now existing outside in the realm of history, might become the higher man within himself. Then we would have attained, in a European way, the psychological state corresponding to Eastern enlightenment.

82   All this is a step in the evolution of a higher consciousness on its way to unknown goals, and is not metaphysics as ordinarily understood. To that extent it is only "psychology," but to that extent, too, it is experienceable, understandable and—thank God—real, a reality we can do something with, a living reality full of possibilities. The fact that I am content with what can be experienced psychically, and reject the metaphysical, does not amount, as any intelligent person can see, to a gesture of scepticism or agnosticism aimed at faith and trust in higher powers, but means approximately the same as what Kant meant when he called the thing-in-itself a "merely negative borderline concept." Every statement about the transcendental is to be avoided because it is only a laughable presumption on the part of a human mind unconscious of its limitations. Therefore, when God or the Tao is named an impulse of the soul, or a psychic state, something has been said about the knowable only, but nothing about the unknowable, about which nothing can be determined.

7. CONCLUSION

83   The purpose of my commentary is to attempt to build a bridge of psychological understanding between East and West. The basis of every real understanding is man, and therefore I had to speak of human beings. This must be my excuse for having dealt only with general aspects, and for not having entered into technical details. Technical directions are valuable for those who know, for example, what a camera is, or a combustion engine, but they are useless for anyone who has no idea of such apparatus. Western man for whom I write is in an analogous position. Therefore it seemed to me important above all to emphasize the agreement between the psychic states and symbolisms of East and West. These analogies open a way to the inner chambers of the Eastern mind, a way that does not require the sacrifice of our own nature and does not confront us with the threat of being torn from our roots. Nor is it an intellectual telescope or microscope offering a view of no fundamental concern to us because it does not touch us. It is the way of suffering, seeking, and striving common to all civilized peoples; it is the tremendous experiment of becoming conscious, which nature has laid upon mankind, and which unites the most diverse cultures in a common task.

84   Western consciousness is by no means the only kind of consciousness there is; it is historically conditioned and geographically limited, and representative of only one part of mankind. The widening of our consciousness ought not to proceed at the expense of other kinds of consciousness; it should come about through the development of those elements of our psyche which are analogous to those of the alien psyche, just as the East cannot do without our technology, science, and industry. The European invasion of the East was an act of violence on a grand scale, and it has left us with the duty—*noblesse oblige*—of understanding the mind of the East. This is perhaps more necessary than we realize at present.

PSYCHOLOGICAL COMMENTARY ON
"THE TIBETAN BOOK OF THE DEAD" [1]

⁸³¹ Before embarking upon the psychological commentary, I should like to say a few words about the text itself. The Tibetan Book of the Dead, or the *Bardo Thödol*, is a book of instructions for the dead and dying. Like the Egyptian Book of the Dead, it is meant to be a guide for the dead man during the period of his *Bardo* existence, symbolically described as an intermediate state of forty-nine days' duration between death and rebirth. The text falls into three parts. The first part, called *Chikhai Bardo*, describes the psychic happenings at the moment of death. The second part, or *Chönyid Bardo*, deals with the dream-state which supervenes immediately after death, and with what are called "karmic illusions." The third part, or *Sidpa Bardo*, concerns the onset of the birth-instinct and of prenatal

1 [Originally published as "Psychologischer Kommentar zum Bardo Thödol" (preceded by an "Einführung," partially translated in the first two pars. here), in *Das Tibetanische Totenbuch*, translated into German by Louise Göpfert-March (Zurich, 1935). As ultimately revised for the 5th (revised and expanded) Swiss edition (1953), the commentary was translated by R. F. C. Hull for publication in the 3rd (revised and expanded) English edition (the original) of *The Tibetan Book of the Dead, or The After-Death Experience on the "Bardo" Plane*, according to Lama Kazi Dawa-Samdup's English rendering, edited by W. Y. Evans-Wentz, with foreword by Sir John Woodroffe (London and New York, 1957). With only minor alterations, it is the translation presented here.—EDITORS.]

events. It is characteristic that supreme insight and illumination, and hence the greatest possibility of attaining liberation, are vouchsafed during the actual process of dying. Soon afterward, the "illusions" begin which lead eventually to reincarnation, the illuminative lights growing ever fainter and more multifarious, and the visions more and more terrifying. This descent illustrates the estrangement of consciousness from the liberating truth as it approaches nearer and nearer to physical rebirth. The purpose of the instruction is to fix the attention of the dead man, at each successive stage of delusion and entanglement, on the ever-present possibility of liberation, and to explain to him the nature of his visions. The text of the *Bardo Thödol* is recited by the lama in the presence of the corpse.

832   I do not think I could better discharge my debt of thanks to the two previous translators of the *Bardo Thödol*, the late Lama Kazi Dawa-Samdup and Dr. Evans-Wentz, than by attempting, with the aid of a psychological commentary, to make the magnificent world of ideas and the problems contained in this treatise a little more intelligible to the Western mind. I am sure that all who read this book with open eyes, and who allow it to impress itself upon them without prejudice, will reap a rich reward.

*

833   The *Bardo Thödol*, fitly named by its editor, Dr. W. Y. Evans-Wentz, "The Tibetan Book of the Dead," caused a considerable stir in English-speaking countries at the time of its first appearance in 1927. It belongs to that class of writings which are not only of interest to specialists in Mahayana Buddhism, but which also, because of their deep humanity and their still deeper insight into the secrets of the human psyche, make an especial appeal to the layman who is seeking to broaden his knowledge of life. For years, ever since it was first published, the *Bardo Thödol* has been my constant companion, and to it I owe not only many stimulating ideas and discoveries, but also many fundamental insights. Unlike the Egyptian Book of the Dead, which always prompts one to say too much or too little, the *Bardo Thödol* offers one an intelligible philosophy addressed to human beings rather than to gods or primitive savages. Its philosophy contains the quintessence of Buddhist psychological criticism; and, as such, one can truly say that it is of an unex-

ampled sublimity. Not only the "wrathful" but also the "peaceful" deities are conceived as samsaric projections of the human psyche, an idea that seems all too obvious to the enlightened European, because it reminds him of his own banal simplifications. But though the European can easily explain away these deities as projections, he would be quite incapable of positing them at the same time as real. The *Bardo Thödol* can do that, because, in certain of its most essential metaphysical premises, it has the enlightened as well as the unenlightened European at a disadvantage. The ever-present, unspoken assumption of the *Bardo Thödol* is the antinomian character of all metaphysical assertions, and also the idea of the qualitative difference of the various levels of consciousness and of the metaphysical realities conditioned by them. The background of this unusual book is not the niggardly European "either-or," but a magnificently affirmative "both-and." This statement may appear objectionable to the Western philosopher, for the West loves clarity and unambiguity; consequently, one philosopher clings to the position, "God is," while another clings equally fervently to the negation, "God is not." What would these hostile brethren make of an assertion like the following [p. 96]:

Recognizing the voidness of thine own intellect to be Buddhahood, and knowing it at the same time to be thine own consciousness, thou shalt abide in the state of the divine mind of the Buddha.

834   Such an assertion is, I fear, as unwelcome to our Western philosophy as it is to our theology. The *Bardo Thödol* is in the highest degree psychological in its outlook; but, with us, philosophy and theology are still in the medieval, pre-psychological stage where only the assertions are listened to, explained, defended, criticized and disputed, while the authority that makes them has, by general consent, been deposed as outside the scope of discussion.

835   Metaphysical assertions, however, are *statements of the psyche,* and are therefore psychological. To the Western mind, which compensates its well-known feelings of resentment by a slavish regard for "rational" explanations, this obvious truth seems all too obvious, or else it is seen as an inadmissible negation of metaphysical "truth." Whenever the Westerner hears the word "psychological," it always sounds to him like *"only*

61

psychological." For him the "soul" is something pitifully small, unworthy, personal, subjective, and a lot more besides. He therefore prefers to use the word "mind" instead, though he likes to pretend at the same time that a statement which may in fact be very subjective indeed is made by the "mind," naturally by the "Universal Mind," or even—at a pinch—by the "Absolute" itself. This rather ridiculous presumption is probably a compensation for the regrettable smallness of the soul. It almost seems as if Anatole France had uttered a truth which were valid for the whole Western world when, in his *Penguin Island,* Cathérine d'Alexandrie offers this advice to God: "Donnez-leur une âme, mais une petite!"

836   It is the psyche which, by the divine creative power inherent in it, makes the metaphysical assertion; it posits the distinctions between metaphysical entities. Not only is it the condition of all metaphysical reality, it *is* that reality.

837   With this great psychological truth the *Bardo Thödol* opens. The book is not a ceremonial of burial, but a set of instructions for the dead, a guide through the changing phenomena of the *Bardo* realm, that state of existence which continues for forty-nine days after death until the next incarnation. If we disregard for the moment the supratemporality of the soul—which the East accepts as a self-evident fact—we, as readers of the *Bardo Thödol,* shall be able to put ourselves without difficulty in the position of the dead man, and shall consider attentively the teaching set forth in the opening section, which is outlined in the quotation above. At this point, the following words are spoken, not presumptuously, but in a courteous manner [pp. 95f.]:

O nobly born (so and so), listen. Now thou art experiencing the Radiance of the Clear Light of Pure Reality. Recognize it. O nobly-born, thy present intellect, in real nature void, not formed into anything as regards characteristics or colour, naturally void, is the very Reality, the All-Good.

Thine own intellect, which is now voidness, yet not to be regarded as of the voidness of nothingness, but as being the intellect itself, unobstructed, shining, thrilling, and blissful, is the very consciousness, the All-good Buddha.

838   This realization is the *Dharmakāya* state of perfect enlightenment; or, as we should express it in our own language, the

creative ground of all metaphysical assertion is consciousness, as the invisible, intangible manifestation of the soul. The "Voidness" is the state transcendent over all assertion and all predication. The fulness of its discriminative manifestations still lies latent in the soul.

839   The text continues:

Thine own consciousness, shining, void, and inseparable from the Great Body of Radiance, hath no birth, nor death, and is the Immutable Light—Buddha Amitābha.

840   The soul is assuredly not small, but the radiant Godhead itself. The West finds this statement either very dangerous, if not downright blasphemous, or else accepts it unthinkingly and then suffers from a theosophical inflation. Somehow we always have a wrong attitude to these things. But if we can master ourselves far enough to refrain from our chief error of always wanting to *do* something with things and put them to practical use, we may perhaps succeed in learning an important lesson from these teachings, or at least in appreciating the greatness of the *Bardo Thödol*, which vouchsafes to the dead man the ultimate and highest truth, that even the gods are the radiance and reflection of our own souls. No sun is thereby eclipsed for the Oriental as it would be for the Christian, who would feel robbed of his God; on the contrary, his soul is the light of the Godhead, and the Godhead is the soul. The East can sustain this paradox better than the unfortunate Angelus Silesius, who even today would be psychologically far in advance of his time.

841   It is highly sensible of the *Bardo Thödol* to make clear to the dead man the primacy of the psyche, for that is the one thing which life does not make clear to us. We are so hemmed in by things which jostle and oppress that we never get a chance, in the midst of all these "given" things, to wonder by whom they are "given." It is from this world of "given" things that the dead man liberates himself; and the purpose of the instruction is to help him towards this liberation. We, if we put ourselves in his place, shall derive no lesser reward from it, since we learn from the very first paragraphs that the "giver" of all "given" things dwells within us. This is a truth which in the face of all evidence, in the greatest things as in the smallest, is never known, although it is often so very necessary, indeed vital, for us to

know it. Such knowledge, to be sure, is suitable only for contemplatives who are minded to understand the purpose of existence, for those who are Gnostics by temperament and therefore believe in a saviour who, like the saviour of the Mandaeans, is called "knowledge of life" (Manda d'Hayye). Perhaps it is not granted to many of us to see the world as something "given." A great reversal of standpoint, calling for much sacrifice, is needed before we can see the world as "given" by the very nature of the psyche. It is so much more straightforward, more dramatic, impressive, and therefore more convincing, to see all the things that happen to me than to observe how I make them happen. Indeed, the animal nature of man makes him resist seeing himself as the maker of his circumstances. That is why attempts of this kind were always the object of secret initiations, culminating as a rule in a figurative death which symbolized the total character of this reversal. And, in point of fact, the instruction given in the *Bardo Thödol* serves to recall to the dead man the experiences of his initiation and the teachings of his guru, for the instruction is, at bottom, nothing less than an initiation of the dead into the *Bardo* life, just as the initiation of the living was a preparation for the Beyond. Such was the case, at least, with all the mystery cults in ancient civilizations from the time of the Egyptian and Eleusinian mysteries. In the initiation of the living, however, this "Beyond" is not a world beyond death, but a reversal of the mind's intentions and outlook, a psychological "Beyond" or, in Christian terms, a "redemption" from the trammels of the world and of sin. Redemption is a separation and deliverance from an earlier condition of darkness and unconsciousness, and leads to a condition of illumination and releasedness, to victory and transcendence over everything "given."

842   Thus far the *Bardo Thödol* is, as Dr. Evans-Wentz also feels, an initiation process whose purpose it is to restore to the soul the divinity it lost at birth. Now it is a characteristic of Oriental religious literature that the teaching invariably begins with the most important item, with the ultimate and highest principles which, with us, would come last—as for instance in Apuleius, where Lucius is worshipped as Helios only right at the end. Accordingly, in the *Bardo Thödol*, the initiation is a series of diminishing climaxes ending with rebirth in the womb. The

only "initiation process" that is still alive and practised today in the West is the analysis of the unconscious as used by doctors for therapeutic purposes. This penetration into the ground-layers of consciousness is a kind of rational maieutics in the Socratic sense, a bringing forth of psychic contents that are still germinal, subliminal, and as yet unborn. Originally, this therapy took the form of Freudian psychoanalysis and was mainly concerned with sexual fantasies. This is the realm that corresponds to the last and lowest region of the *Bardo,* known as the *Sidpa Bardo,* where the dead man, unable to profit by the teachings of the *Chikhai* and *Chönyid Bardo,* begins to fall a prey to sexual fantasies and is attracted by the vision of mating couples. Eventually he is caught by a womb and born into the earthly world again. Meanwhile, as one might expect, the Oedipus complex starts functioning. If his karma destines him to be reborn as a man, he will fall in love with his mother-to-be and will find his father hateful and disgusting. Conversely, the future daughter will be highly attracted by her father-to-be and repelled by her mother. The European passes through this specifically Freudian domain when his unconscious contents are brought to light under analysis, but he goes in the reverse direction. He journeys back through the world of infantile-sexual fantasy to the womb. It has even been suggested in psychoanalytical circles that the trauma par excellence is the birth-experience it-self—nay more, psychoanalysts even claim to have probed back to memories of intra-uterine origin. Here Western reason reaches its limit, unfortunately. I say "unfortunately," because one rather wishes that Freudian psychoanalysis could have happily pursued these so-called intra-uterine experiences still further back. Had it succeeded in this bold undertaking, it would surely have come out beyond the *Sidpa Bardo* and penetrated from behind into the lower reaches of the *Chönyid Bardo.* It is true that, with the equipment of our existing biological ideas, such a venture would not have been crowned with success; it would have needed a wholly different kind of philosophical preparation from that based on current scientific assumptions. But, had the journey back been consistently pursued, it would undoubt-edly have led to the postulate of a pre-uterine existence, a true *Bardo* life, if only it had been possible to find at least some trace of an experiencing subject. As it was, the psychoanalysts never got beyond purely conjectural traces of intra-uterine experiences, and even the famous "birth trauma" has remained such an obvious truism that it can no longer explain anything, any more than can the hypothesis that life is a disease with a bad prognosis because its outcome is always fatal.

843   Freudian psychoanalysis, in all essential aspects, never went beyond the experiences of the *Sidpa Bardo;* that is, it was unable to extricate itself from sexual fantasies and similar "incompatible" tendencies which cause anxiety and other affective states. Nevertheless, Freud's theory is the first attempt made by the West to investigate, as if from below, from the animal sphere of instinct, the psychic territory that corresponds in Tantric Lamaism to the *Sidpa Bardo.* A very justifiable fear of metaphysics prevented Freud from penetrating into the sphere of the "occult." In addition to this, the *Sidpa* state, if we are to accept the psychology of the *Sidpa Bardo,* is characterized by the fierce wind of karma, which whirls the dead man along until he comes to the "womb-door." In other words, the *Sidpa* state permits of no going back, because it is sealed off against the *Chönyid* state by an intense striving downwards, towards the animal sphere of instinct and physical rebirth. That is to say, anyone who penetrates into the unconscious with purely biological assumptions will become stuck in the instinctual sphere and be unable to advance beyond it, for he will be pulled back again and again into physical existence. It is therefore not possible for Freudian theory to reach anything except an essentially negative valuation of the unconscious. It is a "nothing but." At the same time, it must be admitted that this view of the psyche is typically Western, only it is expressed more blatantly, more plainly, and more ruthlessly than others would have dared to express it, though at bottom they think no differently. As to what "mind" means in this connection, we can only cherish the hope that it will carry conviction. But, as even Max Scheler [2] noted with regret, the power of this "mind" is, to say the least of it, doubtful.

844   I think, then, we can state it as a fact that with the aid of psychoanalysis the rationalizing mind of the West has pushed forward into what one might call the neuroticism of the *Sidpa*

----

[2] [German philosopher and sociologist (1874–1928) working mainly in the field of values.—EDITORS.]

state, and has there been brought to an inevitable standstill by the uncritical assumption that everything psychological is subjective and personal. Even so, this advance has been a great gain, inasmuch as it has enabled us to take one more step behind our conscious lives. This knowledge also gives us a hint of how we ought to read the *Bardo Thödol*—that is, backwards. If, with the help of our Western science, we have to some extent succeeded in understanding the psychological character of the *Sidpa Bardo,* our next task is to see if we can make anything of the preceding *Chönyid Bardo.*

845   The *Chönyid* state is one of karmic illusion—that is to say, illusions which result from the psychic residua of previous existences. According to the Eastern view, karma implies a sort of psychic theory of heredity based on the hypothesis of reincarnation, which in the last resort is an hypothesis of the supratemporality of the soul. Neither our scientific knowledge nor our reason can keep in step with this idea. There are too many if's and but's. Above all, we know desperately little about the possibilities of continued existence of the individual soul after death, so little that we cannot even conceive how anyone could prove anything at all in this respect. Moreover, we know only too well, on epistemological grounds, that such a proof would be just as impossible as the proof of God. Hence we may cautiously accept the idea of karma only if we understand it as *psychic heredity* in the very widest sense of the word. Psychic heredity does exist—that is to say, there is inheritance of psychic characteristics such as predisposition to disease, traits of character, special gifts, and so forth. It does no violence to the psychic nature of these complex facts if natural science reduces them to what appear to be physical aspects (nuclear structures in cells, and so on). They are essential phenomena of life which express themselves, in the main, psychically, just as there are other inherited characteristics which express themselves, in the main, physiologically, on the physical level. Among these inherited psychic factors there is a special class which is not confined either to family or to race. These are the universal dispositions of the mind, and they are to be understood as analogous to Plato's forms (*eidola*), in accordance with which the mind organizes its contents. One could also describe these forms as *categories* analogous to the logical categories which are

always and everywhere present as the basic postulates of reason. Only, in the case of our "forms," we are not dealing with categories of reason but with categories of the *imagination*. As the products of imagination are always in essence visual, their forms must, from the outset, have the character of images and moreover of *typical* images, which is why, following St. Augustine, I call them "archetypes." Comparative religion and mythology are rich mines of archetypes, and so is the psychology of dreams and psychoses. The astonishing parallelism between these images and the ideas they serve to express has frequently given rise to the wildest migration theories, although it would have been far more natural to think of the remarkable similarity of the human psyche at all times and in all places. Archetypal fantasy-forms are, in fact, reproduced spontaneously anytime and anywhere, without there being any conceivable trace of direct transmission. The original structural components of the psyche are of no less surprising a uniformity than are those of the visible body. The archetypes are, so to speak, organs of the pre-rational psyche. They are eternally inherited forms and ideas which have at first no specific content. Their specific content only appears in the course of the individual's life, when personal experience is taken up in precisely these forms. If the archetypes were not pre-existent in identical form everywhere, how could one explain the fact, postulated at almost every turn by the *Bardo Thödol*, that the dead do not know that they are dead, and that this assertion is to be met with just as often in the dreary, half-baked literature of European and American Spiritualism? Although we find the same assertion in Swedenborg, knowledge of his writings can hardly be sufficiently widespread for this little bit of information to have been picked up by every small-town medium. And a connection between Swedenborg and the *Bardo Thödol* is completely unthinkable. It is a primordial, universal idea that the dead simply continue their earthly existence and do not know that they are disembodied spirits—an archetypal idea which enters into immediate, visible manifestation whenever anyone sees a ghost. It is significant, too, that ghosts all over the world have certain features in common. I am naturally aware of the unverifiable spiritualistic hypothesis, though I have no wish to make it my own. I must content myself with the hypothesis of an omnipresent, but differentiated, psychic structure which is inherited and which necessarily gives a certain form and direction to all experience. For, just as the organs of the body are not mere lumps of indifferent, passive matter, but are dynamic, functional complexes which assert themselves with imperious urgency, so also the archetypes, as organs of the psyche, are dynamic, instinctual complexes which determine psychic life to an extraordinary degree. That is why I also call them *dominants* of the unconscious. The layer of unconscious psyche which is made up of these universal dynamic forms I have termed the *collective unconscious*.

846   So far as I know, there is no inheritance of individual prenatal, or pre-uterine, memories, but there are undoubtedly inherited archetypes which are, however, devoid of content, because, to begin with, they contain no personal experiences. They only emerge into consciousness when personal experiences have rendered them visible. As we have seen, *Sidpa* psychology consists in wanting to live and to be born. (The *Sidpa Bardo* is the "*Bardo* of Seeking Rebirth.") Such a state, therefore, precludes any experience of transubjective psychic realities, unless the dead man refuses categorically to be born back again into the world of consciousness. According to the teachings of the *Bardo Thödol*, it is still possible for him, in each of the *Bardo* states, to reach the *Dharmakāya* by transcending the four-faced Mount Meru, provided that he does not yield to his desire to follow the "dim lights." This is as much as to say that the individual must desperately resist the dictates of reason, as we understand it, and give up the supremacy of egohood, regarded by reason as sacrosanct. What this means in practice is complete capitulation to the objective powers of the psyche, with all that this entails; a kind of figurative death, corresponding to the Judgment of the Dead in the *Sidpa Bardo*. It means the end of all conscious, rational, morally responsible conduct of life, and a voluntary surrender to what the *Bardo Thödol* calls "karmic illusion." Karmic illusion springs from belief in a visionary world of an extremely irrational nature, which neither accords with nor derives from our rational judgments but is the exclusive product of uninhibited imagination. It is sheer dream or "fantasy," and every well-meaning person will instantly caution us against it; nor indeed can one

69

see at first sight what is the difference between fantasies of this kind and the phantasmagoria of a lunatic. Very often only a slight *abaissement du niveau mental* is needed to unleash this world of illusion. The terror and darkness of this moment are reflected in the experiences described in the opening sections of the *Sidpa Bardo*. But the contents of the *Chönyid Bardo* reveal the archetypes, the karmic images which appear first in their terrifying form. The *Chönyid* state is equivalent to a deliberately induced psychosis.

847   One often hears and reads about the dangers of yoga, particularly of the ill-reputed *kundalini* yoga. The deliberately induced psychotic state, which in certain unstable individuals might easily lead to a real psychosis, is a danger that needs to be taken very seriously indeed. These things really are dangerous and ought not to be meddled with in our typically Western way. It is a meddling with fate, which strikes at the very roots of human existence and can let loose a flood of sufferings of which no sane person ever dreamed. These sufferings correspond to the hellish torments of the *Chönyid* state, described in the text as follows:

> Then the Lord of Death will place round thy neck a rope and drag thee along; he will cut off thy head, tear out thy heart, pull out thy intestines, lick up thy brain, drink thy blood, eat thy flesh, and gnaw thy bones; but thou wilt be incapable of dying. Even when thy body is hacked to pieces, it will revive again. The repeated hacking will cause intense pain and torture.[3]

848   These tortures aptly describe the real nature of the danger: it is a disintegration of the wholeness of the *Bardo* body, which is a kind of "subtle body" constituting the visible envelope of the psychic self in the after-death state. The psychological equivalent of this dismemberment is psychic dissociation. In its deleterious form it would be schizophrenia (split mind). This most common of all mental illnesses consists essentially in a marked *abaissement du niveau mental* which abolishes the normal checks imposed by the conscious mind and thus gives unlimited scope to the play of the unconscious "dominants."

849   The transition, then, from the *Sidpa* state to the *Chönyid*

3 [Actually from the *Sidpa Bardo* section (p. 166), but similar torments figure in the "Wrathful Deities" section (pp. 131ff.) of the *Chönyid Bardo*.—EDITORS.]

state is a dangerous reversal of the aims and intentions of the conscious mind. It is a sacrifice of the ego's stability and a surrender to the extreme uncertainty of what must seem like a chaotic riot of phantasmal forms. When Freud coined the phrase that the ego was "the true seat of anxiety," he was giving voice to a very true and profound intuition. Fear of self-sacrifice lurks deep in every ego, and this fear is often only the precariously controlled demand of the unconscious forces to burst out in full strength. No one who strives for selfhood (individuation) is spared this dangerous passage, for that which is feared also belongs to the wholeness of the self—the sub-human, or supra-human, world of psychic "dominants" from which the ego originally emancipated itself with enormous effort, and then only partially, for the sake of a more or less illusory freedom. This liberation is certainly a very necessary and very heroic undertaking, but it represents nothing final: it is merely the creation of a *subject,* who, in order to find fulfilment, has still to be confronted by an *object.* This, at first sight, would appear to be the world, which is swelled out with projections for that very purpose. Here we seek and find our difficulties, here we seek and find our enemy, here we seek and find what is dear and precious to us; and it is comforting to know that all evil and all good is to be found out there, in the visible object, where it can be conquered, punished, destroyed, or enjoyed. But nature herself does not allow this paradisal state of innocence to continue for ever. There are, and always have been, those who cannot help but see that the world and its experiences are in the nature of a symbol, and that it really reflects something that lies hidden in the subject himself, in his own transubjective reality. It is from this profound intuition, according to lamaist doctrine, that the *Chönyid* state derives its true meaning, which is why the *Chönyid Bardo* is entitled "The *Bardo* of the Experiencing of Reality."

850   The reality experienced in the *Chönyid* state is, as the last section [pp. 143ff.] of this *Bardo* teaches, the reality of thought. The "thought-forms" appear as realities, fantasy takes on real form, and the terrifying dream evoked by karma and played out by the unconscious "dominants" begins. The first to appear (if we read the text backwards) is the all-destroying God of Death, the epitome of all terrors; he is followed by the

twenty-eight "power-holding" and sinister goddesses and the fifty-eight "blood-drinking" goddesses. In spite of their demonic aspect, which appears as a confusing chaos of terrifying attributes and monstrosities, a certain order is already discernible. We find that there are companies of gods and goddesses who are arranged according to the four directions and are distinguished by typical mystic colours. It gradually becomes clearer that all these deities are organized into mandalas, or circles, containing a cross of the four colours. The colours are coordinated with the four aspects of wisdom:

(1) White = the light-path of the mirror-like wisdom;
(2) Yellow = the light-path of the wisdom of equality;
(3) Red = the light-path of the discriminative wisdom;
(4) Green = the light-path of the all-performing wisdom.

851   On a higher level of insight, the dead man knows that the real thought-forms all emanate from himself, and that the four light-paths of wisdom which appear before him are the radiations of his own psychic faculties. This takes us straight to the psychology of the lamaistic mandala, which I have already discussed in the book I brought out with the late Richard Wilhelm, *The Secret of the Golden Flower.*

852   Continuing our ascent backwards through the region of the *Chönyid Bardo,* we come finally to the vision of the Four Great Ones: the green Amogha-Siddhi, the red Amitābha, the yellow Ratna-Sambhava, and the white Vajra-Sattva. The ascent ends with the effulgent blue light of the *Dharmadhātu,* the Buddha-body, which glows in the midst of the mandala from the heart of Vairochana.

853   With this final vision the karmic illusions cease; consciousness, weaned away from all form and from all attachment to objects, returns to the timeless, inchoate state of the *Dharma-kāya.* Thus (reading backwards) the *Chikhai* state, which appeared at the moment of death, is reached.

854   I think these few hints will suffice to give the attentive reader some idea of the psychology of the *Bardo Thödol.* The book describes a way of initiation in reverse, which, unlike the eschatological expectations of Christianity, prepares the soul for a descent into physical being. The thoroughly intellectualistic and rationalistic worldly-mindedness of the European makes it advisable for us to reverse the sequence of the *Bardo Thödol* and

to regard it as an account of Eastern initiation experiences, though one is perfectly free, if one chooses, to substitute Christian symbols for the gods of the *Chönyid Bardo*. At any rate, the sequence of events as I have described it offers a close parallel to the phenomenology of the European unconscious when it is undergoing an "initiation process," that is to say, when it is being analysed. The transformation of the unconscious that occurs under analysis makes it the natural analogue of the religious initiation ceremonies, which do, however, differ in principle from the natural process in that they anticipate the natural course of development and substitute for the spontaneous production of symbols a deliberately selected set of symbols prescribed by tradition. We can see this in the *Exercitia* of Ignatius Loyola, or in the yoga meditations of the Buddhists and Tantrists.

855   The reversal of the order of the chapters, which I have suggested here as an aid to understanding, in no way accords with the original intention of the *Bardo Thödol*. Nor is the psychological use we make of it anything but a secondary intention, though one that is possibly sanctioned by lamaist custom. The real purpose of this singular book is the attempt, which must seem very strange to the educated European of the twentieth century, to enlighten the dead on their journey through the regions of the *Bardo*. The Catholic Church is the only place in the world of the white man where any provision is made for the souls of the departed. Inside the Protestant camp, with its world-affirming optimism, we only find a few mediumistic "rescue circles," whose main concern is to make the dead aware of the fact that they *are* dead.[4] But, generally speaking, we have nothing in the West that is in any way comparable to the *Bardo Thödol*, except for certain secret writings which are inaccessible to the wider public and to the ordinary scientist. According to tradition, the *Bardo Thödol*, too, seems to have been included among the "hidden" books, as Dr. Evans-Wentz makes clear in his Introduction. As such, it forms a special chapter in the magical "cure of the soul" which extends even beyond death. This cult of the dead is rationally based on the belief in the supra-temporality of the soul, but its irrational basis is to be found in the psychological need of the living to do something for the de-

4 Information on this spiritualistic activity will be found in Lord Dowding's writings: *Many Mansions* (1943), *Lychgate* (1945), *God's Magic* (1946).

parted. This is an elementary need which forces itself upon even the most "enlightened" individuals when faced by the death of relatives and friends. That is why, enlightenment or no enlightenment, we still have all manner of ceremonies for the dead. If Lenin had to submit to being embalmed and put on show in a sumptuous mausoleum like an Egyptian pharaoh, we may be quite sure it was not because his followers believed in the resurrection of the body. Apart, however, from the Masses said for the soul in the Catholic Church, the provisions we make for the dead are rudimentary and on the lowest level, not because we cannot convince ourselves of the soul's immortality, but because we have rationalized the above-mentioned psychological need out of existence. We behave as if we did not have this need, and because we cannot believe in a life after death we prefer to do nothing about it. Simpler-minded people follow their own feelings, and, as in Italy, build themselves funeral monuments of gruesome beauty. The Catholic Masses for the soul are on a level considerably above this, because they are expressly intended for the psychic welfare of the deceased and are not a mere gratification of lachrymose sentiments. But the highest application of spiritual effort on behalf of the departed is surely to be found in the instructions of the *Bardo Thödol*. They are so detailed and thoroughly adapted to the apparent changes in the dead man's condition that every serious-minded reader must ask himself whether these wise old lamas might not, after all, have caught a glimpse of the fourth dimension and twitched the veil from the greatest of life's secrets.

856   Even if the truth should prove to be a disappointment, one almost feels tempted to concede at least some measure of reality to the vision of life in the *Bardo*. At any rate, it is unexpectedly original, if nothing else, to find the after-death state, of which our religious imagination has formed the most grandiose conceptions, painted in lurid colours as a terrifying dream-state of a progressively degenerative character.[5] The supreme vision comes not at the end of the *Bardo*, but right at the beginning, at the moment of death; what happens afterward is an ever-deepening descent into illusion and obscuration, down to the ultimate degradation of new physical birth. The spiritual

[5] A similar view in Aldous Huxley, *Time Must Have a Stop* (1945).

climax is reached at the moment when life ends. Human life, therefore, is the vehicle of the highest perfection it is possible to attain; it alone generates the karma that makes it possible for the dead man to abide in the perpetual light of the Voidness without clinging to any object, and thus to rest on the hub of the wheel of rebirth, freed from all illusion of genesis and decay. Life in the *Bardo* brings no eternal rewards or punishments, but merely a descent into a new life which shall bear the individual nearer to his final goal. But this eschatological goal is what he himself brings to birth as the last and highest fruit of the labours and aspirations of earthly existence. This view is not only lofty, it is manly and heroic.

857   The degenerative character of *Bardo* life is corroborated by the spiritualistic literature of the West, which again and again gives one a sickening impression of the utter inanity and banality of communications from the "spirit world." The scientific mind does not hesitate to explain these reports as emanations from the unconscious of the mediums and of those taking part in the séance, and even to extend this explanation to the description of the Hereafter given in the Tibetan Book of the Dead. And it is an undeniable fact that the whole book is created out of the archetypal contents of the unconscious. Behind these there lie—and in this our Western reason is quite right— no physical or metaphysical realities, but "merely" the reality of psychic facts, the data of psychic experience. Now whether a thing is "given" subjectively or objectively, the fact remains that it *is*. The *Bardo Thödol* says no more than this, for its five Dhyāni-Buddhas are themselves no more than psychic data. That is just what the dead man has to recognize, if it has not already become clear to him during life that his own psychic self and the giver of all data are one and the same. The world of gods and spirits is truly "nothing but" the collective unconscious inside me. To turn this sentence round so that it reads "The collective unconscious is the world of gods and spirits outside me," no intellectual acrobatics are needed, but a whole human lifetime, perhaps even many lifetimes of increasing completeness. Notice that I do not say "of increasing perfection," because those who are "perfect" make another kind of discovery altogether.

858   The *Bardo Thödol* began by being a "closed" book, and so it has remained, no matter what kind of commentaries may be written upon it. For it is a book that will only open itself to spiritual understanding, and this is a capacity which no man is born with, but which he can only acquire through special training and special experience. It is good that such to all intents and purposes "useless" books exist. They are meant for those "queer folk" who no longer set much store by the uses, aims, and meaning of present-day "civilization."

YOGA AND THE WEST [1]

859   Less than a century has passed since yoga became known to
the West. Although all sorts of miraculous tales had come to
Europe two thousand years before from the fabled land of India,
with its wise men, its gymnosophists and omphalosceptics, yet
no real knowledge of Indian philosophy and philosophical practices can be said to have existed until, thanks to the efforts of
the Frenchman, Anquetil du Perron, the Upanishads were transmitted to the West. A general and more profound knowledge
was first made possible by Max Müller, of Oxford, and the
Sacred Books of the East edited by him. To begin with, this
knowledge remained the preserve of Sanskrit scholars and philosophers. But it was not so very long before the theosophical
movement inaugurated by Mme. Blavatsky possessed itself of
the Eastern traditions and promulgated them among the general public. For several decades after that, knowledge of yoga
in the West developed along two separate lines. On the one
hand it was regarded as a strictly academic science, and on the
other it became something very like a religion, though it did not
develop into an organized Church—despite the endeavours of
Annie Besant and Rudolf Steiner. Although he was the founder
of the anthroposophical secession, Steiner was originally a fol-
lower of Mme. Blavatsky.

1 [Originally published in *Prabuddha Bharata* (Calcutta), February 1936, Shri
Ramakrishna Centenary Number, Sec. III, in a translation by Cary F. Baynes,
upon which the present translation is based.—EDITORS.]

77

860   The peculiar product resulting from this Western development can hardly be compared with what yoga means in India.
In the West, Eastern teaching encountered a special situation,
a condition of mind such as the earlier India, at any rate, had
never known. This was the strict line of division between science and philosophy, which had already existed, to a greater or
lesser degree, for some three hundred years before yoga teachings
began to be known in the West. The beginning of this split—
a specifically Western phenomenon—really set in with the
Renaissance, in the fifteenth century. At that time, there arose
a widespread and passionate interest in antiquity, stimulated by
the fall of the Byzantine Empire under the onslaught of Islam.
Then, for the first time, knowledge of the Greek language and
of Greek literature was carried to every corner of Europe. As a
direct result of this invasion of so-called pagan philosophy, there
arose the great schism in the Roman Church—Protestantism,
which soon covered the whole of northern Europe. But not even
this renewal of Christianity was able to hold the liberated minds
in thrall.

861   The period of world discovery in the geographical and scientific sense had begun, and to an ever-increasing degree thought
emancipated itself from the shackles of religious tradition. The
Churches, of course, continued to exist because they were maintained by the strictly religious needs of the public, but they lost
their leadership in the cultural sphere. While the Church of
Rome, thanks to her unsurpassed organization, remained a
unity, Protestantism split into nearly four hundred denomina-
tions. This is a proof on the one hand of its bankruptcy, and,
on the other, of a religious vitality which refuses to be stifled.
Gradually, in the course of the nineteenth century, this led to
syncretistic outgrowths and to the importation on a mass scale
of exotic religious systems, such as the religion of Abdul Baha,
the Sufi sects, the Ramakrishna Mission, Buddhism, and so on.
Many of these systems, for instance anthroposophy, were syn-
cretized with Christian elements. The resultant picture corresponds roughly to the Hellenistic syncretism of the third and
fourth centuries A.D., which likewise showed traces of Indian
thought. (Cf. Apollonius of Tyana, the Orphic-Pythagorean
secret doctrines, the Gnosis, etc.)

862   All these systems moved on the religious plane and recruited

the great majority of their adherents from Protestantism. They are thus, fundamentally, Protestant sects. By directing its main attack against the authority of the Roman Church, Protestantism largely destroyed belief in the Church as the indispensable agent of divine salvation. Thus the burden of authority fell to the individual, and with it a religious responsibility that had never existed before. The decline of confession and absolution sharpened the moral conflict of the individual and burdened him with problems which previously the Church had settled for him, since her sacraments, particularly that of the Mass, guaranteed his salvation through the priest's enactment of the sacred rite. The only things the individual had to contribute were confession, repentance, and penance. With the collapse of the rite, which did the work for him, he had to do without God's answer to his plans. This dissatisfaction explains the demand for systems that promise an answer—the visible or at least noticeable favour of another (higher, spiritual, or divine) power.

863   European science paid no attention to these hopes and expectations. It lived its intellectual life unconcerned with religious needs and convictions. This—historically inevitable —split in the Western mind also affected yoga so far as this had gained a footing in the West, and led to its being made an object of scientific study on the one hand, while on the other it was welcomed as a way of salvation. But inside the religious movement there were any number of attempts to combine science with religious belief and practice, as for instance Christian Science, theosophy, and anthroposophy. The last-named, especially, likes to give itself scientific airs and has, therefore, like Christian Science, penetrated into intellectual circles.

864   Since the way of the Protestant is not laid down for him in advance, he gives welcome, one might say, to practically any system which holds out the promise of successful development. He must now do for himself the very thing which had always been done by the Church as intermediary, and he does not know *how* to do it. If he is a man who has taken his religious needs seriously, he has also made untold efforts towards faith, because his doctrine sets exclusive store by faith. But faith is a charisma, a gift of grace, and not a method. The Protestant is so entirely without a method that many of them have seriously interested themselves in the rigorously Catholic exercises of Ignatius

Loyola. Yet, do what they will, the thing that disturbs them most is naturally the contradiction between religious and scientific truth, the conflict between faith and knowledge, which reaches far beyond Protestantism into Catholicism itself. This conflict is due solely to the historical split in the European mind. Had it not been for the—psychologically speaking—unnatural compulsion to believe, and an equally unnatural belief in science, this conflict would have had no reason to exist. One can easily imagine a state of mind in which one simply *knows* and in addition *believes* a thing which seems probable for such and such reasons. There are no grounds whatsoever for any conflict between these two things. Both are necessary, for knowledge alone, like faith alone, is always insufficient.

865   When, therefore, a "religious" method recommends itself at the same time as "scientific," it can be sure of finding a public in the West. Yoga fulfils this expectation. Quite apart from the charm of the new and the fascination of the half-understood, there is good reason for yoga to have many adherents. It offers not only the much-sought way, but also a philosophy of unrivalled profundity. It holds out the possibility of controllable experience, and thus satisfies the scientist's need for "facts." Moreover, by reason of its breadth and depth, its venerable age, its teachings and methods which cover every sphere of life, it promises undreamt of possibilities which the missionaries of yoga seldom omit to emphasize.

866   I will remain silent on the subject of what yoga means for India, because I cannot presume to judge something I do not know from personal experience. I can, however, say something about what it means for the West. Our lack of direction borders on psychic anarchy. Therefore, any religious or philosophical practice amounts to a psychological discipline; in other words, it is a method of psychic hygiene. The numerous purely physical procedures of yoga are a physiological hygiene as well, which is far superior to ordinary gymnastics or breathing exercises in that it is not merely mechanistic and scientific but, at the same time, philosophical. In its training of the parts of the body, it unites them with the whole of the mind and spirit, as is quite clear, for instance, in the *prānayāma* exercises, where *prāna* is both the breath and the universal dynamics of the cosmos. When the doing of the individual is at the same time a cosmic happen-

ing, the elation of the body (innervation) becomes one with the elation of the spirit (the universal idea), and from this there arises a living whole which no technique, however scientific, can hope to produce. Yoga practice is unthinkable, and would also be ineffectual, without the ideas on which it is based. It works the physical and the spiritual into one another in an extraordinarily complete way.

867 In the East, where these ideas and practices originated, and where an uninterrupted tradition extending over some four thousand years has created the necessary spiritual conditions, yoga is, as I can readily believe, the perfect and appropriate method of fusing body and mind together so that they form a unity that can hardly be doubted. They thus create a psychological disposition which makes possible intuitions that transcend consciousness. The Indian mentality has no difficulty in operating intelligently with a concept like *prāna*. The West, on the contrary, with its bad habit of wanting to believe on the one hand, and its highly developed scientific and philosophical critique on the other, finds itself in a real dilemma. Either it falls into the trap of faith and swallows concepts like *prāna, atman, chakra, samādhi,* etc., without giving them a thought, or its scientific critique repudiates them one and all as "pure mysticism." The split in the Western mind therefore makes it impossible at the outset for the intentions of yoga to be realized in any adequate way. It becomes either a strictly religious matter, or else a kind of training like Pelmanism, breath-control, eurhythmics, etc., and not a trace is to be found of the unity and wholeness of nature which is characteristic of yoga. The Indian can forget neither the body nor the mind, while the European is always forgetting either the one or the other. With this capacity to forget he has, for the time being, conquered the world. Not so the Indian. He not only knows his own nature, but he knows also how much he himself is nature. The European, on the other hand, has a science of nature and knows astonishingly little of his own nature, the nature within him. For the Indian, it comes as a blessing to know of a method which helps him to control the supreme power of nature within and without. For the European, it is sheer poison to suppress his nature, which is warped enough as it is, and to make out of it a willing robot.

868 It is said of the yogi that he can remove mountains, though

81

it would be difficult to furnish any real proof of this. The power of the yogi operates within limits acceptable to his environment. The European, on the other hand, can blow up mountains, and the World War has given us a bitter foretaste of what he is capable of when free rein is given to an intellect that has grown estranged from human nature. As a European, I cannot wish the European more "control" and more power over the nature within and around us. Indeed, I must confess to my shame that I owe my best insights (and there are some quite good ones among them) to the circumstance that I have always done just the opposite of what the rules of yoga prescribe. Through his historical development, the European has become so far removed from his roots that his mind was finally split into faith and knowledge, in the same way that every psychological exaggeration breaks up into its inherent opposites. He needs to return, not to Nature in the manner of Rousseau, but to his own nature. His task is to find the natural man again. Instead of this, there is nothing he likes better than systems and methods by which he can repress the natural man who is everywhere at cross purposes with him. He will infallibly make a wrong use of yoga because his psychic disposition is quite different from that of the Oriental. I say to whomsoever I can: "Study yoga—you will learn an infinite amount from it—but do not try to apply it, for we Europeans are not so constituted that we apply these methods correctly, just like that. An Indian guru can explain everything and you can imitate everything. But do you know *who* is applying the yoga? In other words, do you know who you are and how you are constituted?"

869   The power of science and technics in Europe is so enormous and indisputable that there is little point in reckoning up all that can be done and all that has been invented. One shudders at the stupendous possibilities. Quite another question begins to loom up: *Who* is applying this technical skill? in *whose* hands does this power lie? For the present, the state is a provisional means of protection, because, apparently, it safeguards the citizen from the enormous quantities of poison gas and other infernal engines of destruction which can be manufactured by the thousand tons at a moment's notice. Our technical skill has grown to be so dangerous that the most urgent question today is not what *more* can be done in this line, but how the man who is

entrusted with the control of this skill should be constituted, or how to alter the mind of Western man so that he would renounce his terrible skill. It is infinitely more important to strip him of the illusion of his power than to strengthen him still further in the mistaken idea that he can do everything he wills. The slogan one hears so often in Germany, "Where there's a will there's a way," has cost the lives of millions of human beings.

870 Western man has no need of more superiority over nature, whether outside or inside. He has both in almost devilish perfection. What he lacks is conscious recognition of his inferiority to the nature around and within him. He must learn that he may not do exactly as he wills. If he does not learn this, his own nature will destroy him. He does not know that his own soul is rebelling against him in a suicidal way.

871 Since Western man can turn everything into a technique, it is true in principle that everything that looks like a method is either dangerous or condemned to futility. In so far as yoga is a form of hygiene, it is as useful to him as any other system. In the deepest sense, however, yoga does not mean this but, if I understand it correctly, a great deal more, namely the final release and detachment of consciousness from all bondage to object and subject. But since one cannot detach oneself from something of which one is unconscious, the European must first learn to know his subject. This, in the West, is what one calls the unconscious. Yoga technique applies itself exclusively to the conscious mind and will. Such an undertaking promises success only when the unconscious has no potential worth mentioning, that is to say, when it does not contain large portions of the personality. If it does, then all conscious effort remains futile, and what comes out of this cramped condition of mind is a caricature or even the exact opposite of the intended result.

872 The rich metaphysic and symbolism of the East express the larger and more important part of the unconscious and in this way reduce its potential. When the yogi says "prāna," he means very much more than mere breath. For him the word *prāna* brings with it the full weight of its metaphysical components, and it is as if he really knew what prāna meant in this respect. He does not know it with his understanding, but with his heart, belly, and blood. The European only imitates and learns ideas

by rote, and is therefore incapable of expressing his subjective facts through Indian concepts. I am more than doubtful whether the European, if he were capable of the corresponding experiences, would choose to express them through intuitive ideas like prāna.

873   Yoga was originally a natural process of introversion, with all manner of individual variations. Introversions of this sort lead to peculiar inner processes which change the personality. In the course of several thousand years these introversions became organized as methods, and along widely differing lines. Indian yoga itself recognizes numerous and extremely diverse forms. The reason for this lies in the original diversity of individual experience. This is not to say that any one of these methods is suited to the peculiar historical structure of the European. It is much more likely that the yoga natural to the European proceeds from historical patterns unknown to the East. As a matter of fact, the two cultural achievements which, in the West, have had to concern themselves most with the psyche in the practical sense, namely medicine and the Catholic cure of souls, have both produced methods comparable to yoga. I have already referred to the exercises of Ignatius Loyola. With respect to medicine, it is the modern psychotherapeutic methods which come closest to yoga. Freud's psychoanalysis leads the conscious mind of the patient back to the inner world of childhood reminiscences on one side, and on the other to wishes and drives which have been repressed from consciousness. The latter technique is a logical development of confession. It aims at an artificial introversion for the purpose of making conscious the unconscious components of the subject.

874   A somewhat different method is the so-called "autogenic training" of Professor Schultz,[2] which consciously links up with yoga. His chief aim is to break down the conscious cramp and the repression of the unconscious this has caused.

875   My method, like Freud's, is built up on the practice of confession. Like him, I pay close attention to dreams, but when it comes to the unconscious our views part company. For Freud it is essentially an appendage of consciousness, in which all the individual's incompatibilities are heaped up. For me the un-

[2] [The German psychiatrist J. H. Schultz. The reference is to his book *Das autogene Training* (Berlin, 1932).—EDITORS.]

conscious is a collective psychic disposition, creative in character. This fundamental difference of viewpoint naturally produces an entirely different evaluation of the symbolism and the method of interpreting it. Freud's procedure is, in the main, analytical and reductive. To this I add a synthesis which emphasizes the purposiveness of unconscious tendencies with respect to personality development. In this line of research important parallels with yoga have come to light, especially with *kundalini* yoga and the symbolism of tantric yoga, lamaism, and Taoistic yoga in China. These forms of yoga with their rich symbolism afford me invaluable comparative material for interpreting the collective unconscious. However, I do not apply yoga methods in principle, because, in the West, nothing ought to be forced on the unconscious. Usually, consciousness is characterized by an intensity and narrowness that have a cramping effect, and this ought not to be emphasized still further. On the contrary, everything must be done to help the unconscious to reach the conscious mind and to free it from its rigidity. For this purpose I employ a method of active imagination, which consists in a special training for switching off consciousness, at least to a relative extent, thus giving the unconscious contents a chance to develop.

876   If I remain so critically averse to yoga, it does not mean that I do not regard this spiritual achievement of the East as one of the greatest things the human mind has ever created. I hope my exposition makes it sufficiently clear that my criticism is directed solely against the application of yoga to the peoples of the West. The spiritual development of the West has been along entirely different lines from that of the East and has therefore produced conditions which are the most unfavourable soil one can think of for the application of yoga. Western civilization is scarcely a thousand years old and must first of all free itself from its barbarous one-sidedness. This means, above all, deeper insight into the nature of man. But no insight is gained by repressing and controlling the unconscious, and least of all by imitating methods which have grown up under totally different psychological conditions. In the course of the centuries the West will produce its own yoga, and it will be on the basis laid down by Christianity.

THE DREAMLIKE WORLD OF INDIA [1]

981   A first impression of a country is very often like meeting a person for the first time: your impression may be quite inaccurate, even definitely wrong in many respects, yet you are likely to perceive certain qualities or certain shadows which would very probably be blurred by the more accurate impressions of a second or third visit. My reader would make a great mistake if he were to take any statements I make about India for gospel truth. Think of a man coming to Europe for the first time in his life; he spends some six to seven weeks travelling from Lisbon to Moscow and from Norway to Sicily, he does not understand a single European language except English and he has a most superficial knowledge of the peoples, their history, and their actual life. Would he be likely to produce anything more than a mildly delirious phantasmagoria of hasty impressions, snapshot sentiments, and impatient opinions? I am afraid he would have little chance of escaping the charge of utter incompetence and inadequacy. I am very much in the same position in daring to say anything about India. I am told that I have the excuse of being a psychologist, and therefore am supposed to see more, or at least something peculiar which other fellows might be expected to overlook. I do not know. I must leave the final verdict to my reader.

982   The flat expanse of Bombay and its low dark green hills, rising almost suddenly above the horizon, give you the feeling of the vastness of a continent behind. This impression explains my first reaction directly I disembarked: I took a car and went out of town, away into the country. That felt a great deal better—yellow grass, dusty fields, native huts, great, dark-green, weird banyan trees, sickly palmyra palms sucked dry of their life-juice

1 [Written in English and first published in *Asia* (New York), XXXIX (1939):1, 5–8. —EDITORS.]

(it is run into bottles near the top to make palm-wine, which I never tasted), emaciated cattle, thin-legged men, the colourful saris of women, all in leisurely haste or in hasty leisure, with no need of being explained or of explaining themselves, because obviously they are what they are. They were unconcerned and unimpressed; I was the only one who did not belong to India. We drove through a strip of jungle near a blue lake. We pulled up suddenly, but instead of having run over a lurking tiger we found ourselves in the midst of a native movie-scene: something presumably was going to happen to a white girl, dressed up as a *dompteuse* escaped from a circus. Cameras, megaphone, and excited shirt-sleeves were in full action—the shock was so great that we instinctively stepped on the gas. After this I felt that I could go back to the city, which I had not yet really seen.

983   The Anglo-Indian style of architecture of the past fifty years is not interesting, but it gives a peculiar character to Bombay, as if one had already seen it somewhere else. It has more to do with the "English character" than with India. I make an exception of the "Gateway of India," that huge portal at the head of the royal road to Delhi. In a way it repeats the splendid ambition to be found in the "Gate of Victory," built by Akbar the Great in Fatehpur-Sikri, that soon-deserted town lying in ruins— red sandstone glowing in the Indian sun for long centuries, past and to come—a wave that crashed on the shore of time and left a strip of foam.

984   That is India, as I saw her: certain things last forever— yellow plains, green spirit-trees, dark-brown boulders of gigantic size, emerald-green watered fields, crowned by that metaphysical fringe of ice and rock away up north, that inexorable barrier beyond human conception. The other things unroll like a film, unimaginably rich in colour and shape, ever-changing, lasting a few days or a few centuries, but essentially transitory, dreamlike, a multi-coloured veil of *maya*. Today it is the still youthful British Empire that is going to leave a mark on India, like the empire of the Moguls, like Alexander the Great, like number- less dynasties of native kings, like the Aryan invaders—yet India somehow never changes her majestic face. Human life appears to be curiously flimsy in every respect. The native town of Bombay seems to be a jumble of incidentally piled-up human habitations. The people carry on an apparently meaningless life,

eagerly, busily, noisily. They die and are born in ceaseless waves, always much the same, a gigantic monotony of endlessly repeated life.

985   In all that flimsiness and vain tumult, one is conscious of immeasurable age with no history. After all why should there be recorded history? In a country like India one does not really miss it. All her native greatness is in any case anonymous and impersonal, like the greatness of Babylon and Egypt. History makes sense in European countries, where, in a relatively recent, barbarous, and unhistorical past, things began to take shape. Castles, temples, and cities were built, roads and bridges were made, and the peoples discovered that they had names, that they lived somewhere, that their cities multiplied and that their world grew bigger every century. When they saw that things developed, they naturally became interested in the changes of things, and it seemed worth while to record beginnings and later developments—for everything was going somewhere, and everybody hoped for unheard-of possibilities and improvements in the future, spiritual as well as secular.

986   But in India there seems to be nothing that has not lived a hundred thousand times before. Even the unique individual of today has already lived innumerable times in past ages. The world itself is nothing but a renewal of world existence, which has happened many times before. Even India's greatest individual, the unique Gautama Buddha, was preceded by more than a score of other Buddhas and is still not the last. No wonder, then, that the gods too have their numerous avatars. *Plus ça change, plus c'est la même chose*—why any history under such circumstances? Moreover, time is relative: the yogi sees the past as well as the future. If you walk the "noble eightfold path," you will remember what you were ten thousand lives ago. Space is relative: the yogi walks in his spirit-body with the speed of thought over lands, seas, and heavens. What you call real—all the good and ill of human life—is illusion. What you call unreal —sentimental, grotesque, obscene, monstrous, blood-curdling gods—unexpectedly becomes self-evident reality when you listen for half a hot night to an incessant, clever drumming that shakes up the dormant solar plexus of the European. He is used to regarding his head as the only instrument for grasping the world, and the *kathakali*, as he follows it with his eyes, would remain

a grotesque dance were it not for the drumming that creates a new reality rising from the bowels.

987   A walk through the bustle of Bombay's bazaars set me thinking. I had felt the impact of the dreamlike world of India. I am convinced that the average Hindu does not feel his world as dreamlike: on the contrary, his every reaction shows how much he is impressed and gripped by its realities. If he were not enthralled by his world, he would not need his religious and philosophic teaching about the Great Illusion, any more than we ourselves would need the Christian message of love if we were other than we are. (The essence of teaching is to convey knowledge of things about which we know too little!) Perhaps I myself had been thrown into a dreamlike state by moving among fairytale figures of the Thousand and One Nights. My own world of European consciousness had become peculiarly thin, like a network of telegraph wires high above the ground, stretching in straight lines all over the surface of an earth looking treacherously like a geographic globe.

988   It is quite possible that India is the real world, and that the white man lives in a madhouse of abstractions. To be born, to die, to be sick, greedy, dirty, childish, ridiculously vain, miserable, hungry, vicious; to be manifestly stuck in illiterate unconsciousness, to be suspended in a narrow universe of good and evil gods and to be protected by charms and helpful *mantras,* that is perhaps the real life, life as it was meant to be, the life of the earth. Life in India has not yet withdrawn into the capsule of the head. It is still the whole body that lives. No wonder the European feels dreamlike: the complete life of India is something of which he merely dreams. When you walk with naked feet, how can you ever forget the earth? It needs all the acrobatics of the higher yoga to make you unconscious of the earth. One would need some sort of yoga if one tried seriously to live in India. But I did not see one European in India who really lived there. They were all living in Europe, that is, in a sort of bottle filled with European air. One would surely go under without the insulating glass wall; one would be drowned in all the things which we Europeans have conquered in our imagination. In India they become formidable realities directly you step beyond the glass wall.

*

989   Northern India is characterized by the fact that it is part of
the immense Asiatic continent. I noticed a frequent note of
harshness in the way the people talked to each other, recalling
harassed camel-drivers or irritable horse-dealers. The variety of
Asiatic costumes here supersedes the immaculate whiteness of
the mild plant-eaters. Women's dresses are gay and provocative.
The many Pathans, proud, unconcerned, and ruthless, and the
bearded Sikhs, with their contradictory character—over-mascu-
line brutality combined with melting sentimentality—give a
strong Asiatic tinge to the appearance of the masses. The architecture shows clearly how much the Hindu element has succumbed to the predominating Asiatic influence. Even the
temples of Benares are small and not very impressive, if it were
not for their noisiness and dirt. Shiva, the destroyer, and the
bloodthirsty and blood-curdling Kali seem to be in the foreground. The fat, elephant-headed Ganesha is also much in demand to bring good luck.

990   In comparison, Islam seems to be a superior, more spiritual,
and more advanced religion. Its mosques are pure and beautiful,
and of course wholly Asiatic. There is not much mind about it,
but a great deal of feeling. The cult is one wailing outcry for
the All-Merciful. It is a desire, an ardent longing and even greed
for God; I would not call it love. But there is love, the most
poetic, most exquisite love of beauty in these old Moguls. In a
world of tyranny and cruelty, a heavenly dream crystallized in
stone: the Taj Mahal. I cannot conceal my unmitigated admiration for this supreme flower, for this jewel beyond price, and I
marvel at that love which discovered the genius of Shah Jehan
and used it as an instrument of self-realization. This is the one
place in the world where the—alas—all too invisible and all too
jealously guarded beauty of the Islamic Eros has been revealed
by a well-nigh divine miracle. It is the delicate secret of the
rose gardens of Shiraz and of the silent patios of Arabian palaces,
torn out of the heart of a great lover by a cruel and incurable
loss. The mosques of the Moguls and their tombs may be pure
and austere, their *divans,* or audience halls, may be of impec-
cable beauty, but the Taj Mahal is a revelation. It is thoroughly
un-Indian. It is more like a plant that could thrive and flower
in the rich Indian earth as it could nowhere else. It is Eros in
its purest form; there is nothing mysterious, nothing symbolic

about it. It is the sublime expression of human love for a human being.

991   On the same plains of Northern India, almost two thousand years before the time of the Moguls, the spirit of India had borne its ripest fruit, the very essence of its life, the perfect Lord Buddha. Not very far from Agra and Delhi is the hill of Sanchi with its famous stupa. We were there on a brisk morning. The intense light and the extraordinary clarity of the air brought out every detail. There on the top of a rocky hill, with a distant view over the plains of India, you behold a huge globe of masonry, half-buried in the earth. According to the *Maha-Parinibbana-Sutta,* Buddha himself indicated the way in which his remains were to be buried. He took two rice bowls and covered the one with the other. The visible stupa is just the bowl on top. One has to imagine the lower one, buried in the earth. The roundness, a symbol of perfection since olden days, seems a suitable as well as an expressive monument for a Tathagata. It is of immense simplicity, austerity, and lucidity, perfectly in keeping with the simplicity, austerity, and lucidity of Buddha's teaching.

992   There is something unspeakably solemn about this place in its exalted loneliness, as if it were still witnessing the moment in the history of India when the greatest genius of her race formulated her supreme truth. This place, together with its architecture, its silence, and its peace beyond all turmoils of the heart, its very forgetfulness of human emotions, is truly and essentially Indian; it is as much the "secret" of India as the Taj Mahal is the secret of Islam. And just as the perfume of Islamic culture still lingers in the air, so Buddha, though forgotten on the surface, is still the secret breath of life in modern Hinduism. He is suffered at least to be an avatar of Vishnu.

*

993   Travelling with the British delegates to the Indian Science Congress in Calcutta, I was hustled through a good many dinners and receptions. I had a chance at these to talk to educated Indian women. This was a novelty. Their costume stamps them as women. It is the most becoming, the most stylish and, at the same time, the most meaningful dress ever devised by women. I hope fervently that the sexual disease of the West, which tries to transform woman into a sort of awkward boy, will not creep into

India in the wake of that fad "scientific education." It would be a loss to the whole world if the Indian woman should cease to wear her native costume. India (and perhaps China, which I do not know) is practically the only civilized country where one can see on living models how women can and should dress.

994   The costume of the Indian woman conveys far more than the meaningless half-nakedness of the Western woman's evening dress. There is something left which can be unveiled or revealed, and, on the other hand, one's taste is not offended by the sight of aesthetic flaws. The European evening dress is one of the most obvious symptoms of our sexual morbidity: it is compounded of shamelessness, exhibitionism, impotent provocation, and a ridiculous attempt to make the relation between the sexes cheap and easy. Yet everybody is, or ought to be, profoundly aware of the fact that the secret of sexual attraction is neither cheap nor easy, but is one of the demons which no "scientific education" has yet mastered. Women's fashions with us are mostly invented by men: you can guess the result. After having exhausted all the means of producing the semblance of a fertile brood-mare with corsets and bustles, they are now trying to create the adolescent hermaphrodite, an athletic, semimasculine body, despite the fact that the body of the Northern woman already has a painful tendency toward bony coarseness. They try coeducation in order to make the sexes equal to each other, instead of stressing the difference. But the worst sight—oh—is the women in trousers parading the decks! I often wondered if they knew how mercilessly ugly they looked. Usually they were very decent middle-class types and were not smart at all, but only touched by the current rage for hermaphroditosis. It is a sad truth, but the European woman, and particularly her hopelessly wrong dress, put up no show at all when compared with the dignity and elegance of the Indian woman and her costume. Even fat women have a chance in India; with us they can only starve themselves to death.

995   Talking of costumes, I must say that the Hindu man is too fond of ease and coolness. He wears a long piece of cotton cloth wound round and between his legs. The front of the legs is well covered, but the back is ridiculously bare. There is something effeminate and babyish about it. You simply cannot imagine a soldier with such garlands of cloth between his legs. Many wear

a shirt over this or a European jacket. It is quaint, but not very masculine. The northern type of costume is Persian and looks fine and manly. The garland type is chiefly southern, perhaps because of the matriarchal trend which prevails in the south. The "garland" looks like a sort of overgrown diaper. It is an essentially unwarlike dress and suits the pacifist mentality of the Hindu perfectly.

996   A real fight, in such a contrivance, is well-nigh impossible. The combatants would be trapped in no time by the many circumvolutions of their ridiculous sheets. Yet they are free with words and gestures, but, when you are expecting the worst, they confine themselves to attacking the other's shirt and diaper. I once watched two boys of about eight or nine having a heated quarrel over a game. They came to blows. We can all remember pretty well what a fight between boys at that age means. But the performance of the Hindu boys was really worth seeing: they struck out violently, but the dangerous-looking fists remained miraculously arrested about an inch from the enemy's face—and afterwards it was exactly as if they had had a really good fight! They are profoundly civilized. This was in the south; the Mohammedan element in the north is probably much nearer the real stuff when it comes to a fight.

*

997   The impression of softness that the Hindu conveys points to a predominance of the feminine element in the family, presumably of the *mother*. It seems to be a style which is dependent on old matriarchal traditions. The educated Hindu has very much the character of the "family boy," of the "good" son, who knows that he has to deal with a mother and, moreover, knows how to do it. But one gets much the same impression from the women. They show a studied and stylish kind of modesty and inconspicuousness, which immediately gives you the feeling of dealing with an extremely domesticated and socialized person. There is no harshness or arrogance, no mannishness or stridency in their voice. This is a most agreeable contrast to certain European women I have known, whose strained, overloud, and spastic voices betray a peculiarly forced and unnatural attitude.

998   I had many opportunities to study the English voice in India. Voices are treacherous; they reveal far too much. You marvel at the fantastic efforts people make to sound gay, fresh,

welcoming, enterprising, jolly, benevolent, full of good comrade-
ship, and so on. And you know it is merely an attempt to cover
up the real truth, which is very much the reverse. It makes you
tired listening to those unnatural sounds, and you long for somebody to say something unkind or brutally offensive. You cannot
help noticing how a great number of perfectly nice and decent
Englishmen elaborately imitate a he-man voice, God knows why.
It sounds as if they were trying to impress the world with their
throaty rumbling tones, or as if they were addressing a political
meeting, which has to be convinced of the profound honesty
and sincerity of the speaker. The usual brand is the bass voice,
of the colonel for instance, or the master of a household of
numerous children and servants who must be duly impressed.
The Father Christmas voice is a special variety, usually affected
by academically trained specimens. I discovered that particularly
terrific boomers were quite modest and decent chaps, with a
noticeable feeling of inferiority. What a superhuman burden it
is to be the overlords of a continent like India!

999   The Indians speak without affectation. They represent nothing. They belong to the three hundred and sixty million people
of India. The women represent less than nothing. They belong
to large families incidentally and geographically living in a
country called India. And you have to adapt yourself to the
family and know how to talk and how to behave, when twenty-
five to thirty members of a family are crowded together in a
small house, with a grandmother on top. That teaches you to
speak modestly, carefully, politely. It explains that small twitter-
ing voice and that flowerlike behaviour. The crowding together
in families has the contrary effect with us. It makes people
nervous, irritable, rough, and even violent. But India takes the
family seriously. There is no amateurishness or sentimentality
about it. It is understood to be the indispensable form of life,
inescapable, necessary, and self-evident. It needs a religion to
break this law and to make "homelessness" the first step to saint-
liness. It certainly seems as if Indians would be unusually pleasant and easy to live with, particularly the women; and, if the
style were the whole man, Indian life would be almost ideal.
But softness of manners and sweetness of voice are also a part of
secrecy and diplomacy. I guess Indians are just human, and so
no generalization is quite true.

1000   As a matter of fact, you stub your toes time and again against a peculiar obliqueness when you ask for definite information. You often find then that people are less concerned with your question than with deliberations about your possible motives or about how it would be possible to wriggle out of a tight corner without getting hurt. Overcrowding has surely much to do with this widespread and very characteristic defect in the Indian character, for only the art of deception can preserve the privacy of the individual in a crowd. The woman's whole manner is directed towards the mother as well as the man. To the former she is a daughter, to the latter the woman whose skilful behaviour gives him a reasonable chance to feel like a man. At least I did not meet a single "battleship," so typical of the Western drawing-room, the sight of which makes a man feel about as comfortable as a mouse drowning before breakfast in cold water.

1001   The Indians mean and are meant to live in India. Therefore they have settled down to a degree of domestication which we cannot attain, even with the aid of ideals and frantic moral efforts. Our migrations have not yet come to an end. It was only a short while ago that the Anglo-Saxons immigrated from northern Germany to their new homeland. The Normans arrived there from Scandinavia, via northern France, quite a while later, and it is much the same with practically every nation in Europe. Our motto is still: *ubi bene, ibi patria*. Because of this truth we are all fervent patriots. Because we still can and will wander, we imagine that we can live more or less anywhere. Not yet convinced that we ought to be able to get along with one another in closely packed families, we feel that we can afford to quarrel, for there is still good open country "out West" if things come to the worst. At least it seems so. But it is no longer quite true. Even the Englishman is not settled in India; he is really condemned to serve his term there and to make the best of it. Hence all those hopeful, jolly, eager, energetic, powerful voices issue from people who are thinking and dreaming of spring in Sussex.

WHAT INDIA CAN TEACH US[1]

1002   India lies between the Asiatic north and the Pacific south, between Tibet and Ceylon. India ends abruptly at the foothills of the Himalaya, and at Adam's Bridge. At one end, a Mongolian world begins, at the other, the "paradise" of a South Sea island. Ceylon is as strangely different from India as is Tibet. Curiously enough, at either end one finds the "spoor of the elephant," as the Pali Canon [2] calls the teaching of the Lord Buddha.

1003   Why has India lost her greatest light, Buddha's path of redemption, that glorious synthesis of philosophy and *opus divinum*? It is common knowledge that mankind can never remain on an apex of illumination and spiritual endeavour. Buddha was an untimely intruder, upsetting the historical process, which afterwards got the better of him. Indian religion is like a *vimana,* or pagoda. The gods climb over one another like ants, from the elephants carved on the base to the abstract lotus which crowns the top of the building. In the long run, the gods become philosophical concepts. Buddha, a spiritual pioneer for the whole world, said, and tried to make it true, that the enlightened man is even the teacher and redeemer of his gods (not their stupid denier, as Western "enlightenment" will have it). This was obviously too much, because the Indian mind was not at all ready to integrate the gods to such an extent as to make them psychologically dependent upon man's mental condition. How Buddha himself could obtain such insight without losing himself in a complete mental inflation borders on a miracle. (But any genius is a miracle.)

1004   Buddha disturbed the historical process by interfering with

1 [Written in English and first published in *Asia* (New York), XXXIX (1939):2, 97–98.—EDITORS.]
2 [The body of Southern Buddhist Sacred Writings.—EDITORS.]

the slow transformation of the gods into ideas. The true genius nearly always intrudes and disturbs. He speaks to a temporal world out of a world eternal. Thus he says the wrong things at the right time. Eternal truths are never true at any given moment in history. The process of transformation has to make a halt in order to digest and assimilate the utterly impractical things that the genius has produced from the storehouse of eternity. Yet the genius is the healer of his time, because anything he reveals of eternal truth is healing.

1005   The remote goal of the transformation process, however, is very much what Buddha intended. But to get there is possible neither in one generation nor in ten. It obviously takes much longer, thousands of years at all events, since the intended transformation cannot be realized without an enormous development of human consciousness. It can only be "believed," which is what Buddha's, as well as Christ's, followers obviously did, assuming—as "believers" always do—that belief is the whole thing. Belief is a great thing, to be sure, but it is a substitute for a conscious reality which the Christians wisely relegate to a life in the hereafter. This "hereafter" is really the intended future of mankind, anticipated by religious intuition.

1006   Buddha has disappeared from Indian life and religion more than we could ever imagine Christ disappearing in the aftermath of some future catastrophe to Christianity, more even than the Greco-Roman religions have disappeared from present-day Christianity. India is not ungrateful to her master minds. There is a considerable revival of interest in classical philosophy. Universities like Calcutta and Benares have important philosophy departments. Yet the main emphasis is laid on classical Hindu philosophy and its vast Sanskrit literature. The Pali Canon is not precisely within their scope. Buddha does not represent a proper philosophy. He challenges man! This is not exactly what philosophy wants. It, like any other science, needs a good deal of intellectual free play, undisturbed by moral and human entanglements. But also, small and fragmentary people must be able to "do something about it" without getting fatally involved in big issues far beyond their powers of endurance and accomplishment. This is on the right road after all, though it is indeed a *longissima via*. The divine impatience of a genius may disturb or even upset the small man. But after a few generations he will reassert himself by sheer force of numbers, and this too seems to be right.

1007   I am now going to say something which may offend my Indian friends, but actually no offence is intended. I have, so it seems to me, observed the peculiar fact that an Indian, inasmuch as he is really Indian, does not think, at least not what we call "think." *He rather perceives the thought.* He resembles the primitive in this respect. I do not say that he *is* primitive, but that the process of his thinking reminds me of the primitive way of thought-production. The primitive's reasoning is mainly an unconscious function, and he perceives its results. We should expect such a peculiarity in any civilization which has enjoyed an almost unbroken continuity from primitive times.

1008   Our western evolution from a primitive level was suddenly interrupted by the invasion of a psychology and spirituality belonging to a much higher level of civilization. Our case was not so bad as that of the Negroes or the Polynesians, who found themselves suddenly confronted with the infinitely higher civilization of the white man, but in essence it was the same. We were stopped in the midst of a still barbarous polytheism, which was eradicated or suppressed in the course of centuries and not so very long ago. I suppose that this fact has given a peculiar twist to the Western mind. Our mental existence was transformed into something which it had not yet reached and which it could not yet truly be. And this could only be brought about by a dissociation between the conscious part of the mind and the unconscious. It was a liberation of consciousness from the burden of irrationality and instinctive impulsiveness at the expense of the totality of the individual. Man became split into a conscious and an unconscious personality. The conscious personality could be domesticated, because it was separated from the natural and primitive man. Thus we became highly disciplined, organized, and rational on one side, but the other side remained a suppressed primitive, cut off from education and civilization.

1009   This explains our many relapses into the most appalling barbarity, and it also explains the really terrible fact that, the higher we climb the mountain of scientific and technical achievement, the more dangerous and diabolical becomes the misuse of our inventions. Think of the great triumph of the human mind, the power to fly: we have accomplished the age-old dream of humanity! And think of the bombing raids of modern warfare! Is this what civilization means? Is it not rather a convincing demonstration of the fact that, when our mind went up to conquer the skies, our other man, that suppressed barbarous individual, went down to hell? Certainly our civilization can be proud of its achievements, yet we have to be ashamed of ourselves.

1010   This surely is not the only way in which man can become civilized, at all events it is not an ideal way. One could think of another more satisfactory possibility. Instead of differentiating only one side of man, one could differentiate the whole man. By burdening the conscious man with the earthbound weight of his primitive side one could avoid that fatal dissociation between an upper and a lower half. Of course it would be no mean *tour de force* to experiment with the white man of today along these lines. It would obviously lead to devilishly intricate moral and intellectual problems. But, if the white man does not succeed in destroying his own race with his brilliant inventions, he will eventually have to settle down to a desperately serious course of self-education.

1011   Whatever the ultimate fate of the white man may be, we can at least behold one example of a civilization which has brought every essential trace of primitivity with it, embracing the whole man from top to bottom. India's civilization and psychology resemble her temples, which represent the universe in their sculptures, including man and all his aspects and activities, whether as saint or brute. That is presumably the reason why India seems so dreamlike: one gets pushed back into the unconscious, into that unredeemed, uncivilized, aboriginal world, of which we only dream, since our consciousness denies it. India represents the other way of civilizing man, the way without suppression, without violence, without rationalism. You see them there side by side, in the same town, in the same street, in the same temple, within the same square mile: the most highly cultivated mind and the primitive. In the mental make-up of the most spiritual you discern the traits of the living primitive, and in the melancholy eyes of the illiterate half-naked villager you divine an unconscious knowledge of mysterious truths.

1012   I say all this in order to explain what I mean by not-thinking. I could just as well say: Thank heaven there is a man left who has not learned to think, but is still able to perceive his thoughts, as if they were visions or living things; a man who has transformed, or is still going to transform, his gods into visible thoughts based upon the reality of the instincts. He has rescued his gods, and they live with him. It is true that it is an irrational life, full of crudeness, gruesomeness, misery, disease, and death, yet somehow complete, satisfactory and of an unfathomable emotional beauty. It is true that the logical processes of India are funny, and it is bewildering to see how fragments of Western science live peacefully side by side with what we, shortsightedly, would call superstitions. Indians do not mind seemingly intolerable contradictions. If they exist, they are the peculiarity of such thinking, and man is not responsible for them. He does not make them, since thoughts appear by themselves. The Indian does not fish out infinitesimal details from the universe. His ambition is to have a vision of the whole. He does not yet know that you can screw the living world up tightly between two concepts. Did you ever stop to think how much of the conqueror (not to say thief or robber) lies in that very term "concept"? It comes from the Latin *concipere*, 'to take something by grasping it thoroughly.' That is how we get at the world. But Indian "thinking" is an increase of vision and not a predatory raid into the yet unconquered realms of nature.

1013   If you want to learn the greatest lesson India can teach you, wrap yourself in the cloak of your moral superiority, go to the Black Pagoda of Konarak, sit down in the shadow of the mighty ruin that is still covered with the most amazing collection of obscenities, read Murray's cunning old *Handbook for India*, which tells you how to be properly shocked by this lamentable state of affairs, and how you should go into the temples in the evening, because in the lamplight they look if possible "more [and how beautifully!] wicked"; and then analyse carefully and with the utmost honesty all your reactions, feelings, and thoughts. It will take you quite a while, but in the end, if you have done good work, you will have learned something about

101

yourself, and about the white man in general, which you have probably never heard from any one else. I think, if you can afford it, a trip to India is on the whole most edifying and, from a psychological point of view, most advisable, although it may give you considerable headaches.

PSYCHOLOGICAL COMMENTARY ON "THE TIBETAN BOOK OF THE GREAT LIBERATION" [1]

1. THE DIFFERENCE BETWEEN EASTERN AND WESTERN THINKING

759   Dr. Evans-Wentz has entrusted me with the task of commenting on a text which contains an important exposition of Eastern "psychology." The very fact that I have to use quotation marks shows the dubious applicability of this term. It is perhaps not superfluous to mention that the East has produced nothing equivalent to what we call psychology, but rather philosophy or metaphysics. Critical philosophy, the mother of modern psychology, is as foreign to the East as to medieval Europe. Thus the word "mind," as used in the East, has the connotation of something metaphysical. Our Western conception of mind has lost this connotation since the Middle Ages, and the word has now come to signify a "psychic function." Despite the fact that we neither know nor pretend to know what "psyche" is, we can deal with the phenomenon of "mind." We do not assume that the mind is a metaphysical entity or that

1 [Written in English in 1939 and first published in *The Tibetan Book of the Great Liberation*, the texts of which were translated from Tibetan by various hands and edited by W. Y. Evans-Wentz (London and New York, 1954), pp. xxix–lxiv. The commentary is republished here with only minor alterations.—EDITORS.]

103

there is any connection between an individual mind and a hypo-thetical Universal Mind. Our psychology is, therefore, a science of mere phenomena without any metaphysical implications. The development of Western philosophy during the last two centuries has succeeded in isolating the mind in its own sphere and in severing it from its primordial oneness with the uni-verse. Man himself has ceased to be the microcosm and eidolon of the cosmos, and his "anima" is no longer the consubstantial *scintilla,* or spark of the *Anima Mundi,* the World Soul.

760   Psychology accordingly treats all metaphysical claims and assertions as mental phenomena, and regards them as statements about the mind and its structure that derive ultimately from certain unconscious dispositions. It does not consider them to be absolutely valid or even capable of establishing a metaphysical truth. We have no intellectual means of ascertaining whether this attitude is right or wrong. We only know that there is no evidence for, and no possibility of proving, the validity of a metaphysical postulate such as "Universal Mind." If the mind asserts the existence of a Universal Mind, we hold that it is merely making an assertion. We do not assume that by such an assertion the existence of a Universal Mind has been established. There is no argument against this reasoning, but no evidence, either, that our conclusion is ultimately right. In other words, it is just as possible that our mind is nothing but a perceptible manifestation of a Universal Mind. Yet we do not know, and we cannot even see, how it would be possible to recognize whether this is so or not. Psychology therefore holds that the mind cannot establish or assert anything beyond itself.

761   If, then, we accept the restrictions imposed upon the capacity of our mind, we demonstrate our common sense. I admit it is something of a sacrifice, inasmuch as we bid farewell to that miraculous world in which mind-created things and beings move and live. This is the world of the primitive, where even inani-mate objects are endowed with a living, healing, magic power, through which they participate in us and we in them. Sooner or later we had to understand that their potency was really ours, and that their significance was our projection. The theory of knowledge is only the last step out of humanity's childhood, out of a world where mind-created figures populated a metaphysical heaven and hell.

762   Despite this inevitable epistemological criticism, however, we have held fast to the religious belief that the organ of faith enables man to know God. The West thus developed a new disease: the conflict between science and religion. The critical philosophy of science became as it were negatively metaphysical —in other words, materialistic—on the basis of an error in judgment; matter was assumed to be a tangible and recognizable reality. Yet this is a thoroughly metaphysical concept hypostatized by uncritical minds. Matter is an hypothesis. When you say "matter," you are really creating a symbol for something unknown, which may just as well be "spirit" or anything else; it may even be God. Religious faith, on the other hand, refuses to give up its pre-critical *Weltanschauung*. In contradiction to the saying of Christ, the faithful try to *remain* children instead of becoming *as* children. They cling to the world of childhood. A famous modern theologian confesses in his autobiography that Jesus has been his good friend "from childhood on." Jesus is the perfect example of a man who preached something different from the religion of his forefathers. But the *imitatio Christi* does not appear to include the mental and spiritual sacrifice which he had to undergo at the beginning of his career and without which he would never have become a saviour.

763   The conflict between science and religion is in reality a misunderstanding of both. Scientific materialism has merely introduced a new hypostasis, and that is an intellectual sin. It has given another name to the supreme principle of reality and has assumed that this created a new thing and destroyed an old thing. Whether you call the principle of existence "God," "matter," "energy," or anything else you like, you have created nothing; you have simply changed a symbol. The materialist is a metaphysician *malgré lui*. Faith, on the other hand, tries to retain a primitive mental condition on merely sentimental grounds. It is unwilling to give up the primitive, childlike relationship to mind-created and hypostatized figures; it wants to go on enjoying the security and confidence of a world still presided over by powerful, responsible, and kindly parents. Faith may include a *sacrificium intellectus* (provided there is an intellect to sacrifice), but certainly not a sacrifice of feeling. In this way the faithful *remain* children instead of becoming *as* children, and they do not gain their life because they have not lost

it. Furthermore, faith collides with science and thus gets its deserts, for it refuses to share in the spiritual adventure of our age.

764   Any honest thinker has to admit the insecurity of all metaphysical positions, and in particular of all creeds. He has also to admit the unwarrantable nature of all metaphysical assertions and face the fact that there is no evidence whatever for the ability of the human mind to pull itself up by its own bootstrings, that is, to establish anything transcendental.

765   Materialism is a metaphysical reaction against the sudden realization that cognition is a mental faculty and, if carried beyond the human plane, a projection. The reaction was "metaphysical" in so far as the man of average philosophical education failed to see through the implied hypostasis, not realizing that "matter" was just another name for the supreme principle. As against this, the attitude of faith shows how reluctant people were to accept philosophical criticism. It also demonstrates how great is the fear of letting go one's hold on the securities of childhood and of dropping into a strange, unknown world ruled by forces unconcerned with man. Nothing really changes in either case; man and his surroundings remain the same. He has only to realize that he is shut up inside his mind and cannot step beyond it, even in insanity; and that the appearance of his world or of his gods very much depends upon his own mental condition.

766   In the first place, the structure of the mind is responsible for anything we may assert about metaphysical matters, as I have already pointed out. We have also begun to understand that the intellect is not an *ens per se,* or an independent mental faculty, but a psychic function dependent upon the conditions of the psyche as a whole. A philosophical statement is the product of a certain personality living at a certain time in a certain place, and not the outcome of a purely logical and impersonal procedure. To that extent it is chiefly subjective; whether it has an objective validity or not depends on whether there are few or many persons who argue in the same way. The isolation of man within his mind as a result of epistemological criticism has naturally led to psychological criticism. This kind of criticism is not popular with the philosophers, since they like to consider the philosophic intellect as the perfect and unconditioned in-

strument of philosophy. Yet this intellect of theirs is a function dependent upon an individual psyche and determined on all sides by subjective conditions, quite apart from environmental influences. Indeed, we have already become so accustomed to this point of view that "mind" has lost its universal character altogether. It has become a more or less individualized affair, with no trace of its former cosmic aspect as the *anima rationalis*. Mind is understood nowadays as a subjective, even an arbitrary, thing. Now that the formerly hypostatized "universal ideas" have turned out to be mental principles, it is dawning upon us to what an extent our whole experience of so-called reality is psychic; as a matter of fact, everything thought, felt, or perceived is a psychic image, and the world itself exists only so far as we are able to produce an image of it. We are so deeply impressed with the truth of our imprisonment in, and limitation by, the psyche that we are ready to admit the existence in it even of things we do *not* know: we call them "the unconscious."

767   The seemingly universal and metaphysical scope of the mind has thus been narrowed down to the small circle of individual consciousness, profoundly aware of its almost limitless subjectivity and of its infantile-archaic tendency to heedless projection and illusion. Many scientifically-minded persons have even sacrificed their religious and philosophical leanings for fear of uncontrolled subjectivism. By way of compensation for the loss of a world that pulsed with our blood and breathed with our breath, we have developed an enthusiasm for *facts*—mountains of facts, far beyond any single individual's power to survey. We have the pious hope that this incidental accumulation of facts will form a meaningful whole, but nobody is quite sure, because no human brain can possibly comprehend the gigantic sum total of this mass-produced knowledge. The facts bury us, but whoever dares to speculate must pay for it with a bad conscience—and rightly so, for he will instantly be tripped up by the facts.

768   Western psychology knows the mind as the mental functioning of a psyche. It is the "mentality" of an individual. An impersonal Universal Mind is still to be met with in the sphere of philosophy, where it seems to be a relic of the original human "soul." This picture of our Western outlook may seem a little drastic, but I do not think it is far from the truth. At all events,

something of the kind presents itself as soon as we are confronted with the Eastern mentality. In the East, mind is a cosmic factor, the very essence of existence; while in the West we have just begun to understand that it is the essential condition of cognition, and hence of the cognitive existence of the world. There is no conflict between religion and science in the East, because no science is there based upon the passion for facts, and no religion upon mere faith; there is religious cognition and cognitive religion.[2] With us, man is incommensurably small and the grace of God is everything; but in the East, man is God and he redeems himself. The gods of Tibetan Buddhism belong to the sphere of illusory separateness and mind-created projections, and yet they exist; but so far as we are concerned an illusion remains an illusion, and thus is nothing at all. It is a paradox, yet nevertheless true, that with us a thought has no proper reality; we treat it as if it were a nothingness. Even though the thought be true in itself, we hold that it exists only by virtue of certain facts which it is said to formulate. We can produce a most devastating fact like the atom bomb with the help of this ever-changing phantasmagoria of virtually non-existent thoughts, but it seems wholly absurd to us that one could ever establish the reality of thought itself.

769   "Psychic reality" is a controversial concept, like "psyche" or "mind." By the latter terms some understand consciousness and its contents, others allow the existence of "dark" or "subconscious" representations. Some include instincts in the psychic realm, others exclude them. The vast majority consider the psyche to be a result of biochemical processes in the brain cells. A few conjecture that it is the psyche that makes the cortical cells function. Some identify "life" with psyche. But only an insignificant minority regards the psychic phenomenon as a category of existence *per se* and draws the necessary conclusions. It is indeed paradoxical that *the* category of existence, the indispensable *sine qua non* of all existence, namely the psyche, should be treated as if it were only semi-existent. Psychic existence is the only category of existence of which we have *immediate* knowledge, since nothing can be known unless it first appears as a psychic image. Only psychic existence is immediately verifiable. To the extent that the world does not assume the form of

2 I am purposely leaving out of account the modernized East.

a psychic image, it is virtually non-existent. This is a fact which, with few exceptions—as for instance in Schopenhauer's philosophy—the West has not yet fully realized. But Schopenhauer was influenced by Buddhism and by the Upanishads.

770   Even a superficial acquaintance with Eastern thought is sufficient to show that a fundamental difference divides East and West. The East bases itself upon psychic reality, that is, upon the psyche as the main and unique condition of existence. It seems as if this Eastern recognition were a psychological or temperamental fact rather than a result of philosophical reasoning. It is a typically introverted point of view, contrasted with the equally typical extraverted point of view of the West.[3] Introversion and extraversion are known to be temperamental or even constitutional attitudes which are never intentionally adopted in normal circumstances. In exceptional cases they may be produced at will, but only under very special conditions. Introversion is, if one may so express it, the "style" of the East, an habitual and collective attitude, just as extraversion is the "style" of the West. Introversion is felt here as something abnormal, morbid, or otherwise objectionable. Freud identifies it with an autoerotic, "narcissistic" attitude of mind. He shares his negative position with the National Socialist philosophy of modern Germany,[4] which accuses introversion of being an offence against community feeling. In the East, however, our cherished extraversion is depreciated as illusory desirousness, as existence in the *samsāra*, the very essence of the *nidāna*-chain which culminates in the sum of the world's sufferings.[5] Anyone with practical knowledge of the mutual depreciation of values between introvert and extravert will understand the emotional conflict between the Eastern and the Western standpoint. For those who know something of the history of European philosophy the bitter wrangling about "universals" which began with Plato will provide an instructive example. I do not wish to go into all the ramifications of this conflict between introversion and extraversion, but I must mention the religious aspects of the problem. The Christian West considers man to be wholly dependent upon the grace of God, or at least upon the Church as the exclusive and divinely sanctioned earthly instrument of

---

3 *Psychological Types*, Defs. 19 and 34.   4 Written in the year 1939.
5 *Samyutta-nikāya* 12, *Nidāna-samyutta*.

man's redemption. The East, however, insists that man is the sole cause of his higher development, for it believes in "self-liberation."

771   The religious point of view always expresses and formulates the essential psychological attitude and its specific prejudices, even in the case of people who have forgotten, or who have never heard of, their own religion. In spite of everything, the West is thoroughly Christian as far as its psychology is concerned. Tertullian's *anima naturaliter christiana* holds true throughout the West—not, as he thought, in the religious sense, but in a psychological one. Grace comes from elsewhere; at all events from outside. Every other point of view is sheer heresy. Hence it is quite understandable why the human psyche is suffering from undervaluation. Anyone who dares to establish a connection between the psyche and the idea of God is immediately accused of "psychologism" or suspected of morbid "mysticism." The East, on the other hand, compassionately tolerates those "lower" spiritual stages where man, in his blind ignorance of karma, still bothers about sin and tortures his imagination with a belief in absolute gods, who, if he only looked deeper, are nothing but the veil of illusion woven by his own unenlightened mind. The psyche is therefore all-important; it is the all-pervading Breath, the Buddha-essence; it is the Buddha-Mind, the One, the *Dharmakāya*. All existence emanates from it, and all separate forms dissolve back into it. This is the basic psychological prejudice that permeates Eastern man in every fibre of his being, seeping into all his thoughts, feelings, and deeds, no matter what creed he professes.

772   In the same way Western man is Christian, no matter to what denomination his Christianity belongs. For him man is small inside, he is next to nothing; moreover, as Kierkegaard says, "before God man is always wrong." By fear, repentance, promises, submission, self-abasement, good deeds, and praise he propitiates the great power, which is not himself but *totaliter aliter*, the Wholly Other, altogether perfect and "outside," the only reality.[6] If you shift the formula a bit and substitute for God some other power, for instance the world or money, you get a complete picture of Western man—assiduous, fearful, devout, self-abasing, enterprising, greedy, and violent in his pur-

6 [Cf. Otto, *The Idea of the Holy*, pp. 26ff.—EDITORS.]

suit of the goods of this world: possessions, health, knowledge, technical mastery, public welfare, political power, conquest, and so on. What are the great popular movements of our time? Attempts to grab the money or property of others and to protect our own. The mind is chiefly employed in devising suitable "isms" to hide the real motives or to get more loot. I refrain from describing what would happen to Eastern man should he forget his ideal of Buddhahood, for I do not want to give such an unfair advantage to my Western prejudices. But I cannot help raising the question of whether it is possible, or indeed advisable, for either to imitate the other's standpoint. The difference between them is so vast that one can see no reasonable possibility of this, much less its advisability. You cannot mix fire and water. The Eastern attitude stultifies the Western, and vice versa. You cannot be a good Christian and redeem yourself, nor can you be a Buddha and worship God. It is much better to accept the conflict, for it admits only of an irrational solution, if any.

773   By an inevitable decree of fate the West is becoming acquainted with the peculiar facts of Eastern spirituality. It is useless either to belittle these facts, or to build false and treacherous bridges over yawning gaps. Instead of learning the spiritual techniques of the East by heart and imitating them in a thoroughly Christian way—*imitatio Christi!*—with a correspondingly forced attitude, it would be far more to the point to find out whether there exists in the unconscious an introverted tendency similar to that which has become the guiding spiritual principle of the East. We should then be in a position to build on our own ground with our own methods. If we snatch these things directly from the East, we have merely indulged our Western acquisitiveness, confirming yet again that "everything good is outside," whence it has to be fetched and pumped into our barren souls.[7] It seems to me that we have really learned something from the East when we understand that the psyche contains riches enough without having to be primed from outside, and when we feel capable of evolving out of ourselves with

---

[7] "Whereas who holdeth not God as such an inner possession, but with every means must fetch Him from without . . . verily such a man hath Him not, and easily something cometh to trouble him." Meister Eckhart (Büttner, II, p. 185). Cf. *Meister Eckhart*, trans. by Evans, II, p. 8.

or without divine grace. But we cannot embark upon this ambitious enterprise until we have learned how to deal with our spiritual pride and blasphemous self-assertiveness. The Eastern attitude violates the specifically Christian values, and it is no good blinking this fact. If our new attitude is to be genuine, i.e., grounded in our own history, it must be acquired with full consciousness of the Christian values and of the conflict between them and the introverted attitude of the East. We must get at the Eastern values from within and not from without, seeking them in ourselves, in the unconscious. We shall then discover how great is our fear of the unconscious and how formidable are our resistances. Because of these resistances we doubt the very thing that seems so obvious to the East, namely, the *self-liberating power of the introverted mind.*

774   This aspect of the mind is practically unknown to the West, though it forms the most important component of the unconscious. Many people flatly deny the existence of the unconscious, or else they say that it consists merely of instincts, or of repressed or forgotten contents that were once part of the conscious mind. It is safe to assume that what the East calls "mind" has more to do with our "unconscious" than with mind as we understand it, which is more or less identical with consciousness. To us, consciousness is inconceivable without an ego; it is equated with the relation of contents to an ego. If there is no ego there is nobody to be conscious of anything. The ego is therefore indispensable to the conscious process. The Eastern mind, however, has no difficulty in conceiving of a consciousness without an ego. Consciousness is deemed capable of transcending its ego condition; indeed, in its "higher" forms, the ego disappears altogether. Such an ego-less mental condition can only be unconscious to us, for the simple reason that there would be nobody to witness it. I do not doubt the existence of mental states transcending consciousness. But they lose their consciousness to exactly the same degree that they transcend consciousness. I cannot imagine a conscious mental state that does not relate to a subject, that is, to an ego. The ego may be depotentiated— divested, for instance, of its awareness of the body—but so long as there is awareness of something, there must be somebody who is aware. The unconscious, however, is a mental condition of which no ego is aware. It is only by indirect means that we even-

tually become conscious of the existence of an unconscious. We can observe the manifestation of unconscious fragments of the personality, detached from the patient's consciousness, in insanity. But there is no evidence that the unconscious contents are related to an unconscious centre analogous to the ego; in fact there are good reasons why such a centre is not even probable.

775   The fact that the East can dispose so easily of the ego seems to point to a mind that is not to be identified with our "mind." Certainly the ego does not play the same role in Eastern thought as it does with us. It seems as if the Eastern mind were less egocentric, as if its contents were more loosely connected with the subject, and as if greater stress were laid on mental states which include a depotentiated ego. It also seems as if *hatha* yoga were chiefly useful as a means for extinguishing the ego by fettering its unruly impulses. There is no doubt that the higher forms of yoga, in so far as they strive to reach samādhi, seek a mental condition in which the ego is practically dissolved. Consciousness in our sense of the word is rated a definitely inferior condition, the state of *avidyā* (ignorance), whereas what we call the "dark background of consciousness" is understood to be a "higher" consciousness.[8] Thus our concept of the "collective unconscious" would be the European equivalent of *buddhi,* the enlightened mind.

776   In view of all this, the Eastern form of "sublimation" amounts to a withdrawal of the centre of psychic gravity from ego-consciousness, which holds a middle position between the body and the ideational processes of the psyche. The lower, semi-physiological strata of the psyche are subdued by *askesis,* i.e., exercises, and kept under control. They are not exactly denied or suppressed by a supreme effort of the will, as is customary in Western sublimation. Rather, the lower psychic strata are adapted and shaped through the patient practice of *hatha* yoga until they no longer interfere with the development of "higher" consciousness. This peculiar process seems to be aided by the fact that the ego and its desires are checked by the greater

8 In so far as "higher" and "lower" are categorical judgments of consciousness, Western psychology does not differentiate unconscious contents in this way. It appears that the East recognizes subhuman psychic conditions, a real "subconsciousness" comprising the instincts and semi-physiological psychisms, but classed as a "higher consciousness."

importance which the East habitually attaches to the "subjective factor." [9] By this I mean the "dark background" of consciousness, the unconscious. The introverted attitude is characterized in general by an emphasis on the *a priori* data of apperception. As is well known, the act of apperception consists of two phases: first the perception of the object, second the assimilation of the perception to a preexisting pattern or concept by means of which the object is "comprehended." The psyche is not a nonentity devoid of all quality; it is a definite system made up of definite conditions and it reacts in a specific way. Every new representation, be it a perception or a spontaneous thought, arouses associations which derive from the storehouse of memory. These leap immediately into consciousness, producing the complex picture of an "impression," though this is already a sort of interpretation. The unconscious disposition upon which the quality of the impression depends is what I call the "subjective factor." It deserves the qualification "subjective" because objectivity is hardly ever conferred by a first impression. Usually a rather laborious process of verification, comparison, and analysis is needed to modify and adapt the immediate reactions of the subjective factor.

777   The prominence of the subjective factor does not imply a *personal subjectivism,* despite the readiness of the extraverted attitude to dismiss the subjective factor as "nothing but" subjective. The psyche and its structure are real enough. They even transform material objects into psychic images, as we have said. They do not perceive waves, but sound; not wave-lengths, but colours. Existence is as we see and understand it. There are innumerable things that can be seen, felt, and understood in a great variety of ways. Quite apart from merely personal prejudices, the psyche assimilates external facts in its own way, which is based ultimately upon the laws or patterns of apperception. These laws do not change, although different ages or different parts of the world call them by different names. On a primitive level people are afraid of witches; on the modern level we are apprehensively aware of microbes. There everybody believes in ghosts, here everybody believes in vitamins. Once upon a time men were possessed by devils, now they are not less obsessed by ideas, and so on.

[9] *Psychological Types,* pars. 621ff.

778   The subjective factor is made up, in the last resort, of the eternal patterns of psychic functioning. Anyone who relies upon the subjective factor is therefore basing himself on the reality of psychic law. So he can hardly be said to be wrong. If by this means he succeeds in extending his consciousness downwards, to touch the basic laws of psychic life, he is in possession of that truth which the psyche will naturally evolve if not fatally interfered with by the non-psychic, i.e., the external, world. At any rate, his truth could be weighed against the sum of all knowledge acquired through the investigation of externals. We in the West believe that a truth is satisfactory only if it can be verified by external facts. We believe in the most exact observation and exploration of nature; our truth must coincide with the behaviour of the external world, otherwise it is merely "subjective." In the same way that the East turns its gaze from the dance of *prakriti* (physis) and from the multitudinous illusory forms of *māyā*, the West shuns the unconscious and its futile fantasies. Despite its introverted attitude, however, the East knows very well how to deal with the external world. And despite its extraversions the West, too, has a way of dealing with the psyche and its demands; it has an institution called the Church, which gives expression to the unknown psyche of man through its rites and dogmas. Nor are natural science and modern techniques by any means the invention of the West. Their Eastern equivalents are somewhat old-fashioned, or even primitive. But what we have to show in the way of spiritual insight and psychological technique must seem, when compared with yoga, just as backward as Eastern astrology and medicine when compared with Western science. I do not deny the efficacy of the Christian Church; but, if you compare the *Exercitia* of Ignatius Loyola with yoga, you will take my meaning. There is a difference, and a big one. To jump straight from that level into Eastern yoga is no more advisable than the sudden transformation of Asian peoples into half-baked Europeans. I have serious doubts as to the blessings of Western civilization, and I have similar misgivings as to the adoption of Eastern spirituality by the West. Yet the two contradictory worlds have met. The East is in full transformation; it is thoroughly and fatally disturbed. Even the most efficient methods of European warfare have been successfully imitated. The trouble with us seems to

be far more psychological. Our blight is ideologies—they are the long-expected Antichrist! National Socialism comes as near to being a religious movement as any movement since A.D. 622.[9a] Communism claims to be paradise come to earth again. We are far better protected against failing crops, inundations, epidemics, and invasions from the Turk than we are against our own deplorable spiritual inferiority, which seems to have little resistance to psychic epidemics.

779   In its religious attitude, too, the West is extraverted. Nowadays it is gratuitously offensive to say that Christianity implies hostility, or even indifference, to the world and the flesh. On the contrary, the good Christian is a jovial citizen, an enterprising business man, an excellent soldier, the very best in every profession there is. Worldly goods are often interpreted as special rewards for Christian behaviour, and in the Lord's Prayer the adjective ἐπιούσιος, *supersubstantialis*,[10] referring to the bread, has long since been omitted, for the real bread obviously makes so very much more sense! It is only logical that extraversion, when carried to such lengths, cannot credit man with a psyche which contains anything not imported into it from outside, either by human teaching or divine grace. From this point of view it is downright blasphemy to assert that man has it in him to accomplish his own redemption. Nothing in our religion encourages the idea of the self-liberating power of the mind. Yet a very modern form of psychology—"analytical" or "complex" psychology—envisages the possibility of there being certain processes in the unconscious which, by virtue of their symbolism, compensate the defects and anfractuosities of the conscious attitude. When these unconscious compensations are made conscious through the analytical technique, they produce such a change in the conscious attitude that we are entitled to speak of a new level of consciousness. The method cannot, however, produce the actual process of unconscious compensation; for that we depend upon the unconscious psyche or the "grace of God"—names make no difference. But the unconscious process itself hardly ever reaches consciousness without technical aid. When brought to the surface, it reveals contents that offer

---

[9a] [Date of Mohammed's flight (*hegira*) to Medina: beginning of Moslem era.]
[10] This is not the unacceptable translation of ἐπιούσιος by Jerome but the ancient spiritual interpretation by Tertullian, Origen, and others.

a striking contrast to the general run of conscious thinking and feeling. If that were not so, they would not have a compensatory effect. The first effect, however, is usually a conflict, because the conscious attitude resists the intrusion of apparently incompatible and extraneous tendencies, thoughts, feelings, etc. Schizophrenia yields the most startling examples of such intrusions of utterly foreign and unacceptable contents. In schizophrenia it is, of course, a question of pathological distortions and exaggerations, but anybody with the slightest knowledge of the normal material will easily recognize the sameness of the underlying patterns. It is, as a matter of fact, the same imagery that one finds in mythology and other archaic thought-forms.

780   Under normal conditions, every conflict stimulates the mind to activity for the purpose of creating a satisfactory solution. Usually—i.e., in the West—the conscious standpoint arbitrarily decides against the unconscious, since anything coming from inside suffers from the prejudice of being regarded as inferior or somehow wrong. But in the cases with which we are here concerned it is tacitly agreed that the apparently incompatible contents shall not be suppressed again, and that the conflict shall be accepted and suffered. At first no solution appears possible, and this fact, too, has to be borne with patience. The suspension thus created "constellates" the unconscious—in other words, the conscious suspense produces a new compensatory reaction in the unconscious. This reaction (usually manifested in dreams) is brought to conscious realization in its turn. The conscious mind is thus confronted with a new aspect of the psyche, which arouses a different problem or modifies an old one in an unexpected way. The procedure is continued until the original conflict is satisfactorily resolved. The whole process is called the "transcendent function." It is a process and a method at the same time. The production of unconscious compensations is a spontaneous *process;* the conscious realization is a *method.* The function is called "transcendent" because it facilitates the transition from one psychic condition to another by means of the mutual confrontation of opposites.

781   This is a very sketchy description of the transcendent function, and for details I must refer the reader to the relevant literature.[11] But I felt it necessary to call attention to these

11 *Psychological Types,* Def. 51. [Cf. also "The Transcendent Function."]

psychological observations and methods because they indicate
the way by which we may find access to the sort of "mind" referred to in our text. This is the image-creating mind, the
matrix of all those patterns that give apperception its peculiar
character. These patterns are inherent in the unconscious
"mind"; they are its structural elements, and they alone can
explain why certain mythological motifs are more or less ubiqui-
tous, even where migration as a means of transmission is exceedingly improbable. Dreams, fantasies, and psychoses produce
images to all appearances identical with mythological motifs of
which the individuals concerned had absolutely no knowledge,
not even indirect knowledge acquired through popular figures
of speech or through the symbolic language of the Bible.[12] The
psychopathology of schizophrenia, as well as the psychology of
the unconscious, demonstrate the production of archaic material
beyond a doubt. Whatever the structure of the unconscious may
be, one thing is certain: it contains an indefinite number of
motifs or patterns of an archaic character, in principle identical
with the root ideas of mythology and similar thought-forms.

782   Because the unconscious is the matrix mind, the quality of
creativeness attaches to it. It is the birthplace of thought-forms
such as our text considers the Universal Mind to be. Since we
cannot attribute any particular form to the unconscious, the
Eastern assertion that the Universal Mind is without form, the
arupaloka, yet is the source of all forms, seems to be psychologically justified. In so far as the forms or patterns of the unconscious belong to no time in particular, being seemingly eternal,
they convey a peculiar feeling of timelessness when consciously
realized. We find similar statements in primitive psychology:
for instance, the Australian word *aljira* [13] means 'dream' as well
as 'ghostland' and the 'time' in which the ancestors lived and
still live. It is, as they say, the 'time when there was no time.'
This looks like an obvious concretization and projection of the

12 Some people find such statements incredible. But either they have no knowledge of primitive psychology, or they are ignorant of the results of psychopathological research. Specific observations occur in my *Symbols of Transformation*
and *Psychology and Alchemy,* Part II; Nelken, "Analytische Beobachtungen
über Phantasien eines Schizophrenen," pp. 504ff.; Spielrein, "Über den psycho-
logischen Inhalt eines Falls von Schizophrenie," pp. 329ff.; and C. A. Meier,
"Spontanmanifestationen des kollektiven Unbewussten."
13 Lévy-Bruhl, *La Mythologie primitive,* pp. xxiii ff.

unconscious with all its characteristic qualities—its dream manifestations, its ancestral world of thought-forms, and its timelessness.

783   An introverted attitude, therefore, which withdraws its emphasis from the external world (the world of consciousness) and localizes it in the subjective factor (the background of consciousness) necessarily calls forth the characteristic manifestations of the unconscious, namely, archaic thought-forms imbued with "ancestral" or "historic" feeling, and, beyond them, the sense of indefiniteness, timelessness, oneness. The extraordinary feeling of oneness is a common experience in all forms of "mysticism" and probably derives from the general contamination of contents, which increases as consciousness dims. The almost limitless contamination of images in dreams, and particularly in the products of insanity, testifies to their unconscious origin. In contrast to the clear distinction and differentiation of forms in consciousness, unconscious contents are incredibly vague and for this reason capable of any amount of contamination. If we tried to conceive of a state in which nothing is distinct, we should certainly feel the whole as one. Hence it is not unlikely that the peculiar experience of oneness derives from the subliminal awareness of all-contamination in the unconscious.

784   By means of the transcendent function we not only gain access to the "One Mind" but also come to understand why the East believes in the possibility of self-liberation. If, through introspection and the conscious realization of unconscious compensations, it is possible to transform one's mental condition and thus arrive at a solution of painful conflicts, one would seem entitled to speak of "self-liberation." But, as I have already hinted, there is a hitch in this proud claim to self-liberation, for a man cannot produce these unconscious compensations at will. He has to rely upon the possibility that they *may* be produced. Nor can he alter the peculiar character of the compensation: *est ut est aut non est*—'it is as it is or it isn't at all.' It is a curious thing that Eastern philosophy seems to be almost unaware of this highly important fact. And it is precisely this fact that provides the psychological justification for the Western point of view. It seems as if the Western mind had a most penetrating intuition of man's fateful dependence upon some dark power which must co-operate if all is to be well. Indeed, when-

ever and wherever the unconscious fails to co-operate, man is instantly at a loss, even in his most ordinary activities. There may be a failure of memory, of co-ordinated action, or of interest and concentration; and such failure may well be the cause of serious annoyance, or of a fatal accident, a professional disaster, or a moral collapse. Formerly, men called the gods unfavourable; now we prefer to call it a neurosis, and we seek the cause in lack of vitamins, in endocrine disturbances, overwork, or sex. The co-operation of the unconscious, which is something we never think of and always take for granted, is, when it suddenly fails, a very serious matter indeed.

785   In comparison with other races—the Chinese for instance —the white man's mental equilibrium, or, to put it bluntly, his brain, seems to be his tender spot. We naturally try to get as far away from our weaknesses as possible, a fact which may explain the sort of extraversion that is always seeking security by dominating its surroundings. Extraversion goes hand in hand with mistrust of the inner man, if indeed there is any consciousness of him at all. Moreover, we all tend to undervalue the things we are afraid of. There must be some such reason for our absolute conviction that *nihil est in intellectu quod non antea fuerit in sensu,* which is the motto of Western extraversion. But, as we have emphasized, this extraversion is psychologically justified by the vital fact that unconscious compensation lies beyond man's control. I know that yoga prides itself on being able to control even the unconscious processes, so that nothing can happen in the psyche as a whole that is not ruled by a supreme consciousness. I have not the slightest doubt that such a condition is more or less possible. But it is possible only at the price of becoming identical with the unconscious. Such an identity is the Eastern equivalent of our Western fetish of "complete objectivity," the machine-like subservience to one goal, to one idea or cause, at the cost of losing every trace of inner life. From the Eastern point of view this complete objectivity is appalling, for it amounts to complete identity with the samsāra; to the West, on the other hand, samādhi is nothing but a meaningless dream-state. In the East, the inner man has always had such a firm hold on the outer man that the world had no chance of tearing him away from his inner roots; in the West, the outer man gained the ascendancy to such an extent

that he was alienated from his innermost being. The One Mind, Oneness, indefiniteness, and eternity remained the prerogative of the One God. Man became small, futile, and essentially in the wrong.

786   I think it is becoming clear from my argument that the two standpoints, however contradictory, each have their psychological justification. Both are one-sided in that they fail to see and take account of those factors which do not fit in with their typical attitude. The one underrates the world of consciousness, the other the world of the One Mind. The result is that, in their extremism, both lose one half of the universe; their life is shut off from total reality, and is apt to become artificial and inhuman. In the West, there is the mania for "objectivity," the asceticism of the scientist or of the stockbroker, who throw away the beauty and universality of life for the sake of the ideal, or not so ideal, goal. In the East, there is the wisdom, peace, detachment, and inertia of a psyche that has returned to its dim origins, having left behind all the sorrow and joy of existence as it is and, presumably, ought to be. No wonder that one-sidedness produces very similar forms of monasticism in both cases, guaranteeing to the hermit, the holy man, the monk or the scientist unswerving singleness of purpose. I have nothing against one-sidedness as such. Man, the great experiment of nature, or his own great experiment, is evidently entitled to all such undertakings—if he can endure them. Without one-sidedness the spirit of man could not unfold in all its diversity. But I do not think there is any harm in trying to understand both sides.

787   The extraverted tendency of the West and the introverted tendency of the East have one important purpose in common: both make desperate efforts to conquer the mere naturalness of life. It is the assertion of mind over matter, the *opus contra naturam*, a symptom of the youthfulness of man, still delighting in the use of the most powerful weapon ever devised by nature: the conscious mind. The afternoon of humanity, in a distant future, may yet evolve a different ideal. In time, even conquest will cease to be the dream.

2. COMMENTS ON THE TEXT

788   Before embarking upon the commentary proper, I must not omit to call the reader's attention to the very marked difference between the tenor of a psychological dissertation and that of a sacred text. A scientist forgets all too easily that the impartial handling of a subject may violate its emotional values, often to an unpardonable degree. The scientific intellect is inhuman and cannot afford to be anything else; it cannot avoid being ruthless in effect, though it may be well-intentioned in motive. In dealing with a sacred text, therefore, the psychologist ought at least to be aware that his subject represents an inestimable religious and philosophical value which should not be desecrated by profane hands. I confess that I myself venture to deal with such a text only because I know and appreciate its value. In commenting upon it I have no intention whatsoever of anatomizing it with heavy-handed criticism. On the contrary, my endeavour will be to amplify its symbolic language so that it may yield itself more easily to our understanding. To this end, it is necessary to bring down its lofty metaphysical concepts to a level where it is possible to see whether any of the psychological facts known to us have parallels in, or at least border upon, the sphere of Eastern thought. I hope this will not be misunderstood as an attempt to belittle or to banalize; my aim is simply to bring ideas which are alien to our way of thinking within reach of Western psychological experience.

789   What follows is a series of notes and comments which should be read together with the textual sections indicated by the titles.

The Obeisance

790   Eastern texts usually begin with a statement which in the West would come at the end, as the *conclusio finalis* to a long argument. We would begin with things generally known and accepted, and would end with the most important item of our investigation. Hence our dissertation would conclude with the sentence: "Therefore the *Trikāya* is the All-Enlightened Mind itself." In this respect, the Eastern mentality is not so very different from the medieval. As late as the eighteenth century our books on history or natural science began, as here, with God's

decision to create a world. The idea of a Universal Mind is a commonplace in the East, since it aptly expresses the introverted Eastern temperament. Put into psychological language, the above sentence could be paraphrased thus: The unconscious is the root of all experience of oneness (*dharmakāya*), the matrix of all archetypes or structural patterns (*sambhogakāya*), and the *conditio sine qua non* of the phenomenal world (*nirmānakāya*).

The Foreword

791   The gods are archetypal thought-forms belonging to the *sambhogakāya*.[14] Their peaceful and wrathful aspects, which play a great role in the meditations of the Tibetan Book of the Dead, symbolize the opposites. In the *nirmānakāya* these opposites are no more than human conflicts, but in the *sambhogakāya* they are the positive and negative principles united in one and the same figure. This corresponds to the psychological experience, also formulated in Lao-tzu's *Tao Teh Ching*, that there is no position without its negation. Where there is faith, there is doubt; where there is doubt, there is credulity; where there is morality, there is temptation. Only saints have diabolical visions, and tyrants are the slaves of their *valets de chambre*. If we carefully scrutinize our own character we shall inevitably find that, as Lao-tzu says, "high stands on low," which means that the opposites condition one another, that they are really one and the same thing. This can easily be seen in persons with an inferiority complex: they foment a little megalomania somewhere. The fact that the opposites appear as gods comes from the simple recognition that they are exceedingly powerful. Chinese philosophy therefore declared them to be cosmic principles, and named them *yang* and *yin*. Their power increases the more one tries to separate them. "When a tree grows up to heaven its roots reach down to hell," says Nietzsche. Yet, above as below, it is the same tree. It is characteristic of our Western mentality that we should separate the two aspects into antagonistic personifications: God and the Devil. And it is equally characteristic of the worldly optimism of Protestantism that it should have hushed up the Devil in a tactful sort of way, at any

14 Cf. the *Shrī-Chakra-Sambhara Tantra*, in Avalon, ed., *Tantric Texts*, VII.

rate in recent times. *Omne bonum a Deo, omne malum ab homine* is the uncomfortable consequence.

792   The "seeing of reality" clearly refers to Mind as the supreme reality. In the West, however, the unconscious is considered to be a fantastic irreality. The "seeing of the Mind" implies self-liberation. This means, psychologically, that the more weight we attach to unconscious processes the more we detach ourselves from the world of desires and of separated opposites, and the nearer we draw to the state of unconsciousness with its qualities of oneness, indefiniteness, and timelessness. This is truly a liberation of the self from its bondage to strife and suffering. "By this method, one's mind is understood." Mind in this context is obviously the individual's mind, that is, his psyche. Psychology can agree in so far as the understanding of the unconscious is one of its foremost tasks.

Salutation to the One Mind

793   This section shows very clearly that the One Mind is the unconscious, since it is characterized as "eternal, unknown, not visible, not recognized." But it also displays positive features which are in keeping with Eastern experience. These are the attributes "ever clear, ever existing, radiant and unobscured." It is an undeniable psychological fact that the more one concentrates on one's unconscious contents the more they become charged with energy; they become vitalized, as if illuminated from within. In fact they turn into something like a substitute reality. In analytical psychology we make methodical use of this phenomenon. I have called the method "active imagination." Ignatius Loyola also made use of active imagination in his *Exercitia*. There is evidence that something similar was used in the meditations of alchemical philosophy.[15]

The Result of Not Knowing the One Mind

794   "Knowledge of that which is vulgarly called mind is widespread." This clearly refers to the conscious mind of everybody, in contrast to the One Mind which is unknown, i.e., unconscious. These teachings "will also be sought after by ordi-

---

15 Cf. *Psychology and Alchemy*, pars. 390ff. [Also *Mysterium Coniunctionis*, pars. 706, 753ff.]

nary individuals who, not knowing the One Mind, do not know themselves." Self-knowledge is here definitely identified with "knowing the One Mind," which means that knowledge of the unconscious is essential for any understanding of one's own psychology. The desire for such knowledge is a well-established fact in the West, as evidenced by the rise of psychology in our time and a growing interest in these matters. The public desire for more psychological knowledge is largely due to the suffering which results from the disuse of religion and from the lack of spiritual guidance. "They wander hither and thither in the Three Regions . . . suffering sorrow." As we know what a neurosis can mean in moral suffering, this statement needs no comment. This section formulates the reasons why we have such a thing as the psychology of the unconscious today.

795   Even if one wishes "to know the mind as it is, one fails." The text again stresses how hard it is to gain access to the basic mind, because it is unconscious.

The Results of Desires

796   Those "fettered by desires cannot perceive the Clear Light." The "Clear Light" again refers to the One Mind. Desires crave for external fulfilment. They forge the chain that fetters man to the world of consciousness. In that condition he naturally cannot become aware of his unconscious contents. And indeed there is a healing power in withdrawing from the conscious world—up to a point. Beyond that point, which varies with individuals, withdrawal amounts to neglect and repression.

797   Even the "Middle Path" finally becomes "obscured by desires." This is a very true statement, which cannot be dinned too insistently into European ears. Patients and normal individuals, on becoming acquainted with their unconscious material, hurl themselves upon it with the same heedless desirousness and greed that before had engulfed them in their extraversion. The problem is not so much a withdrawal from the objects of desire, as a more detached attitude to desire as such, no matter what its object. We cannot compel unconscious compensation through the impetuousness of uncontrolled desire. We have to wait patiently to see whether it will come of its own accord, and put up with whatever form it takes. Hence we are forced

into a sort of contemplative attitude which, in itself, not rarely has a liberating and healing effect.

The Transcendent At-one-ment

798   "There being really no duality, pluralism is untrue." This is certainly one of the most fundamental truths of the East. There are no opposites—it is the same tree above and below. The *Tabula smaragdina* says: "Quod est inferius est sicut quod est superius. Et quod est superius est sicut quod est inferius, ad perpetranda miracula rei unius." [16] Pluralism is even more illusory, since all separate forms originate in the indistinguishable oneness of the psychic matrix, deep down in the unconscious. The statement made by our text refers psychologically to the subjective factor, to the material immediately constellated by a stimulus, i.e., the first impression which, as we have seen, interprets every new perception in terms of previous experience. "Previous experience" goes right back to the instincts, and thus to the inherited and inherent patterns of psychic functioning, the ancestral and "eternal" laws of the human mind. But the statement entirely ignores the possible transcendent reality of the physical world as such, a problem not unknown to Sankhya philosophy, where *prakriti* and *purusha*—so far as they are a polarization of Universal Being—form a cosmic dualism that can hardly be circumvented. One has to close one's eyes to dualism and pluralism alike, and forget all about the existence of a world, as soon as one tries to identify oneself with the monistic origin of life. The questions naturally arise: "Why should the One appear as the Many, when ultimate reality is All-One? What is the cause of pluralism, or of the illusion of pluralism? If the One is pleased with itself, why should it mirror itself in the Many? Which after all is the more real, the one that mirrors itself, or the mirror it uses?" Probably we should not ask such questions, seeing that there is no answer to them.

799   It is psychologically correct to say that "At-one-ment" is attained by withdrawal from the world of consciousness. In the stratosphere of the unconscious there are no more thunder-

---

[16] "What is below is like what is above. And what is above is like what is below. so that the miracle of the One may be accomplished." Cf. Ruska, *Tabula Smaragdina*, p. 2.

storms, because nothing is differentiated enough to produce tensions and conflicts. These belong to the surface of our reality.

800   The Mind in which the irreconcilables—samsāra and nir-vāna—are united is ultimately our mind. Does this statement spring from profound modesty or from overweening hybris? Does it mean that the Mind is "nothing but" our mind? Or that our mind is the Mind? Assuredly it means the latter, and from the Eastern point of view there is no hybris in this; on the contrary, it is a perfectly acceptable truth, whereas with us it would amount to saying "I am God." This is an incontestable "mystical" experience, though a highly objectionable one to the Westerner; but in the East, where it derives from a mind that has never lost touch with the instinctual matrix, it has a very different value. The collective introverted attitude of the East did not permit the world of the senses to sever the vital link with the unconscious; psychic reality was never seriously disputed, despite the existence of so-called materialistic speculations. The only known analogy to this fact is the mental condition of the primitive, who confuses dream and reality in the most bewildering way. Naturally we hesitate to call the Eastern mind primitive, for we are deeply impressed with its remarkable civilization and differentiation. Yet the primitive mind is its matrix, and this is particularly true of that aspect of it which stresses the validity of psychic phenomena, such as relate to ghosts and spirits. The West has simply cultivated the other aspect of primitivity, namely, the scrupulously accurate observation of nature at the expense of abstraction. Our natural science is the epitome of primitive man's astonishing powers of observation. We have added only a moderate amount of abstraction, for fear of being contradicted by the facts. The East, on the other hand, cultivates the psychic aspect of primitivity together with an inordinate amount of abstraction. Facts make excellent stories but not much more.

801   Thus, if the East speaks of the Mind as being inherent in everybody, no more hybris or modesty is involved than in the European's belief in facts, which are mostly derived from man's own observation and sometimes from rather less than his observation, to wit, his interpretation. He is, therefore, quite right to be afraid of too much abstraction.

The Great Self-Liberation

802   I have mentioned more than once that the shifting of the
basic personality-feeling to the less conscious mental sphere has
a liberating effect. I have also described, somewhat cursorily,
the transcendent function which produces the transformation
of personality, and I have emphasized the importance of spontaneous unconscious compensation. Further, I have pointed out
the neglect of this crucial fact in yoga. This section tends to
confirm my observations. The grasping of "the whole essence
of these teachings" seems also to be the whole essence of "self-
liberation." The Westerner would take this to mean: "Learn
your lesson and repeat it, and then you will be self-liberated."
That, indeed, is precisely what happens with most Western
practitioners of yoga. They are very apt to "do" it in an extraverted fashion, oblivious of the inturning of the mind which
is the essence of such teachings. In the East, the "truths" are so
much a part of the collective consciousness that they are at least
intuitively grasped by the pupil. If the European could turn
himself inside out and live as an Oriental, with all the social,
moral, religious, intellectual, and aesthetic obligations which
such a course would involve, he might be able to benefit by
these teachings. But you cannot be a good Christian, either in
your faith or in your morality or in your intellectual make-up,
and practise genuine yoga at the same time. I have seen too
many cases that have made me sceptical in the highest degree.
The trouble is that Western man cannot get rid of his history as
easily as his short-legged memory can. History, one might say,
is written in the blood. I would not advise anyone to touch yoga
without a careful analysis of his unconscious reactions. What is
the use of imitating yoga if your dark side remains as good a
medieval Christian as ever? If you can afford to seat yourself
on a gazelle skin under a Bo-tree or in the cell of a *gompa* for
the rest of your life without being troubled by politics or the
collapse of your securities, I will look favourably upon your
case. But yoga in Mayfair or Fifth Avenue, or in any other place
which is on the telephone, is a spiritual fake.

803   Taking the mental equipment of Eastern man into account,
we may suppose that the teaching is effective. But unless one is
prepared to turn away from the world and to disappear into the

unconscious for good, mere teaching has no effect, or at least not the desired one. For this the union of opposites is necessary, and in particular the difficult task of reconciling extraversion and introversion by means of the transcendent function.

The Nature of Mind

804   This section contains a valuable piece of psychological information. The text says: "The mind is of intuitive ("quick-knowing") Wisdom." Here "mind" is understood to be identical with immediate awareness of the "first impression" which conveys the whole sum of previous experience based upon instinctual patterns. This bears out our remarks about the essentially introverted prejudice of the East. The formula also draws attention to the highly differentiated character of Eastern intuition. The intuitive mind is noted for its disregard of facts in favour of possibilities.[17]

805   The assertion that the Mind "has no existence" obviously refers to the peculiar "potentiality" of the unconscious. A thing seems to exist only to the degree that we are aware of it, which explains why so many people are disinclined to believe in the existence of an unconscious. When I tell a patient that he is chock full of fantasies, he is often astonished beyond all measure, having been completely unaware of the fantasy-life he was leading.

The Names Given to the Mind

806   The various terms employed to express a "difficult" or "obscure" idea are a valuable source of information about the ways in which that idea can be interpreted, and at the same time an indication of its doubtful or controversial nature even in the country, religion, or philosophy to which it is indigenous. If the idea were perfectly straightforward and enjoyed general acceptance, there would be no reason to call it by a number of different names. But when something is little known, or ambiguous, it can be envisaged from different angles, and then a multiplicity of names is needed to express its peculiar nature. A classical example of this is the philosophers' stone; many of the old alchemical treatises give long lists of its names.

17 Cf. *Psychological Types*, Def. 35.

807   The statement that "the various names given to it [the Mind] are innumerable" proves that the Mind must be something as vague and indefinite as the philosophers' stone. A substance that can be described in "innumerable" ways must be expected to display as many qualities or facets. If these are really "innumerable," they cannot be counted, and it follows that the substance is well-nigh indescribable and unknowable. It can never be realized completely. This is certainly true of the unconscious, and a further proof that the Mind is the Eastern equivalent of our concept of the unconscious, more particularly of the collective unconscious.

808   In keeping with this hypothesis, the text goes on to say that the Mind is also called the "Mental Self." The "self" is an important concept in analytical psychology, where much has been said that I need not repeat here. I would refer the interested reader to the literature given below.[18] Although the symbols of the "self" are produced by unconscious activity and are mostly manifested in dreams,[19] the facts which the idea covers are not merely mental; they include aspects of physical existence as well. In this and other Eastern texts the "Self" represents a purely spiritual idea, but in Western psychology the "self" stands for a totality which comprises instincts, physiological and semi-physiological phenomena. To us a purely spiritual totality is inconceivable for the reasons mentioned above.[20]

809   It is interesting to note that in the East, too, there are "heretics" who identify the Self with the ego.[21] With us this heresy is pretty widespread and is subscribed to by all those who firmly believe that ego-consciousness is the only form of psychic life.

810   The Mind as "the means of attaining the Other Shore" points to a connection between the transcendent function and the idea of the Mind or Self. Since the unknowable substance of the Mind, i.e., of the unconscious, always represents itself to consciousness in the form of symbols—the self being one such

[18] Cf. *Two Essays on Analytical Psychology*, index, s.v. "self"; *Psychological Types*, Def. 16 [and 46 in *Coll. Works*, 6]; *Psychology and Alchemy*, Part II; *Aion*, ch. IV.
[19] One such case is described in Part II of *Psychology and Alchemy*.
[20] This is no criticism of the Eastern point of view *in toto*; for, according to the *Amitāyur-dhyāna Sūtra*, the Buddha's body is included in the meditation.
[21] Cf. for instance, *Chhāndogya Upanishad*, viii. 8.

symbol—the symbol functions as a "means of attaining the Other Shore," in other words, as a means of transformation. In my essay on psychic energy I said that the symbol acts as a transformer of energy.[22]

811   My interpretation of the Mind or Self as a symbol is not arbitrary; the text itself calls it "The Great Symbol."

812   It is also remarkable that our text recognizes the "potentiality" of the unconscious, as formulated above, by calling the Mind the "Sole Seed" and the "Potentiality of Truth."

813   The matrix-character of the unconscious comes out in the term "All-Foundation."

The Timelessness of Mind

814   I have already explained this "timelessness" as a quality inherent in the experience of the collective unconscious. The application of the "yoga of self-liberation" is said to reintegrate all forgotten knowledge of the past with consciousness. The motif of ἀποκατάστασις (restoration, restitution) occurs in many redemption myths and is also an important aspect of the psychology of the unconscious, which reveals an extraordinary amount of archaic material in the dreams and spontaneous fantasies of normal and insane people. In the systematic analysis of an individual the spontaneous reawakening of ancestral patterns (as a compensation) has the effect of a restoration. It is also a fact that premonitory dreams are relatively frequent, and this substantiates what the text calls "knowledge of the future."

815   The Mind's "own time" is very difficult to interpret. From the psychological point of view we must agree with Dr. Evans-Wentz's comment here.[23] The unconscious certainly has its "own time" inasmuch as past, present, and future are blended together in it. Dreams of the type experienced by J. W. Dunne,[24] where he dreamed the night before what he ought logically to have dreamed the night after, are not infrequent.

22 "On Psychic Energy," p. 48.
23 Cf. his *Tibetan Book of the Great Liberation*, p. 210, n. 3.
24 *An Experiment with Time.* [Cf. Jung's "Synchronicity: An Acausal Connecting Principle," p. 433.—EDITORS].

Mind in Its True State

816   This section describes the state of detached consciousness [25] which corresponds to a psychic experience very common throughout the East. Similar descriptions are to be found in Chinese literature, as, for instance, in the *Hui Ming Ch'ing:*

A luminosity surrounds the world of spirit.
We forget one another when, still and pure, we draw strength from
    the Void.
The Void is filled with the light of the Heart of Heaven . . .
Consciousness dissolves in vision.[26]

817   The statement "Nor is one's own mind separable from other minds" is another way of expressing the fact of "all-contamination." Since all distinctions vanish in the unconscious condition, it is only logical that the distinction between separate minds should disappear too. Wherever there is a lowering of the conscious level we come across instances of unconscious identity,[27] or what Lévy-Bruhl calls "participation mystique." [28] The realization of the One Mind is, as our text says, the "at-one-ment of the *Trikāya*"; in fact it creates the at-one-ment. But we are unable to imagine how such a realization could ever be complete in any human individual. There must always be somebody or something left over to experience the realization, to say "I know at-one-ment, I know there is no distinction." The very fact of the realization proves its inevitable incompleteness. One cannot know something that is not distinct from oneself. Even

[25] I have explained this in my "Commentary on *The Secret of the Golden Flower,*" pars. 64ff.   [26] From the [German] trans. of L. C. Lo, I, p. 114. [Cf. *Golden Flower,* 1962, pp. 77f.]   [27] *Psychological Types,* Def. 25.
[28] Cf. Lévy-Bruhl, *How Natives Think.* Recently this concept as well as that of the *état prélogique* have been severely criticized by ethnologists, and moreover Lévy-Bruhl himself began to doubt their validity in the last years of his life. First he cancelled the adjective "mystique," growing afraid of the term's bad reputation in intellectual circles. It is rather to be regretted that he made such a concession to rationalistic superstition, since "mystique" is just the right word to characterize the peculiar quality of "unconscious identity." There is always something numinous about it. Unconscious identity is a well-known psychological and psychopathological phenomenon (identity with persons, things, functions, roles, positions, creeds, etc.), which is only a shade more characteristic of the primitive than of the civilized mind. Lévy-Bruhl, unfortunately having no psychological knowledge, was not aware of this fact, and his opponents ignore it.

when I say "I know myself," an infinitesimal ego—the knowing "I"—is still distinct from "myself." In this as it were atomic ego, which is completely ignored by the essentially non-dualist standpoint of the East, there nevertheless lies hidden the whole unabolished pluralistic universe and its unconquered reality.

818   The experience of "at-one-ment" is one example of those "quick-knowing" realizations of the East, an intuition of what it would be like if one could exist and not exist at the same time. If I were a Moslem, I should maintain that the power of the All-Compassionate is infinite, and that He alone can make a man to be and not to be at the same time. But for my part I cannot conceive of such a possibility. I therefore assume that, in this point, Eastern intuition has overreached itself.

Mind Is Non-Created

819   This section emphasizes that as the Mind is without characteristics, one cannot assert that it is created. But then, it would be illogical to assert that it is non-created, for such a qualification would amount to a "characteristic." As a matter of fact you can make no assertion whatever about a thing that is indistinct, void of characteristics and, moreover, "unknowable." For precisely this reason Western psychology does not speak of the One Mind, but of the unconscious, regarding it as a thing-in-itself, a noumenon, "a merely negative borderline concept," to quote Kant.[29] We have often been reproached for using such a negative term, but unfortunately intellectual honesty does not allow a positive one.

The Yoga of Introspection

820   Should there be any doubt left concerning the identity of the One Mind and the unconscious, this section certainly ought to dispel it. "The One Mind being verily of the Voidness and without any foundation, one's mind is, likewise, as vacuous as the sky." The One Mind and the individual mind are equally void and vacuous. Only the collective and the personal unconscious can be meant by this statement, for the conscious mind is in no circumstances "vacuous."

29 Cf. *The Critique of Pure Reason*, sec. i, Part I, 2, 3 (cf. trans. by Meiklejohn, p. 188).

821   As I have said earlier, the Eastern mind insists first and foremost upon the subjective factor, and in particular upon the
intuitive "first impression," or the psychic disposition. This is
borne out by the statement that "All appearances are verily one's
own concepts, self-conceived in the mind."

The Dharma Within

522   *Dharma,* law, truth, guidance, is said to be "nowhere save in
the mind." Thus the unconscious is credited with all those
faculties which the West attributes to God. The transcendent
function, however, shows how right the East is in assuming that
the complex experience of *dharma* comes from "within,". i.e.,
from the unconscious. It also shows that the phenomenon of
spontaneous compensation, being beyond the control of man, is
quite in accord with the formula "grace" or the "will of God."

823   This and the preceding section insist again and again that
introspection is the only source of spiritual information and
guidance. If introspection were something morbid, as certain
people in the West opine, we should have to send practically the
whole East, or such parts of it as are not yet infected with the
blessings of the West, to the lunatic asylum.

The Wondrousness of These Teachings

824   This section calls the mind "Natural Wisdom," which is very
much the same expression that I used in order to designate the
symbols produced by the unconscious. I called them "natural
symbols." [30] I chose the term before I had any knowledge of this
text. I mention this fact simply because it illustrates the close
parallelism between the findings of Eastern and Western psychology.

825   The text also confirms what we said earlier about the im-
possibility of a "knowing" ego. "Although it is Total Reality,
there is no perceiver of it. Wondrous is this." Wondrous indeed,
and incomprehensible; for how could such a thing ever be
realized in the true sense of the word? "It remains undefiled by
evil" and "it remains unallied to good." One is reminded of
Nietzsche's "six thousand feet beyond good and evil." But the
consequences of such a statement are usually ignored by the

30 Cf. the first paper in this volume, chs. 2 and 3.

emulators of Eastern wisdom. While one is safely ensconced in one's cosy flat, secure in the favour of the Oriental gods, one is free to admire this lofty moral indifference. But does it agree with our temperament, or with our history, which is not thereby conquered but merely forgotten? I think not. Anyone who affects the higher yoga will be called upon to prove his professions of moral indifference, not only as the doer of evil but, even more, as its victim. As psychologists well know, the moral conflict is not to be settled merely by a declaration of superiority bordering on inhumanity. We are witnessing today some terrifying examples of the Superman's aloofness from moral principles.

826   I do not doubt that the Eastern liberation from vices, as well as from virtues, is coupled with detachment in every respect, so that the yogi is translated beyond this world, and quite inoffensive. But I suspect every European attempt at detachment of being mere liberation from moral considerations. Anybody who tries his hand at yoga ought therefore to be conscious of its far-reaching consequences, or else his so-called quest will remain a futile pastime.

The Fourfold Great Path

827   The text says: "This meditation [is] devoid of mental concentration." The usual assumption about yoga is that it chiefly consists in intense concentration. We think we know what concentration means, but it is very difficult to arrive at a real understanding of Eastern concentration. Our sort may well be just the opposite of the Eastern, as a study of Zen Buddhism will show.[31] However, if we take "devoid of mental concentration" literally, it can only mean that the meditation does not centre upon anything. Not being centred, it would be rather like a dissolution of consciousness and hence a direct approach to the unconscious condition. Consciousness always implies a certain degree of concentration, without which there would be no clarity of mental content and no consciousness of anything. Meditation without concentration would be a waking but empty condition, on the verge of falling asleep. Since our text calls this "the most excellent of meditations" we must suppose the existence of less excellent meditations which, we infer, would be characterized

31 Cf. Suzuki, Essays in Zen Buddhism.

by more concentration. The meditation our text has in mind seems to be a sort of Royal Road to the unconscious.

The Great Light

828   The central mystical experience of enlightenment is aptly symbolized by Light in most of the numerous forms of mysticism. It is a curious paradox that the approach to a region which seems to us the way into utter darkness should yield the light of illumination as its fruit. This is, however, the usual *enantio-dromia per tenebras ad lucem*. Many initiation ceremonies [32] stage a κατάβασις εἰς ἄντρον (descent into the cave), a diving down into the depths of the baptismal water, or a return to the womb of rebirth. Rebirth symbolism simply describes the union of opposites—conscious and unconscious—by means of concretistic analogies. Underlying all rebirth symbolism is the transcendent function. Since this function results in an increase of consciousness (the previous condition augmented by the addition of formerly unconscious contents), the new condition carries more insight, which is symbolized by more light.[33] It is therefore a more enlightened state compared with the relative darkness of the previous state. In many cases the Light even appears in the form of a vision.

The Yoga of the Nirvanic Path

829   This section gives one of the best formulations of the complete dissolution of consciousness, which appears to be the goal of this yoga: "There being no two such things as action and performer of action, if one seeks the performer of action and no performer of action be found anywhere, thereupon the goal of all fruit-obtaining is reached and also the final consummation itself."

830   With this very complete formulation of the method and its aim, I reach the end of my commentary. The text that follows, in Book II, is of great beauty and wisdom, and contains nothing

[32] As in the Eleusinian mysteries and the Mithras and Attis cults.
[33] In alchemy the philosophers' stone was called, among other things, *lux moderna, lux lucis, lumen luminum*, etc.

that requires further comment. It can be translated into psychological language and interpreted with the help of the principles I have here set forth in Part I and illustrated in Part II.

FOREWORD TO SUZUKI'S
"INTRODUCTION TO ZEN BUDDHISM"[1]

877   Daisetz Teitaro Suzuki's works on Zen Buddhism are among
the best contributions to the knowledge of living Buddhism that
recent decades have produced, and Zen itself is the most important fruit to have sprung from the tree whose roots are the
collections of the Pali Canon.[2] We cannot be sufficiently grateful to the author, first for having brought Zen closer to Western
understanding, and secondly for the manner in which he has
performed this task. Oriental religious conceptions are usually
so very different from our Western ones that even the bare
translation of the words often presents the greatest difficulties,
quite apart from the meaning of the terms used, which in certain circumstances are better left untranslated. I need only
mention the Chinese "tao," which no European translation has

1 [Originally published as a foreword to Suzuki, *Die grosse Befreiung: Einführung
in den Zen-Buddhismus* (Leipzig, 1939). The Suzuki text had been translated into
German by Heinrich Zimmer from the original edition of *An Introduction to
Zen Buddhism*. The foreword by Jung was published in an earlier translation by
Constance Rolfe in a new edition of the Suzuki work (London and New York,
1949).—EDITORS.]
2 The origin of Zen, as Oriental authors themselves admit, is to be found in
Buddha's Flower Sermon. On this occasion he held up a flower to a gathering of
disciples without uttering a word. Only Kasyapa understood him. Cf. Shuei
Ohazama, *Zen: Der lebendige Buddhismus in Japan*, p. 3.

yet got near. The original Buddhist writings contain views and
ideas which are more or less unassimilable for ordinary Europeans. I do not know, for instance, just what kind of mental (or
perhaps climatic?) background or preparation is necessary before
one can form any completely clear idea of what is meant by the
Buddhist "kamma." Judging by all we know of the nature of
Zen, here too we are up against a central conception of unsurpassed singularity. This strange conception is called "satori,"
which may be translated as "enlightenment." "Satori is the
raison d'être of Zen without which Zen is not Zen," says Suzuki.[3]
It should not be too difficult for the Western mind to grasp what
a mystic understands by "enlightenment," or what is known as
such in religious parlance. Satori, however, designates a special
kind and way of enlightenment which it is practically impossible
for the European to appreciate. By way of illustration, I would
refer the reader to the enlightenment of Hyakujo (Pai-chang
Huai-hai, A.D. 724–814) and of the Confucian poet and states-
man Kozankoku (Huang Shan-ku),[4] as described by Suzuki.

878   The following may serve as a further example: A monk
once went to Gensha, and wanted to learn where the entrance
to the path of truth was. Gensha asked him, "Do you hear the
murmuring of the brook?" "Yes, I hear it," answered the monk.
"There is the entrance," the Master instructed him.

879   I will content myself with these few examples, which aptly
illustrate the opacity of satori experiences. Even if we take example after example, it still remains exceedingly obscure how
any enlightenment comes and of what it consists—in other
words, by what or about what one is enlightened. Kaiten
Nukariya, who was himself a professor at the So-to-shu Buddhist
College in Tokyo, says, speaking of enlightenment:

Having set ourselves free from the mistaken conception of self, next
we must awaken our innermost wisdom, pure and divine, called the
Mind of Buddha, or Bodhi, or Prajna by Zen masters. It is the divine
light, the inner heaven, the key to all moral treasures, the centre of
thought and consciousness, the source of all influence and power,
the seat of kindness, justice, sympathy, impartial love, humanity,
and mercy, the measure of all things. When this innermost wisdom
is fully awakened, we are able to realize that each and every one
of us is identical in spirit, in essence, in nature with the universal

3 *Introduction to Zen Buddhism* (1949), p. 95.   4 Ibid., pp. 89 and 92f.

life or Buddha, that each ever lives face to face with Buddha, that each is beset by the abundant grace of the Blessed One, that He arouses his moral nature, that He opens his spiritual eyes, that He unfolds his new capacity, that He appoints his mission, and that life is not an ocean of birth, disease, old age, and death, nor the vale of tears, but the holy temple of Buddha, the Pure Land, where he can enjoy the bliss of Nirvana.[5]

880   That is how an Oriental, himself an adept in Zen, describes the essence of enlightenment. One must admit that this passage would need only a few trifling alterations in order to find its way into a Christian mystical book of devotion. Yet somehow it sends us away empty as regards understanding the satori experience described again and again in the literature. Presumably Nukariya is addressing himself to Western rationalism, of which he himself acquired a good dose, and that is why it all sounds so flatly edifying. The abstruse obscurity of the Zen anecdotes is distinctly preferable to this adaptation *ad usum Delphini:* it conveys a great deal more by saying less.

881   Zen is anything but a philosophy in the Western sense of the word.[6] This is also the opinion of Rudolf Otto, who says in his foreword to Ohazama's book on Zen that Nukariya has "imported the magical world of Oriental ideas into our Western philosophical categories" and confused it with these. "If psychophysical parallelism, that most wooden of all doctrines, is invoked in order to explain this mystical intuition of Non-duality and Oneness and the *coincidentia oppositorum,* then one is completely outside the sphere of the *koan,* the *kwatsu,* and *satori.*"[7] It is far better to allow oneself to become deeply imbued at the outset with the exotic obscurity of the Zen anecdotes, and to bear in mind the whole time that satori is a *mysterium ineffabile,* as indeed the Zen masters wish it to be. Between the anecdote and the mystical enlightenment there is, to our way of thinking, a gulf, and the possibility of bridging it can at best be hinted but never in practice achieved.[8] One has

[5] *The Religion of the Samurai,* p. 133.

[6] "Zen is neither psychology nor philosophy."   [7] In Ohazama, p. viii.

[8] If in spite of this I attempt "explanations" in what follows, I am nevertheless fully aware that in the sense of satori I have said nothing valid. All the same, I had to make an attempt to manoeuvre our Western understanding into at least the proximity of an understanding—a task so difficult that in doing it one must take upon oneself certain crimes against the spirit of Zen.

the feeling of touching upon a true secret, and not one that is merely imagined or pretended. It is not a question of mystification and mumbo-jumbo, but rather of an experience which strikes the experient dumb. Satori comes upon one unawares, as something utterly unexpected.

882   When, in the sphere of Christianity, visions of the Holy Trinity, the Madonna, the Crucified, or of the patron saint are vouchsafed after long spiritual preparation, one has the impression that this is all more or less as it should be. That Jakob Böhme should obtain a glimpse into the *centrum naturae* by means of a sunbeam reflected in a tin platter is also understandable. It is harder to digest Meister Eckhart's vision of the "little naked boy," not to speak of Swedenborg's "man in the purple coat," who wanted to dissuade him from overeating, and whom, in spite—or perhaps because—of this, he recognized as the Lord God.[9] Such things are difficult to swallow, bordering as they do on the grotesque. Many of the Zen anecdotes, however, not only border on the grotesque but are right there in the middle of it, and sound like the most crashing nonsense.

883   For anyone who has devoted himself, with love and sympathetic understanding, to studying the flowerlike mind of the Far East, many of these puzzling things, which drive the naïve European from one perplexity to another, simply disappear. Zen is indeed one of the most wonderful blossoms of the Chinese spirit [10]—a spirit fertilized by the immense world of Buddhist thought. Anyone who has really tried to understand Buddhist doctrine—even if only to the extent of giving up certain Western prejudices—will begin to suspect treacherous depths beneath the bizarre surface of individual satori experiences, or will sense disquieting difficulties which the religion and philosophy of the West have up to now thought fit to disregard. If he is a philosopher, he is exclusively concerned with the kind of understanding that has nothing to do with life. And if he is a Christian, he has of course no truck with heathens ("God, I thank thee that I

9 Cf. Spamer, ed., *Texte aus der deutschen Mystik des 14. und 15. Jahrhunderts*, p. 143; Evans, *Meister Eckhart*, I, p. 438; William White, *Emanuel Swedenborg*, I, p. 243.

10 "There is no doubt that Zen is one of the most precious and in many respects the most remarkable [of the] spiritual possessions bequeathed to Eastern people." Suzuki, *Essays on Zen Buddhism*, I, p. 264.

am not as other men are"). There is no satori within these Western limits—that is a purely Oriental affair. But is this really so? Have we in fact no satori?

884   When one reads the Zen texts attentively, one cannot escape the impression that, however bizarre, satori is a *natural occurrence,* something so very simple,[11] even, that one fails to see the wood for the trees, and in attempting to explain it invariably says the very thing that throws others into the greatest confusion. Nukariya is therefore right when he says that any attempt to explain or analyse the content of Zen, or of the enlightenment, is futile. Nevertheless he does venture to assert that enlightenment "implies an insight into the nature of self," [12] and that it is an "emancipation of mind from illusion concerning self." [13] The illusion concerning the nature of self is the common confusion of the self with the ego. Nukariya understands by "self" the All-Buddha, i.e., total consciousness of life. He quotes Pan Shan, who says: "The moon of mind comprehends all the universe in its light," adding: "It is Cosmic life and Cosmic spirit, and at the same time individual life and individual spirit." [14]

885   However one may define the self, it is always something other than the ego, and inasmuch as a higher insight of the ego leads over to the self, the self is a more comprehensive thing which includes the experience of the ego and therefore transcends it. Just as the ego is a certain experience I have of myself, so is the self an experience of my ego. It is, however, no longer experienced in the form of a broader or higher ego, but in the form of a non-ego.

886   Such thoughts were familiar to the anonymous author of the *Theologia Germanica:*

> In whatsoever creature the Perfect shall be known, therein creature-nature, created state, I-hood, selfhood, and the like must all be given up and done away.[15]

---

[11] "Before a man studies Zen, to him mountains are mountains and waters are waters; after he gets an insight into the truth of Zen, through the instruction of a good master, mountains to him are not mountains and waters are not waters; after this when he really attains to the abode of rest, mountains are once more mountains and waters are waters." Ibid., pp. 22f.

[12] *Religion of the Samurai,* p. 123.   [13] Ibid., p. 124.   [14] Ibid., p. 132.

[15] *Theologia Germanica,* ed. by Trask, p. 115.

Now that I arrogate anything good to myself, as if I were, or had done, or knew, or could perform any good thing, or that it were mine; that is all out of blindness and folly. For if the real truth were in me, I should understand that I am not that good thing, and that it is not mine nor of me.

Then the man says: "Behold! I, poor fool that I was, thought it was I, but behold! it is, and was, of a truth, God!" [16]

887   This tells us a good deal about the "content of enlightenment." The occurrence of satori is interpreted and formulated as a *break-through,* by a consciousness limited to the ego-form, into the non-ego-like self. This view is in accord not only with the essence of Zen, but also with the mysticism of Meister Eckhart:

When I flowed out from God, all things declared, "God is!" Now this cannot make me blessed, for thereby I acknowledge myself a creature. But in the breakthrough [17] I stand empty in the will of God, and empty also of God's will, and of all his works, even of God himself—then I am more than all creatures, then I am neither God nor creature: I am what I was, and that I shall remain, now and ever more! Then I receive a thrust which carries me above all angels. By this thrust I become so rich that God cannot suffice me, despite all that he is as God and all his godly works; for in this breakthrough I receive what God and I have in common. I am what I was, [18] I neither increase nor diminish, for I am the unmoved mover that moves all things. Here God can find no more place in man, for man by his emptiness has won back that which he was eternally and ever shall remain. [19]

888   Here the Master may actually be describing a satori experience, a supersession of the ego by the self, which is endued with the "Buddha nature" or divine universality. Since, out of scientific modesty, I do not presume to make a metaphysical statement, but am referring only to a change of consciousness that can be experienced, I treat satori first of all as a psychological

16 Ibid., pp. 120–21.
17 There is a similar image in Zen: When a Master was asked what Buddhahood consisted in, he answered, "The bottom of a pail is broken through" (Suzuki, *Essays,* I, p. 229). Another analogy is the "bursting of the bag" (*Essays,* II, p. 117).
18 Cf. Suzuki, *Essays,* I, pp. 231, 255. Zen means catching a glimpse of the original nature of man, or the recognition of the original man (p. 157).
19 Cf. Evans, *Meister Eckhart,* p. 221; also *Meister Eckhart: A Modern Translation,* by Blakney, pp. 231f.

problem. For anyone who does not share or understand this point of view, the "explanation" will consist of nothing but words which have no tangible meaning. He is then incapable of throwing a bridge from these abstractions to the facts reported; that is to say, he cannot understand how the scent of the blossoming laurel or the tweaked nose [20] could bring about so formidable a change of consciousness. Naturally the simplest thing would be to relegate all these anecdotes to the realm of amusing fairytales, or, if one accepts the facts as they are, to write them off as instances of self-deception. (Another favourite explanation is "auto-suggestion," that pathetic white elephant from the arsenal of intellectual inadequacies!) But no serious and responsible investigation can pass over these facts unheedingly. Of course, we can never decide definitely whether a person is *really* "enlightened" or "released," or whether he merely imagines it. We have no criteria to go on. Moreover, we know well enough that an imaginary pain is often far more agonizing than a so-called real one, since it is accompanied by a subtle moral suffering caused by a dull feeling of secret self-accusation. In this sense, therefore, it is not a question of "actual fact" but of *psychic reality,* i.e., the psychic process known as satori.

889   Every psychic process is an image and an "imagining," otherwise no consciousness could exist and the occurrence would lack phenomenality. Imagination itself is a psychic process, for which reason it is completely irrelevant whether the enlightenment be called "real" or "imaginary." The person who has the enlightenment, or alleges that he has it, thinks at all events that he is enlightened. What others think about it decides nothing whatever for him in regard to his experience. Even if he were lying, his lie would still be a psychic fact. Indeed, even if all the reports of religious experiences were nothing but deliberate inventions and falsifications, a very interesting psychological treatise could still be written about the incidence of such lies, and with the same scientific objectivity with which one describes the psychopathology of delusional ideas. The fact that there is a religious movement upon which many brilliant minds have worked over a period of many centuries is sufficient reason for at least venturing a serious attempt to bring such processes within the realm of scientific understanding.

[20] Suzuki, *Introduction,* pp. 93, 84.

890   Earlier, I raised the question of whether we have anything like satori in the West. If we discount the sayings of our Western mystics, a superficial glance discloses nothing that could be likened to it in even the faintest degree. The possibility that there are stages in the development of consciousness plays no role in our thinking. The mere thought that there is a tremendous psychological difference between consciousness of the existence of an object and "consciousness of the consciousness" of an object borders on a quibble that hardly needs answering. For the same reason, one could hardly bring oneself to take such a problem seriously enough to consider the psychological conditions in which it arose. It is significant that questions of this kind do not, as a rule, arise from any intellectual need, but, where they exist, are nearly always rooted in an originally religious practice. In India it was yoga and in China Buddhism which supplied the driving force for these attempts to wrench oneself free from bondage to a state of consciousness that was felt to be incomplete. So far as Western mysticism is concerned, its texts are full of instructions as to how man can and must release himself from the "I-ness" of his consciousness, so that through knowledge of his own nature he may rise above it and attain the inner (godlike) man. John of Ruysbroeck makes use of an image which was also known to Indian philosophy, that of the tree whose roots are above and its branches below: [21] "And he must climb up into the tree of faith, which grows from above downwards, for its roots are in the Godhead." [22] He also says, like the yogi: "Man must be free and without ideas, released from all attachments and empty of all creatures." [23] "He must be untouched by joy and sorrow, profit and loss, rising and falling, concern for others, pleasure and fear, and not be attached to any creature." [24] It is in this that the "unity" of his being consists, and this means "being turned inwards." Being turned inwards means that "a man is turned within, into his own heart, that he may understand and feel the inner working

---

[21] "Its root is above, its branches below—this eternal fig-tree! . . . That is Brahma, that is called the Immortal." Katha Upanishad, 6, 1, trans. by Hume, *The Thirteen Principal Upanishads*, p. 358.
[22] John of Ruysbroeck, *The Adornment of the Spiritual Marriage*, p. 47. One can hardly suppose that this Flemish mystic, who was born in 1273, borrowed this image from any Indian text.   [23] Ibid., p. 51.   [24] P. 57, modified.

145

and the inner words' of God." [25] This new state of consciousness born of religious practice is distinguished by the fact that
outward things no longer affect an ego-bound consciousness,
thus giving rise to mutual attachment, but that an empty consciousness stands open to another influence. This "other" influence is no longer felt as one's own activity, but as that of a
non-ego which has the conscious mind as its object.[26] It is as if
the subject-character of the ego had been overrun, or taken over,
by another subject which appears in place of the ego.[27] This is a
well-known religious experience, already formulated by St.
Paul.[28] Undoubtedly a new state of consciousness is described
here, separated from the earlier state by an incisive process of
religious transformation.

891   It could be objected that consciousness in itself has not
changed, only the consciousness of something, just as though one
had turned over the page of a book and now saw a different picture with the same eyes. I am afraid this is no more than an
arbitrary interpretation, for it does not fit the facts. The fact is
that in the texts it is not merely a different picture or object
that is described, but rather an experience of transformation,
often occurring amid the most violent psychic convulsions. The
blotting out of one picture and its replacement by another is
an everyday occurrence which has none of the attributes of a
transformation experience. *It is not that something different is
seen, but that one sees differently.* It is as though the spatial act
of seeing were changed by a new dimension. When the Master
asks: "Do you hear the murmuring of the brook?" he obviously
means something quite different from ordinary "hearing." [29]
Consciousness is something like perception, and like the latter
is subject to conditions and limitations. You can, for instance,
be conscious at various levels, within a narrower or wider field,

25 Ibid., p. 62, modified.
26 "O Lord . . . instruct me in the doctrine of the non-ego, which is grounded
in the self-nature of mind." Cited from the Lankavatāra Sutra, in Suzuki,
Essays, I, p. 89.
27 A Zen Master says: "Buddha is none other than the mind, or rather, him who
strives to see this mind."
28 Galatians 2:20: "It is no longer I who live, but Christ who lives in me."
29 Suzuki says of this change, "The old way of viewing things is abandoned and
the world acquires a new signification . . . a new beauty which exists in the
'refreshing breeze' and in the 'shining jewel.' " *Essays*, I, p. 249. See also p. 138.

more on the surface or deeper down. These differences in degree are often differences in kind as well, since they depend on the development of the personality as a whole; that is to say, on the nature of the perceiving subject.

892   The intellect has no interest in the nature of the perceiving subject so far as the latter only thinks logically. The intellect is essentially concerned with elaborating the contents of consciousness and with methods of elaboration. A rare philosophic passion is needed to compel the attempt to get beyond intellect and break through to a "knowledge of the knower." Such a passion is practically indistinguishable from the driving force of religion; consequently this whole problem belongs to the religious transformation process, which is incommensurable with intellect. Classical philosophy subserves this process on a wide scale, but this can be said less and less of the newer philosophy. Schopenhauer is still—with qualifications—classical, but Nietzsche's *Zarathustra* is no longer philosophy at all: it is a dramatic process of transformation which has completely swallowed up the intellect. It is no longer concerned with thought, but, in the highest sense, with the thinker of thought—and this on every page of the book. A new man, a completely transformed man, is to appear on the scene, one who has broken the shell of the old and who not only looks upon a new heaven and a new earth, but has created them. Angelus Silesius puts it rather more modestly than Zarathustra:

My body is a shell in which a chick lies closed about;
Brooded by the spirit of eternity, it waits its hatching out.[30]

893   Satori corresponds in the Christian sphere to an experience of religious transformation. As there are different degrees and kinds of such an experience, it may not be superfluous to define more accurately the category which corresponds most closely to the Zen experience. This is without doubt the mystic experience, which differs from other types in that its preliminary stages consist in "letting oneself go," in "emptying oneself of images and ideas," as opposed to those religious experiences which, like the exercises of Ignatius Loyola, are based on the practice of envisaging sacred images. In this latter class I would

30 From *Der Cherubinischer Wandersmann*. [Trans. by W. R. Trask (unpub.).]

include transformation through faith and prayer and through collective experience in Protestantism, since a very definite expectation plays the decisive role here, and not by any means "emptiness" or "freeness." The characteristically Eckhartian assertion that "God is Nothingness" may well be incompatible in principle with the contemplation of the Passion, with faith and collective expectations.

894   Thus the correspondence between satori and Western experience is limited to those few Christian mystics whose paradoxical statements skirt the edge of heterodoxy or actually overstep it. As we know, it was this that drew down on Meister Eckhart's writings the condemnation of the Church. If Buddhism were a "Church" in our sense of the word, she would undoubtedly find Zen an insufferable nuisance. The reason for this is the extreme individualism of its methods, and also the iconoclastic attitude of many of the Masters.[31] To the extent that Zen is a movement, collective forms have arisen in the course of the centuries, as can be seen from Suzuki's *Training of the Zen Buddhist Monk* (Kyoto, 1934). But these concern externals only. Apart from the typical mode of life, the spiritual training or development seems to lie in the method of the *koan*. The koan is understood to be a paradoxical question, statement, or action of the Master. Judging by Suzuki's description, it seems to consist chiefly of master-questions handed down in the form of anecdotes. These are submitted by the teacher to the student for meditation. A classic example is the Wu anecdote. A monk once asked the Master: "Has a dog a Buddha nature too?" Whereupon the Master replied: "Wu!" As Suzuki remarks, this "Wu" means quite simply "bow-wow," obviously just what the dog himself would have said in answer to such a question.[32]

895   At first sight it seems as if the posing of such a question as

31 *Satori* is the most intimate individual experience." *Essays*, I, p. 261.

    A Master says to his pupil: "I have really nothing to impart to you, and if I tried to do so you might have occasion to make me an object of ridicule. Besides, whatever I can tell you is my own and can never be yours." *Introduction*, p. 91.

    A monk says to the Master: "I have been seeking for the Buddha, but do not yet know how to go on with my research." Said the Master: "It is very much like looking for an ox when riding on one." *Essays*, II, p. 74.

    A Master says: "The mind that does not understand is the Buddha: there is no other." Ibid., p. 72.   32 *Essays*, II, pp. 84, 90.

an object of meditation would anticipate or prejudice the end-result, and that it would therefore determine the content of the experience, just as in the Jesuit exercises or in certain yoga meditations the content is determined by the task set by the teacher. The koans, however, are so various, so ambiguous, and above all so boundlessly paradoxical that even an expert must be completely in the dark as to what might be considered a suitable solution. In addition, the descriptions of the final result are so obscure that in no single case can one discover any rational connection between the koan and the experience of enlightenment. Since no logical sequence can be demonstrated, it remains to be supposed that the koan method puts not the smallest restraint upon the freedom of the psychic process and that the end-result therefore springs from nothing but the individual disposition of the pupil. The complete destruction of the rational intellect aimed at in the training creates an almost perfect lack of conscious presuppositions. These are excluded as far as possible, but not unconscious presuppositions—that is, the existing but unrecognized psychological disposition, which is anything but empty or a *tabula rasa*. It is a nature-given factor, and when it answers—this being obviously the satori experience—it is an answer of Nature, who has succeeded in conveying her reaction direct to the conscious mind.[33] What the unconscious nature of the pupil presents to the teacher or to the koan by way of an answer is, manifestly, satori. This seems, at least to me, to be the view which, to judge by the descriptions, formulates the nature of satori more or less correctly. It is also supported by the fact that the "glimpse into one's own nature," the "original man," and the depths of one's being are often a matter of supreme concern to the Zen master.[34]

[33] "Zen consciousness is to be nursed to maturity. When it is fully matured, it is sure to break out as satori, which is an insight into the unconscious." *Essays*, II, p. 60.

[34] The fourth maxim of Zen is "Seeing into one's nature and the attainment of Buddhahood" (I, p. 18). When a monk asked Hui-neng for instruction, the Master told him: "Show me your original face before you were born" (I, p. 224). A Japanese Zen book says: "If you wish to seek the Buddha, you ought to see into your own nature; for this nature is the Buddha himself" (I, p. 231). A satori experience shows a Master the "original man" (I, p. 255). Hui-neng said: "Think not of good, think not of evil, but see what at the moment your own original features are, which you had even before coming into existence" (II, p. 42).

896   Zen differs from all other exercises in meditation, whether philosophical or religious, in its total lack of presuppositions. Often Buddha himself is sternly rejected, indeed, almost blasphemously ignored, although—or perhaps just because—he could be the strongest spiritual presupposition of the whole exercise. But he too is an image and must therefore be set aside. Nothing must be present except what is actually there: that is, man with all his unconscious presuppositions, of which, precisely because they are unconscious, he can never, never rid himself. The answer which appears to come from the void, the light which flares up from the blackest darkness, these have always been experienced as a wonderful and blessed illumination.

897   The world of consciousness is inevitably a world full of restrictions, of walls blocking the way. It is of necessity one-sided, because of the nature of consciousness itself. No consciousness can harbour more than a very small number of simultaneous perceptions. All else must lie in shadow, withdrawn from sight. Any increase in the simultaneous contents immediately produces a dimming of consciousness, if not confusion to the point of disorientation. Consciousness not only requires, but is of its very nature strictly limited to, the few and hence the distinct. We owe our general orientation simply and solely to the fact that through attention we are able to register a fairly rapid succession of images. But attention is an effort of which we are not capable all the time. We have to make do, so to speak, with a minimum of simultaneous perceptions and successions of images. Hence in wide areas possible perceptions are continuously excluded, and consciousness is always bound to the narrowest circle. What would happen if an individual consciousness were able to take in at a single glance a simultaneous picture of every possible perception is beyond imagining. If man has already succeeded in building up the structure of the world from the few distinct things that he can perceive at one and the same time, what godlike spectacle would present itself to his eyes if he were able to perceive a great deal more all at once and distinctly? This question applies only to perceptions that are *possible* to us. If we now add to these the unconscious contents—i.e., contents which are not yet, or no longer, capable of consciousness—and then try to imagine a total vision, why, this is beyond the most

audacious fantasy. It is of course completely unimaginable in any conscious form, but in the unconscious it is a fact, since everything subliminal holds within it the ever-present possibility of being perceived and represented in consciousness. The unconscious is an irrepresentable totality of all subliminal psychic factors, a "total vision" *in potentia*. It constitutes the total disposition from which consciousness singles out tiny fragments from time to time.

898   Now if consciousness is emptied as far as possible of its contents, they will fall into a state of unconsciousness, at least for the time being. In Zen, this displacement usually results from the energy being withdrawn from conscious contents and transferred either to the conception of "emptiness" or to the koan. As both of these must be static, the succession of images is abolished and with it the energy which maintains the kinetics of consciousness. The energy thus saved goes over to the unconscious and reinforces its natural charge to bursting point. This increases the readiness of the unconscious contents to break through into consciousness. But since the emptying and shutting down of consciousness is no easy matter, a special training of indefinite duration [35] is needed in order to set up that maximum tension which leads to the final break-through of unconscious contents.

899   The contents that break through are far from being random ones. As psychiatric experience with insane patients shows, specific relations exist between the conscious contents and the delusional ideas that break through in delirium. They are the same relations as exist between the dreams and the waking consciousness of normal people. The connection is an essentially compensatory relationship: [36] the unconscious contents bring to the surface everything that is necessary [37] in the broadest sense

---

[35] Bodhidarma, the founder of Zen in China, says: "The incomparable doctrine of Buddhism can be comprehended only after a long hard discipline and by enduring what is most difficult to endure, and by practising what is most difficult to practise. Men of inferior virtue and wisdom are not allowed to understand anything about it. All the labours of such ones will come to naught." (Ibid., I, p. 188.)

[36] This is more probable than one that is merely "complementary."

[37] This "necessity" is a working hypothesis. People can, and do, hold very different views on this point. For instance, are religious ideas "necessary"? Only the course of the individual's life can decide this, i.e., his individual experience. There are no abstract criteria.

for the completion and wholeness of conscious orientation. If the fragments offered by, or forced up from, the unconscious are meaningfully built into conscious life, a form of psychic existence results which corresponds better to the whole of the individual's personality, and so abolishes the fruitless conflicts between his conscious and unconscious self. Modern psychotherapy is based on this principle, in so far as it has been able to free itself from the historical prejudice that the unconscious consists only of infantile and morally inferior contents. There is certainly an inferior corner in it, a lumber-room full of dirty secrets, though these are not so much unconscious as hidden and only half forgotten. But all this has about as much to do with the whole of the unconscious as a decayed tooth has with the total personality. The unconscious is the matrix of all metaphysical statements, of all mythology, of all philosophy (so far as this is not merely critical), and of all expressions of life that are based on psychological premises.

900   Every invasion of the unconscious is an answer to a definite conscious situation, and this answer follows from the totality of possible ideas present, i.e., from the total disposition which, as explained above, is a simultaneous picture *in potentia* of psychic existence. The splitting up into single units, its one-sided and fragmentary character, is of the essence of consciousness. The reaction coming from the disposition always has a total character, as it reflects a nature which has not been divided up by any discriminating consciousness.[38] Hence its overpowering effect. It is the unexpected, all-embracing, completely illuminating answer, which works all the more as illumination and revelation since the conscious mind has got itself wedged into a hopeless blind alley.[39]

901   When, therefore, after many years of the hardest practice and the most strenuous demolition of rational understanding, the Zen devotee receives an answer—the only true answer—from Nature herself, everything that is said of satori can be understood. As one can see for oneself, it is the *naturalness* of the answer that strikes one most about the Zen anecdotes. Yes, one

[38] "When the mind discriminates, there is manifoldness of things; when it does not it looks into the true state of things." *Essays,* I, p. 99.
[39] See the passage beginning "Have your mind like unto space. . . ." Suzuki, *Essays,* I, p. 223.

can accept with a sort of old-roguish satisfaction the story of the enlightened pupil who gave his Master a slap in the face as a reward.[40] And how much wisdom there is in the Master's "Wu," the answer to the question about the Buddha-nature of the dog! One must always bear in mind, however, that there are a great many people who cannot distinguish between a metaphysical joke and nonsense, and just as many who are so convinced of their own cleverness that they have never in their lives met any but fools.

902 Great as is the value of Zen Buddhism for understanding the religious transformation process, its use among Western people is very problematical. The mental education necessary for Zen is lacking in the West. Who among us would place such implicit trust in a superior Master and his incomprehensible ways? This respect for the greater human personality is found only in the East. Could any of us boast that he believes in the possibility of a boundlessly paradoxical transformation experience, to the extent, moreover, of sacrificing many years of his life to the wearisome pursuit of such a goal? And finally, who would dare to take upon himself the responsibility for such an unorthodox transformation experience—except a man who was little to be trusted, one who, maybe for pathological reasons, has too much to say for himself? Just such a person would have no cause to complain of any lack of following among us. But let a "Master" set us a hard task, which requires more than mere parrot-talk, and the European begins to have doubts, for the steep path of self-development is to him as mournful and gloomy as the path to hell.

903 I have no doubt that the satori experience does occur also in the West, for we too have men who glimpse ultimate goals and spare themselves no pains to draw near to them. But they will keep silent, not only out of shyness, but because they know that any attempt to convey their experience to others is hopeless. There is nothing in our civilization to foster these strivings, not even the Church, the custodian of religious values. Indeed, it is the function of the Church to oppose all original experience, because this can only be unorthodox. The only movement inside our civilization which has, or should have, some understanding of these endeavours is psychotherapy. It is therefore

40 *Introduction to Zen Buddhism*, p. 94.

no accident that it is a psychotherapist who is writing this foreword.

904   Psychotherapy is at bottom a dialectical relationship between doctor and patient. It is an encounter, a discussion between two psychic wholes, in which knowledge is used only as a tool. The goal is transformation—not one that is predetermined, but rather an indeterminable change, the only criterion of which is the disappearance of egohood. No efforts on the part of the doctor can compel this experience. The most he can do is to smooth the path for the patient and help him to attain an attitude which offers the least resistance to the decisive experience. If knowledge plays no small part in our Western procedure, this is equivalent to the importance of the traditional spiritual atmosphere of Buddhism in Zen. Zen and its technique could only have arisen on the basis of Buddhist culture, which it presupposes at every turn. You cannot annihilate a rationalistic intellect that was never there—no Zen adept was ever the product of ignorance and lack of culture. Hence it frequently happens with us also that a conscious ego and a cultivated understanding must first be produced through analysis before one can even think about abolishing egohood or rationalism. What is more, psychotherapy does not deal with men who, like Zen monks, are ready to make any sacrifice for the sake of truth, but very often with the most stubborn of all Europeans. Thus the tasks of psychotherapy are much more varied, and the individual phases of the long process much more contradictory, than is the case in Zen.

905   For these and many other reasons a direct transplantation of Zen to our Western conditions is neither commendable nor even possible. All the same, the psychotherapist who is seriously concerned with the question of the aim of his therapy cannot remain unmoved when he sees the end towards which this Eastern method of psychic "healing"—i.e., "making whole"—is striving. As we know, this question has occupied the most adventurous minds of the East for more than two thousand years, and in this respect methods and philosophical doctrines have been developed which simply put all Western attempts along these lines into the shade. Our attempts have, with few exceptions, all stopped short at either magic (mystery cults, amongst which we must include Christianity) or intellectualism (philos-

ophy from Pythagoras to Schopenhauer). It is only the tragedies of Goethe's *Faust* and Nietzsche's *Zarathustra* which mark the first glimmerings of a break-through of total experience in our Western hemisphere.[41] And we do not know even today what these most promising of all products of the Western mind may at length signify, so overlaid are they with the materiality and concreteness of our thinking, as moulded by the Greeks.[42] Despite the fact that our intellect has developed almost to perfection the capacity of the bird of prey to espy the tiniest mouse from the greatest height, yet the pull of the earth drags it down, and the *samskaras* entangle it in a world of confusing images the moment it no longer seeks for booty but turns one eye inwards *to find him who seeks*. Then the individual falls into the throes of a daemonic rebirth, beset with unknown terrors and dangers and menaced by deluding mirages in a labyrinth of error. The worst of all fates threatens the venturer: mute, abysmal loneliness in the age he calls his own. What do we know of the hidden motives for Goethe's "main business," as he called his *Faust,* or of the shudders of the "Dionysus experience"? One has to read the *Bardo Thödol*, the Tibetan Book of the Dead, backwards, as I have suggested,[43] in order to find an Eastern parallel to the torments and catastrophes of the Western "way of release" to wholeness. This is the issue here—not good intentions, clever imitations, or intellectual acrobatics. And this, in shadowy hints or in greater or lesser fragments, is what the psychotherapist is faced with when he has freed himself from over-hasty and short-sighted doctrinal opinions. If he is a slave to his quasi-biological credo he will always try to reduce what he has glimpsed to the banal and the known, to a rationalistic denominator which satisfies only those who are content with illusions. But the foremost of all illusions is that anything can ever satisfy anybody. That illusion stands behind all that is unendurable in life and in front of all progress, and it is one of the most difficult things to overcome. If the psychotherapist can take time off from his helpful activities for a little reflection,

---

[41] In this connection I must also mention the English mystic, William Blake. Cf. an excellent account in Percival, *William Blake's Circle of Destiny.*

[42] The genius of the Greeks lay in the break-through of consciousness into the materiality of the world, thus robbing the world of its original dreamlike quality.

[43] [Cf. above, par. 844.]

or if by any chance he is forced into seeing through his own illusions, it may dawn on him how hollow and flat, how inimical to life, are all rationalistic reductions when they come upon something that is alive, that wants to grow. Should he follow this up he will soon get an idea of what it means to "open wide that gate / Past which man's steps have ever flinching trod." [44]

906   I would not under any circumstances like it to be understood that I am making any recommendations or offering any advice. But when one begins to talk about Zen in the West I consider it my duty to show the European where our entrance lies to that "longest road" which leads to satori, and what kind of difficulties bestrew the path which only a few of our great ones have trod—beacons, perhaps, on high mountains, shining out into the dim future. It would be a disastrous mistake to assume that satori or samādhi are to be met with anywhere below these heights. As an experience of totality it cannot be anything cheaper or smaller than the whole. What this means psychologically can be seen from the simple reflection that consciousness is always only a part of the psyche and therefore never capable of psychic wholeness: for that the indefinite extension of the unconscious is needed. But the unconscious can neither be caught with clever formulas nor exorcized by means of scientific dogmas, for something of destiny clings to it—indeed, it is sometimes destiny itself, as *Faust* and *Zarathustra* show all too clearly. The attainment of wholeness requires one to stake one's whole being. Nothing less will do; there can be no easier conditions, no substitutes, no compromises. Considering that both *Faust* and *Zarathustra,* despite the highest recognition, stand on the border-line of what is comprehensible to the European, one could hardly expect the educated public, which has only just begun to hear about the obscure world of the psyche, to form any adequate conception of the spiritual state of a man caught in the toils of the individuation process—which is my term for "becoming whole." People then drag out the vocabulary of pathology and console themselves with the terminology of neurosis and psychosis, or else they whisper about the "creative secret." But what can a man "create" if he doesn't happen to be a poet? This misunderstanding has caused not a few persons in recent times to call themselves—by their own grace—"artists," just as

[44] *Faust*, Part I, trans. by Wayne, p. 54.

if art had nothing to do with ability. But if you have nothing at all to create, then perhaps you create yourself.

907   Zen shows how much "becoming whole" means to the East. Preoccupation with the riddles of Zen may perhaps stiffen the spine of the faint-hearted European or provide a pair of spectacles for his psychic myopia, so that from his "damned hole in the wall" [45] he may enjoy at least a glimpse of the world of psychic experience, which till now lay shrouded in fog. No harm can be done, for those who are too frightened will be effectively protected from further corruption, as also from everything of significance, by the helpful idea of "auto-suggestion." [46] I should like to warn the attentive and sympathetic reader, however, not to underestimate the spiritual depth of the East, or to assume that there is anything cheap and facile about Zen.[47] The assiduously cultivated credulity of the West in regard to Eastern thought is in this case a lesser danger, as in Zen there are fortunately none of those marvellously incomprehensible words that we find in Indian cults. Neither does Zen play about with complicated *hatha*-yoga techniques,[48] which delude the physiologically minded European into the false hope that the spirit can be obtained by just sitting and breathing. On the contrary, Zen demands intelligence and will power, as do all greater things that want to become realities.

---

45 Ibid., p. 44.   46 *Introduction*, p. 95.
47 "It is no pastime but the most serious task in life; no idlers will ever dare attempt it." Suzuki, *Essays*, I, p. 27; cf. also p. 92.
48 Says a Master: "If thou seekest Buddhahood by thus sitting cross-legged, thou murderest him. So long as thou freest thyself not from sitting so, thou never comest to the truth." *Essays*, I, p. 235. Cf. also II, p. 83f.

THE PSYCHOLOGY OF EASTERN MEDITATION [1]

908   The profound relationship between yoga and the hieratic architecture of India has already been pointed out by my friend Heinrich Zimmer, whose unfortunate early death is a great loss to Indology. Anyone who has visited Borobudur or seen the stupas at Bharhut and Sanchi can hardly avoid feeling that an attitude of mind and a vision quite foreign to the European have been at work here—if he has not already been brought to this realization by a thousand other impressions of Indian life. In the overflowing wealth of Indian spirituality there is reflected a vision of the soul which at first appears strange and inaccessible to the Greek-trained European mind. Our minds perceive things, our eyes, as Gottfried Keller says, "drink what the eyelids hold of the golden abundance of the world," and we

[1] [Delivered as a lecture to the Schweizerische Gesellschaft der Freunde ostasiatischer Kultur, in Zurich, Basel, and Bern, during March–May 1943, and published as "Zur Psychologie östlicher Meditation" in the Society's *Mitteilungen* (St. Gallen), V (1943), 33–53; repub. in *Symbolik des Geistes* (Zurich, 1948), pp. 447–72. Previously trans. by Carol Baumann in *Art and Thought*, a volume in honour of Ananda K. Coomaraswamy (London, 1948), pp. 169–79.

[The work of Heinrich Zimmer's which the author refers to in the opening sentence was his *Kunstform und Yoga im indischen Kultbild* (1926), the central argument of which has been restated in his posthumous English works, particularly *Myths and Symbols in Indian Art and Civilization* (1946) and *The Art of Indian Asia* (1955). Cf. also the next paper in this volume.—EDITORS.]

draw conclusions about the inner world from our wealth of outward impressions. We even derive its content from outside on the principle that "nothing is in the mind which was not previously in the senses." This principle seems to have no validity in India. Indian thought and Indian art merely *appear* in the sense-world, but do not derive from it. Although often expressed with startling sensuality, they are, in their truest essence, unsensual, not to say suprasensual. It is not the world of the senses, of the body, of colours and sounds, not human passions that are born anew in transfigured form, or with realistic pathos, through the creativity of the Indian soul, but rather an underworld or an overworld of a metaphysical nature, out of which strange forms emerge into the familiar earthly scene. For instance, if one carefully observes the tremendously impressive impersonations of the gods performed by the Kathakali dancers of southern India, there is not a single *natural* gesture to be seen. Everything is bizarre, subhuman and superhuman at once. The dancers do not walk like human beings—they glide; they do not think with their heads but with their hands. Even their human faces vanish behind blue-enamelled masks. The world we know offers nothing even remotely comparable to this grotesque splendour. Watching these spectacles one is transported to a world of dreams, for that is the only place where we might conceivably meet with anything similar. But the Kathakali dancers, as we see them in the flesh or in the temple sculptures, are no nocturnal phantoms; they are intensely dynamic figures, consistent in every detail, or as if they had grown organically. These are no shadows or ghosts of a bygone reality, they are more like realities which have *not yet been,* potential realities which might at any moment step over the threshold.

909　　Anyone who wholeheartedly surrenders to these impressions will soon notice that these figures do not strike the Indians themselves as dreamlike but as real. And, indeed, they touch upon something in our own depths, too, with an almost terrifying intensity, though we have no words to express it. At the same time, one notices that the more deeply one is stirred the more our sense-world fades into a dream, and that we seem to wake up in a world of gods, so immediate is their reality.

910　　What the European notices at first in India is the outward corporeality he sees everywhere. But that is not India as the

Indian sees it; that is not *his* reality. Reality, as the German word "Wirklichkeit" implies, is that which *works*. For us the essence of that which works is the world of appearance; for the Indian it is the soul. The world for him is a mere show or façade, and his reality comes close to being what we would call a dream.

911   This strange antithesis between East and West is expressed most clearly in religious practice. We speak of religious uplift and exaltation; for us God is the Lord of the universe, we have a religion of brotherly love, and in our heaven-aspiring churches there is a *high altar*. The Indian, on the other hand, speaks of *dhyāna*, of self-immersion, and of *sinking* into meditation; God is within all things and especially within man, and one turns away from the outer world to the inner. In the old Indian temples the altar is sunk six to eight feet deep in the earth, and what we hide most shamefacedly is the holiest symbol to the Indian. We believe in *doing*, the Indian in impassive *being*. Our religious exercises consist of prayer, worship, and singing hymns. The Indian's most important exercise is yoga, an immersion in what we would call an unconscious state, but which he praises as the highest consciousness. Yoga is the most eloquent expression of the Indian mind and at the same time the instrument continually used to produce this peculiar attitude of mind.

912   What, then, is yoga? The word means literally "yoking," i.e., the disciplining of the instinctual forces of the psyche, which in Sanskrit are called *kleshas*. The yoking aims at controlling these forces that fetter human beings to the world. The *kleshas* would correspond, in the language of St. Augustine, to *superbia* and *concupiscentia*. There are many different forms of yoga, but all of them pursue the same goal. Here I will only mention that besides the purely psychic exercises there is also a form called *hatha* yoga, a sort of gymnastics consisting chiefly of breathing exercises and special body postures. In this lecture I have undertaken to describe a yoga text which allows a deep insight into the psychic processes of yoga. It is a little-known Buddhist text, written in Chinese but translated from the original Sanskrit, and dating from A.D. 424. It is called the *Amitā-yur-dhyāna Sūtra,* the Sutra of Meditation on Amitāyus. This

sutra, highly valued in Japan, belongs to the sphere of theistic Buddhism, in which is found the teaching that the Ādi-Buddha or Mahābuddha, the Primordial Buddha, brought forth the five Dhyāni-Buddhas or Dhyāni-Bodhisattvas. One of the five is Amitābha, "the Buddha of the *setting sun* of immeasurable light," the Lord of Sukhāvati, land of supreme bliss. He is the protector of our present world-period, just as Shākyamuni, the historical Buddha, is its teacher. In the cult of Amitābha there is, oddly enough, a kind of Eucharistic feast with consecrated bread. He is sometimes depicted holding in his hand the vessel of the life-giving food of immortality, or the vessel of holy water.

913   The text [2] begins with an introductory story that need not detain us here. A crown prince seeks to take the life of his parents, and in her extremity the Queen calls upon the Buddha for help, praying him to send her his two disciples Maudgalyāyana and Ānanda. The Buddha fulfils her wish, and the two appear at once. At the same time Shākyamuni, the Buddha himself, appears before her eyes. He shows her in a vision all the ten worlds, so that she can choose in which one she wishes to be reborn. She chooses the western realm of Amitābha. He then teaches her the yoga which should enable her to retain rebirth in the Amitābha land, and after giving her various moral instructions he speaks to her as follows:

914   You and all other beings besides ought to make it their only aim, with concentrated thought, to get a perception of the western quarter. You will ask how that perception is to be formed. I will explain it now. All beings, if not blind from birth, are uniformly possessed of sight, and they all see the setting sun. You should sit down properly, looking in the western direction, and prepare your thought for a close meditation on the sun: cause your mind to be firmly fixed on it so as to have an unwavering perception by the exclusive application of your thought, and gaze upon it more particularly when it is about to set and looks like a suspended drum. After you have thus seen the sun, let that image remain clear and fixed, whether your eyes be shut or open. Such is the perception of the sun, which is the First Meditation.

2 In *Buddhist Mahāyāna Sūtras* (Sacred Books of the East, vol. 49), Part II, pp. 159–201, trans. by J. Takakusu, slightly modified.

915   As we have already seen, the setting sun is an allegory of the immortality-dispensing Amitābha. The text continues:

Next you should form the perception of water; gaze on the water clear and pure, and let this image also remain clear and fixed afterwards; never allow your thought to be scattered and lost.

916   As already mentioned, Amitābha is also the dispenser of the water of immortality.

917   When you have thus seen the water you should form the perception of ice. As you see the ice shining and transparent, so you should imagine the appearance of lapis lazuli. After that has been done, you will see the ground consisting of lapis lazuli transparent and shining both within and without. Beneath this ground of lapis lazuli there will be seen a golden banner with the seven jewels, diamonds, and the rest, supporting the ground. It extends to the eight points of the compass, and thus the eight corners of the ground are perfectly filled up. Every side of the eight quarters consists of a hundred jewels, every jewel has a thousand rays, and every ray has eighty-four thousand colours which, when reflected in the ground of lapis lazuli, look like a thousand millions of suns, and it is difficult to see them all one by one. Over the surface of that ground of lapis lazuli there are stretched golden ropes intertwined crosswise; divisions are made by means of [strings of] seven jewels with every part clear and distinct. . . .

When this perception has been formed, you should meditate on its constituents one by one and make the images as clear as possible, so that they may never be scattered and lost, whether your eyes be shut or open. Except only during the time of your sleep, you should always keep this in mind. One who has reached this stage of perception is said to have dimly seen the Land of Highest Happiness [Sukhāvati]. One who has obtained samādhi [the state of supernatural calm] is able to see the land of that Buddha country clearly and distinctly; this state is too much to be explained fully. Such is the perception of the land, and it is the Third Meditation.

918   Samādhi is 'withdrawnness,' i.e., a condition in which all connections with the world are absorbed into the inner world. Samādhi is the eighth phase of the Eightfold Path.

919   After the above comes a meditation on the Jewel Tree of the Amitābha land, and then follows the meditation on water:

In the Land of Highest Happiness there are waters in eight lakes; the water in every lake consists of seven jewels which are soft and yielding. Its source derives from the king of jewels that fulfils every wish [*cintāmani*, the wishing-pearl]. . . . In the midst of each lake there are sixty millions of lotus-flowers, made of seven jewels; all the flowers are perfectly round and exactly equal in circumference. . . . The water of jewels flows amidst the flowers and . . . the sound of the streaming water is melodious and pleasing. It proclaims all the perfect virtues [*pāramitās*], "suffering," "non-existence," "impermanence" and "non-self"; it proclaims also the praise of the signs of perfection, and minor marks of excellence, of all Buddhas. From the king of jewels that fulfils every wish stream forth the golden-coloured rays excessively beautiful, the radiance of which transforms itself into birds possessing the colours of a hundred jewels, which sing out harmonious notes, sweet and delicious, ever praising the remembrance of the Buddha, the remembrance of the Law, and the remembrance of the Church. Such is the perception of the water of eight good qualities, and it is the Fifth Meditation.

920   Concerning the meditation on Amitābha himself, the Buddha instructs the Queen in the following manner: "Form the perception of a lotus-flower on a ground of seven jewels." The flower has 84,000 petals, each petal 84,000 veins, and each vein possesses 84,000 rays, "of which each can clearly be seen."

921   When you have perceived this, you should next perceive the Buddha himself. Do you ask how? Every Buddha Tathāgata is one whose spiritual body is the principle of nature [*Dharmadhātu-kāya*], so that he may enter into the mind of all beings. Consequently, when you have perceived the Buddha, it is indeed that mind of yours that possesses those thirty-two signs of perfection and eighty minor marks of excellence which you see in the Buddha. In fine, it is your mind that becomes the Buddha, nay, it is your mind that is indeed the Buddha. The ocean of true and universal knowledge of all the Buddhas derives its source from one's own mind and thought. Therefore you should apply your thought with undivided attention to a careful meditation on that Buddha Tathāgata, the *Arhat*, the Holy and Fully Enlightened One. In forming the perception of that Buddha, you should first perceive the image of that Buddha; whether your eyes be open or shut, look at him as at an image like to Jambunada [3] gold in colour, sitting on the flower.

3 Jambunadi = Jambu-tree. A river formed of the juice of the fruit of the Jambu-tree flows in a circle round Mount Meru and returns to the tree.

When you have seen the seated figure your mental vision will become clear, and you will be able to see clearly and distinctly the adornment of that Buddha-country, the jewelled ground, etc. In seeing these things let them be clear and fixed just as you see the palms of your hands. . . .

If you pass through this experience, you will at the same time see all the Buddhas of the ten quarters. . . . Those who have practised this meditation are said to have contemplated the bodies of all the Buddhas. Since they have meditated on the Buddha's body, they will also see the Buddha's mind. It is great compassion that is called the Buddha's mind. It is by his absolute compassion that he receives all beings. Those who have practised this meditation will, when they die, be born in the presence of the Buddhas in another life, and obtain a spirit of resignation wherewith to face all the consequences which shall hereafter arise. Therefore those who have wisdom should direct their thought to the careful meditation upon that Buddha Amitāyus.

922   Of those who practise this meditation it is said that they no longer live in an embryonic condition but will "obtain free access to the excellent and admirable countries of Buddhas."

923 After you have had this perception, you should imagine yourself to be born in the World of Highest Happiness in the western quarter, and to be seated, cross-legged, on a lotus-flower there. Then imagine that the flower has shut you in and has afterwards unfolded; when the flower has thus unfolded, five hundred coloured rays will shine over your body, your eyes will be opened so as to see the Buddhas and Bodhisattvas who fill the whole sky; you will hear the sounds of waters and trees, the notes of birds, and the voices of many Buddhas. . . .

924   The Buddha then says to Ānanda and Vaidehi (the Queen):

Those who wish, by means of their serene thoughts, to be born in the western land, should first meditate on an image of the Buddha, which is sixteen cubits high, seated on a lotus-flower in the water of the lake. As was stated before, the real body and its measurements are unlimited, incomprehensible to the ordinary mind. But by the efficacy of the ancient prayer of that Tathāgata, those who think of and remember him shall certainly be able to accomplish their aim. . . .

925   The Buddha's speech continues for many pages, then the text says:

When the Buddha had finished this speech, Vaidehi, together with her five hundred female attendants, guided by the Buddha's words, could see the scene of the far-stretching World of the Highest Happiness, and could also see the body of the Buddha and the bodies of the two Bodhisattvas. With her mind filled with joy she praised them, saying: "Never have I seen such a wonder!" Instantly she became wholly and fully enlightened, and attained a spirit of resignation, prepared to endure whatever consequences might yet arise. Her five hundred female attendants too cherished the thought of obtaining the highest perfect knowledge, and sought to be born in that Buddha-country. The World-Honoured One predicted that they would all be born in that Buddha-country, and be able to obtain samādhi of the presence of many Buddhas.

926   In a digression on the fate of the unenlightened, the Buddha sums up the yoga exercise as follows:

But, being harassed by pains, he will have no time to think of the Buddha. Some good friend will then say to him: "Even if you cannot exercise the remembrance of the Buddha, you may, at least, utter the name, 'Buddha Amitāyus.'" Let him do so serenely with his voice uninterrupted; let him be continually thinking of the Buddha until he has completed ten times the thought, repeating the formula, "Adoration to Buddha Amitāyus." On the strength of his merit in uttering the Buddha's name he will, during every repetition, expiate the sins which involve him in births and deaths during eighty millions of *kalpas*. He will, while dying, see a golden lotus-flower like the disc of the sun appearing before his eyes; in a moment he will be born in the World of Highest Happiness.

927   The above quotations form the essential content of the yoga exercise which interests us here. The text is divided into sixteen meditations, from which I have chosen only certain parts, but they will suffice to portray the intensification of the meditation, culminating in samādhi, the highest ecstasy and enlightenment.

928   The exercise begins with the concentration on the setting sun. In southern latitudes the intensity of the rays of the setting sun is so strong that a few moments of gazing at it are enough to create an intense after-image. With closed eyes one continues to see the sun for some time. As is well known, one method of hypnosis consists in fixating a shining object, such as a diamond or a crystal. Presumably the fixation of the sun is meant to produce a similar hypnotic effect. On the other hand it should not

have a soporific effect, because a "meditation" of the sun must accompany the fixation. This meditation is a reflecting, a "making clear," in fact a *realization* of the sun, its form, its qualities, and its meanings. Since the round form plays such an important role in the subsequent meditations, we may suppose that the sun's disk serves as a model for the later fantasies of circular structures, just as, by reason of its intense light, it prepares the way for the resplendent visions that come afterwards. In this manner, so the text says, "the perception is to be formed."

929   The next meditation, that of the water, is no longer based on any sense-impression but creates through active imagination the image of a reflecting expanse of water. This, as we know, throws back the full light of the sun. It should now be imagined that the water changes into ice, "shining and transparent." Through this procedure the immaterial light of the sun-image is transformed into the substance of water and this in turn into the solidity of ice. A concretization of the vision is evidently aimed at, and this results in a materialization of the fantasy-creation, which appears in the place of physical nature, of the world as we know it. A different reality is created, so to speak, out of soul-stuff. The ice, of a bluish colour by nature, changes into blue lapis lazuli, a solid, stony substance, which then becomes a "ground," "transparent and shining." With this "ground" an immutable, absolutely real foundation has been created. The blue translucent floor is like a lake of glass, and through its transparent layers one's gaze penetrates into the depths below.

930   The so-called "golden banner" then shines forth out of these depths. It should be noted that the Sanskrit word *dhvaja* also means 'sign' or 'symbol' in general. So we could speak just as well of the appearance of the "symbol." It is evident that the symbol "extending to the eight points of the compass" represents the ground plan of an eight-rayed system. As the text says, the "eight corners of the ground are perfectly filled up" by the banner. The system shines "like a thousand millions of suns," so that the shining after-image of the sun has enormously increased its radiant energy, and its illuminative power has now been intensified to an immeasurable degree. The strange idea of the "golden ropes" spread over the system like a net presumably means that the system is tied together and secured in this

way, so that it can no longer fall apart. Unfortunately the text says nothing about a possible failure of the method, or about the phenomena of disintegration which might supervene as the result of a mistake. But disturbances of this kind in an imaginative process are nothing unexpected to an expert—on the contrary, they are a regular occurrence. So it is not surprising that a kind of inner reinforcement of the image is provided in the yoga vision by means of golden ropes.

931   Although not explicitly stated in the text, the eight-rayed system is already the Amitābha land. In it grow wonderful trees, as is meet and proper, for this is paradise. Especial importance attaches to the water of the Amitābha land. In accordance with the octagonal system it is arranged in the form of eight lakes, and the source of these waters is a central jewel, *cintāmani*, the wishing pearl, a symbol of the "treasure hard to attain," [4] the highest value. In Chinese art it appears as a moonlike image, frequently associated with a dragon.[5] The wondrous sounds of the water consist of two pairs of opposites which proclaim the dogmatic ground truths of Buddhism: "suffering and non-existence, impermanence and non-self," signifying that all existence is full of suffering, and that everything that clings to the ego is impermanent. Not-being and not-being-ego deliver us from these errors. Thus the singing water is something like the teaching of the Buddha—a redeeming water of wisdom, an *aqua doctrinae*, to use an expression of Origen. The source of this water, the pearl without peer, is the Tathāgata, the Buddha himself. Hence the imaginative reconstruction of the Buddha-image follows immediately afterwards, and while this structure is being built up in the meditation it is realized that the Buddha is really nothing other than the activating psyche of the yogi—the meditator himself. It is not only that the image of the Buddha is produced out of "one's own mind and thought," but the psyche which produces these thought-forms *is the Buddha himself.*

932   The image of the Buddha sits in the round lotus in the centre of the octagonal Amitābha land. He is distinguished by the great compassion with which he "receives all beings," including the meditator. This means that the inmost being which is the Buddha is bodied forth in the vision and revealed as the

4 Cf. *Symbols of Transformation*, Part II, chs. 6 and 7, especially par. 510.
5 Cf. *Psychology and Alchemy*, fig. 61.

true self of the meditator. He experiences himself as the only thing that exists, as the highest consciousness, even the Buddha. In order to attain this final goal it was necessary to pass through all the laborious exercises of mental reconstruction, to get free of the deluded ego-consciousness which is responsible for the sorrowful illusion of the world, and to reach that other pole of the psyche where the world as illusion is abolished.

*

933   Although it appears exceedingly obscure to the European, this yoga text is not a mere literary museum piece. It lives in the psyche of every Indian, in this form and in many others, so that his life and thinking are permeated by it down to the smallest details. It was not Buddhism that nurtured and educated this psyche, but yoga. Buddhism itself was born of the spirit of yoga, which is older and more universal than the historical reformation wrought by the Buddha. Anyone who seeks to understand Indian art, philosophy, and ethics from the inside must of necessity befriend this spirit. Our habitual understanding from the outside breaks down here, because it is hopelessly inadequate to the nature of Indian spirituality. And I wish particularly to warn against the oft-attempted imitation of Indian practices and sentiments. As a rule nothing comes of it except an artificial stultification of our Western intelligence. Of course, if anyone should succeed in giving up Europe from every point of view, and could actually *be* nothing but a yogi and sit in the lotus position with all the practical and ethical consequences that this entails, evaporating on a gazelle-skin under a dusty banyan tree and ending his days in nameless non-being, then I should have to admit that such a person understood yoga in the Indian manner. But anyone who cannot do this should not behave as if he did. He cannot and should not give up his Western understanding; on the contrary, he should apply it honestly, without imitation or sentimentality, to understanding as much of yoga as is possible for the Western mind. The secrets of yoga mean as much or even more to the Indian than our own Christian mysteries mean to us, and just as we would not allow any foreigner to make our *mysterium fidei* ludicrous, so we should not belittle these strange Indian ideas and practices or scorn them as absurd errors. By so doing we only block the way to a sensible

understanding. Indeed, we in Europe have already gone so far in this direction that the spiritual content of our Christian dogma has disappeared in a rationalistic and "enlightened" fog of alarming density, and this makes it all too easy for us to undervalue those things which we do not know and do not understand.

934 If we wish to understand at all, we can do so only in the European way. One can, it is true, understand many things with the heart, but then the head often finds it difficult to follow up with an intellectual formulation that gives suitable expression to what has been understood. There is also an understanding with the head, particularly of the scientific kind, where there is sometimes too little room for the heart. We must therefore leave it to the good will and co-operation of the reader to use first one and then the other. So let us first attempt, with the head, to find or build that hidden bridge which may lead to a European understanding of yoga.

935 For this purpose we must again take up the series of symbols we have already discussed, but this time we shall consider their sense-content. The *sun*, with which the series begins, is the source of warmth and light, the indubitable central point of our visible world. As the giver of life it is always and everywhere either the divinity itself or an image of the same. Even in the world of Christian ideas, the sun is a favourite allegory of Christ. A second source of life, especially in southern countries, is *water*, which also plays an important role in Christian allegory, for instance as the four rivers of paradise and the waters which issued from the side of the temple (Ezekiel 47). The latter were compared to the blood that flowed from the wound in Christ's side. In this connection I would also mention Christ's talk with the woman of Samaria at the well, and the rivers of living water flowing from the body of Christ (John 7:38). A meditation on sun and water evokes these and similar associations without fail, so that the meditator will gradually be led from the foreground of visible appearances into the background, that is, to the spiritual meaning behind the object of meditation. He is transported to the psychic sphere, where sun and water, divested of their physical objectivity, become symbols of psychic contents, images of the source of life in the individual psyche. For indeed our consciousness does not create itself—it wells up from

unknown depths. In childhood it awakens gradually, and all through life it wakes each morning out of the depths of sleep from an unconscious condition. It is like a child that is born daily out of the primordial womb of the unconscious. In fact, closer investigation reveals that it is not only influenced by the unconscious but continually emerges out of it in the form of numberless spontaneous ideas and sudden flashes of thought. Meditation on the meaning of sun and water is therefore something like a descent into the fountainhead of the psyche, into the unconscious itself.

936   Here, then, is a great difference between the Eastern and the Western mind. It is the same difference as the one we met before: the difference between the high and the low altar. The West is always seeking uplift, but the East seeks a sinking or deepening. Outer reality, with its bodiliness and weight, appears to make a much stronger and sharper impression on the European than it does on the Indian. Therefore the European seeks to raise himself above this world, while the Indian likes to turn back into the maternal depths of Nature.

937   Just as the Christian contemplative, for instance in the *Exercitia spiritualia* of Loyola, strives to comprehend the holy image as concretely as possible, with all the senses, so the yogi solidifies the water he contemplates first to ice and then to lapis lazuli, thereby creating a firm "ground," as he calls it. He makes, so to speak, a solid body for his vision. In this way he endows the figures of his psychic world with a concrete reality which takes the place of the outer world. At first he sees nothing but a reflecting blue surface, like that of a lake or ocean (also a favourite symbol of the unconscious in our Western dreams); but under the shining surface unknown depths lie hidden, dark and mysterious.

938   As the text says, the blue stone is *transparent,* which informs us that the gaze of the meditator can penetrate into the depths of the psyche's secrets. There he sees what could not be seen before, i.e., what was unconscious. Just as sun and water are the physical sources of life, so, as symbols, they express the essential secret of the life of the unconscious. In the *banner,* the symbol the yogi sees through the floor of lapis lazuli, he beholds, as it were, an image of the source of consciousness, which before was invisible and apparently without form. Through *dhyāna,*

through the sinking and deepening of contemplation, the unconscious has evidently taken on form. It is as if the light of consciousness had ceased to illuminate the objects of the outer world of the senses and now illumines the darkness of the unconscious. If the world of the senses and all thought of it are completely extinguished, then the inner world springs into relief more distinctly.

939   Here the Eastern text skips over a psychic phenomenon that is a source of endless difficulties for the European. If a European tries to banish all thought of the outer world and to empty his mind of everything outside, he immediately becomes the prey of his own subjective fantasies, which have nothing whatever to do with the images mentioned in our text. Fantasies do not enjoy a good reputation; they are considered cheap and worthless and are therefore rejected as useless and meaningless. They are the *kleshas,* the disorderly and chaotic instinctual forces which yoga proposes to yoke. The *Exercitia spiritualia* pursue the same goal, in fact both methods seek to attain success by providing the meditator with an object to contemplate and showing him the image he has to concentrate on in order to shut out the allegedly worthless fantasies. Both methods, Eastern as well as Western, try to reach the goal by a direct path. I do not wish to question the possibilities of success when the meditation exercise is conducted in some kind of ecclesiastical setting. But, outside of some such setting, the thing does not as a rule work, or it may even lead to deplorable results. By throwing light on the unconscious one gets first of all into the chaotic sphere of the personal unconscious, which contains all that one would like to forget, and all that one does not wish to admit to oneself or to anybody else, and which one prefers to believe is not true anyhow. One therefore expects to come off best if one looks as little as possible into this dark corner. Naturally anyone who proceeds in that way will never get round this corner and will never obtain even a trace of what yoga promises. Only the man who goes through this darkness can hope to make any further progress. I am therefore in principle against the uncritical appropriation of yoga practices by Europeans, because I know only too well that they hope to avoid their own dark corners. Such a beginning is entirely meaningless and worthless.

940   This is also the deeper reason why we in the West have never

developed anything comparable to yoga, aside from the very limited application of the Jesuit *Exercitia*. We have an abysmal fear of that lurking horror, our personal unconscious. Hence the European much prefers to tell others "how to do it." That the improvement of the whole begins with the individual, even with myself, never enters our heads. Besides, many people think it morbid to glance into their own interiors—it makes you melancholic, a theologian once assured me.

941   I have just said that we have developed nothing that could be compared with yoga. This is not entirely correct. True to our European bias, we have evolved a medical psychology dealing specifically with the kleshas. We call it the "psychology of the unconscious." The movement inaugurated by Freud recognized the importance of the human shadow-side and its influence on consciousness, and then got entangled in this problem. Freudian psychology is concerned with the very thing that our text passes over in silence and assumes is already dealt with. The yogi is perfectly well aware of the world of the kleshas, but his religion is such a natural one that he knows nothing of the *moral conflict* which the kleshas represent for us. An ethical dilemma divides us from our shadow. The spirit of India grows out of nature; with us spirit is opposed to nature.

942   The floor of lapis lazuli is not transparent for us because the question of the *evil in nature* must first be answered. This question *can* be answered, but surely not with shallow rationalistic arguments and intellectual patter. The ethical responsibility of the individual can give a valid answer, but there are no cheap recipes and no licences—one must pay to the last penny before the floor of lapis lazuli can become transparent. Our sutra presupposes that the shadow world of our personal fantasies—the personal unconscious—has been traversed, and goes on to describe a symbolical figure which at first strikes us as very strange. This is a geometrical structure raying out from a centre and divided into eight parts—an ogdoad. In the centre there is a lotus with the Buddha sitting in it, and the decisive experience is the final knowledge that the meditator himself is the Buddha, whereby the fateful knots woven in the opening story are apparently resolved. The concentrically constructed symbol evidently expresses the highest concentration, which can be achieved only when the previously described withdrawal and

canalization of interest away from the impressions of the sense-world and from object-bound ideas is pushed to the limit and applied to the background of consciousness. The conscious world with its attachment to objects, and even the centre of consciousness, the ego, are extinguished, and in their place the splendour of the Amitābha land appears with ever-increasing intensity.

943 Psychologically this means that behind or beneath the world of personal fantasies and instincts a still deeper layer of the unconscious becomes visible, which in contrast to the chaotic disorder of the kleshas is pervaded by the highest order and harmony, and, in contrast to their multiplicity, symbolizes the all-embracing unity of the *bodhimandala,* the magic circle of enlightenment.

944 What has our psychology to say about this Indian assertion of a supra-personal, world-embracing unconscious that appears when the darkness of the personal unconscious grows transparent? Modern psychology knows that the personal unconscious is only the top layer, resting on a foundation of a wholly different nature which we call the collective unconscious. The reason for this designation is the circumstance that, unlike the personal unconscious and its purely personal contents, the images in the deeper unconscious have a distinctly mythological character. That is to say, in form and content they coincide with those widespread primordial ideas which underlie the myths. They are no longer of a personal but of a purely supra-personal nature and are therefore common to all men. For this reason they are to be found in the myths and legends of all peoples and all times, as well as in individuals who have not the slightest knowledge of mythology.

945 Our Western psychology has, in fact, got as far as yoga in that it is able to establish scientifically a deeper layer of unity in the unconscious. The mythological motifs whose presence has been demonstrated by the exploration of the unconscious form in themselves a multiplicity, but this culminates in a concentric or radial order which constitutes the true centre or essence of the collective unconscious. On account of the remarkable agreement between the insights of yoga and the results of psychological research, I have chosen the Sanskrit term *mandala* for this central symbol.

946   You will now surely ask: but how in the world does science come to such conclusions? There are two paths to this end. The first is the historical path. If we study, for instance, the intro-spective method of medieval natural philosophy, we find that it repeatedly used the circle, and in most cases the circle divided into four parts, to symbolize the central principle, obviously borrowing this idea from the ecclesiastical allegory of the quater-nity as found in numerous representations of the *Rex gloriae* with the four evangelists, the four rivers of paradise, the four winds, and so on.

947   The second is the path of empirical psychology. At a cer-tain stage in the psychological treatment patients sometimes paint or draw such mandalas spontaneously, either because they dream them or because they suddenly feel the need to compen-sate the confusion in their psyches through representations of an ordered unity. For instance, our Swiss national saint, the Blessed Brother Nicholas of Flüe, went through a process of this kind, and the result can still be seen in the picture of the Trinity in the parish church at Sachseln. With the help of circular draw-ings in a little book by a German mystic,[6] he succeeded in as-similating the great and terrifying vision that had shaken him to the depths.

948   But what has our empirical psychology to say about the Buddha sitting in the lotus? Logically one would expect Christ to be enthroned in the centre of our Western mandalas. This was once true, as we have already said, in the Middle Ages. But our modern mandalas, spontaneously produced by numerous individuals without any preconceived ideas or suggestions from outside, contain no Christ-figure, still less a Buddha in the lotus position. On the other hand, the equal-armed Greek cross, or even an unmistakable imitation of the swastika, is to be found fairly often. I cannot discuss this strange fact here, though in it-self it is of the greatest interest.[7]

949   Between the Christian and the Buddhist mandala there is a subtle but enormous difference. The Christian during con-templation would never say "*I* am Christ," but will confess with Paul: "Not I, but Christ liveth in me" (Gal. 2:20). Our sutra,

6 Cf. Stoeckli, *Die Visionen des Seligen Bruder Klaus.* Cf. also the sixth paper in this volume, pars. 474ff.

7 Cf. "Psychology and Religion," pars. 136ff.

however, says: "Thou wilt know that *thou* art the Buddha." At bottom the two confessions are identical, in that the Buddhist only attains this knowledge when he is *anātman*, 'without self.' But there is an immeasurable difference in the formulation. The Christian attains his end *in Christ,* the Buddhist knows *he* is the Buddha. The Christian gets *out of* the transitory and ego-bound world of consciousness, but the Buddhist *still* reposes on the eternal ground of his inner nature, whose oneness with Deity, or with universal Being, is confirmed in other Indian testimonies.

THE HOLY MEN OF INDIA [1]

950   Heinrich Zimmer had been interested for years in the
Maharshi of Tiruvannamalai, and the first question he asked me
on my return from India concerned this latest holy and wise
man from southern India. I do not know whether my friend
found it an unforgivable or an incomprehensible sin on my
part that I had not sought out Shri Ramana. I had the feeling
that *he* would certainly not have neglected to pay him a visit, so
warm was his interest in the life and thought of the holy man.
This was scarcely surprising, as I know how deeply Zimmer had
penetrated into the spirit of India. His most ardent wish to see
India in reality was unfortunately never fulfilled, and the one
chance he had of doing so fell through in the last hours before
the outbreak of the second World War. As if in compensation,
his vision of the spiritual India was all the more magnificent.
In our work together he gave me invaluable insights into the
Oriental psyche, not only through his immense technical knowl-

1 [Introduction to Heinrich Zimmer, *Der Weg zum Selbst: Lehre und Leben des
indischen Heiligen Shri Ramana Maharshi aus Tiruvannamalai* (Zurich, 1944),
edited by C. G. Jung. The work consists of 167 pages translated by Zimmer from
English publications of the Sri Ramanasramam Book Depot, Tiruvannamalai,
India, preceded by a brief (non-significant) foreword and this introduction, both
by Jung, an obituary notice by Emil Abegg of Zimmer's death in New York in
1944, and an introduction to the Shri Ramana Maharshi texts by Zimmer.—
EDITORS.]

edge, but above all through his brilliant grasp of the meaning and content of Indian mythology. Unhappily, the early death of those beloved of the gods was fulfilled in him, and it remains for us to mourn the loss of a spirit that overcame the limitations of the specialist and, turning towards humanity, bestowed upon it the joyous gift of "immortal fruit."

951   The carrier of mythological and philosophical wisdom in India has been since time immemorial the "holy man"—a Western title which does not quite render the essence and outward appearance of the parallel figure in the East. This figure is the embodiment of the spiritual India, and we meet him again and again in the literature. No wonder, then, that Zimmer was passionately interested in the latest and best incarnation of this type in the phenomenal personage of Shri Ramana. He saw in this yogi the true avatar of the figure of the *rishi*, seer and philosopher, which strides, as legendary as it is historical, down the centuries and the ages.

952   Perhaps I should have visited Shri Ramana. Yet I fear that if I journeyed to India a second time to make up for my omission, it would fare with me just the same: I simply could not, despite the uniqueness of the occasion, bring myself to visit this undoubtedly distinguished man personally. For the fact is, I doubt his uniqueness; he is of a type which always was and will be. Therefore it was not necessary to seek him out. I saw him all over India, in the pictures of Ramakrishna, in Ramakrishna's disciples, in Buddhist monks, in innumerable other figures of the daily Indian scene, and the words of his wisdom are the *sous-entendu* of India's spiritual life. Shri Ramana is, in a sense, a *hominum homo,* a true "son of man" of the Indian earth. He is "genuine," and on top of that he is a "phenomenon" which, seen through European eyes, has claims to uniqueness. But in India he is merely the whitest spot on a white surface (whose whiteness is mentioned only because there are so many surfaces that are just as black). Altogether, one sees so much in India that in the end one only wishes one could see less: the enormous variety of countries and human beings creates a longing for complete simplicity. This simplicity is there too; it pervades the spiritual life of India like a pleasant fragrance or a melody. It is everywhere the same, but never monotonous, endlessly varied. To get to know it, it is sufficient to read an Upanishad or any

discourse of the Buddha. What is heard there is heard everywhere; it speaks out of a million eyes, it expresses itself in countless gestures, and there is no village or country road where that broad-branched tree cannot be found in whose shade the ego struggles for its own abolition, drowning the world of multiplicity in the All and All-Oneness of Universal Being. This note rang so insistently in my ears that soon I was no longer able to shake off its spell. I was then absolutely certain that no one could ever get beyond this, least of all the Indian holy man himself; and should Shri Ramana say anything that did not chime in with this melody, or claim to know anything that transcended it, his illumination would assuredly be false. The holy man is right when he intones India's ancient chants, but wrong when he pipes any other tune. This effortless drone of argumentation, so suited to the heat of southern India, made me refrain, without regret, from a visit to Tiruvannamalai.

953   Nevertheless, the unfathomableness of India saw to it that I should encounter the holy man after all, and in a form that was more congenial to me, without my seeking him out: in Trivandrum, the capital of Travancore, I ran across a disciple of the Maharshi. He was an unassuming little man, of a social status which we would describe as that of a primary-school teacher, and he reminded me most vividly of the shoemaker of Alexandria who (in Anatole France's story) was presented to St. Anthony by the angel as an example of an even greater saint than he. Like the shoemaker, my little holy man had innumerable children to feed and was making special sacrifices in order that his eldest son might be educated. (I will not enter here into the closely allied question as to whether holy men are always wise, and conversely, whether all wise men are unconditionally holy. In this respect there is room for doubt.) Be that as it may, in this modest, kindly, devout, and childlike spirit I encountered a man who had absorbed the wisdom of the Maharshi with utter devotion, and at the same time had surpassed his master because, notwithstanding his cleverness and holiness, he had "eaten" the world. I acknowledge with deep gratitude this meeting with him; nothing better could have happened to me. The man who is only wise and only holy interests me about as much as the skeleton of a rare saurian, which would not move me to tears. The insane contradiction, on the other hand, be-

tween existence beyond Māyā in the cosmic Self, and that amiable human weakness which fruitfully sinks many roots into the black earth, repeating for all eternity the weaving and rending of the veil as the ageless melody of India—this contradiction fascinates me; for how else can one perceive the light without the shadow, hear the silence without the noise, attain wisdom without foolishness? The experience of holiness may well be the most painful of all. My man—thank God—was only a little holy man; no radiant peak above the dark abysses, no shattering sport of nature, but an example of how wisdom, holiness, *and* humanity can dwell together in harmony, richly, pleasantly, sweetly, peacefully, and patiently, without limiting one another, without being peculiar, causing no surprise, in no way sensational, necessitating no special post-office, yet embodying an age-old culture amid the gentle murmur of the coconut palms fanning themselves in the light sea wind. He has found a meaning in the rushing phantasmagoria of Being, freedom in bondage, victory in defeat.

954   Unadulterated wisdom and unadulterated holiness, I fear, are seen to best advantage in literature, where their reputation remains undisputed. Lao-tzu reads exquisitely, unsurpassably well, in the *Tao Teh Ching;* Lao-tzu with his dancing girl on the Western slope of the mountain, celebrating the evening of life, is rather less edifying. But even less can one approve of the neglected body of the "unadulterated" holy man, especially if one believes that beauty is one of the most excellent of God's creations.

955   Shri Ramana's thoughts are beautiful to read. What we find here is purest India, the breath of eternity, scorning and scorned by the world. It is the song of the ages, resounding, like the shrilling of crickets on a summer's night, from a million beings. This melody is built up on the one great theme, which, veiling its monotony under a thousand colourful reflections, tirelessly and everlastingly rejuvenates itself in the Indian spirit, whose youngest incarnation is Shri Ramana himself. It is the drama of *ahamkāra*, the "I-maker" or ego-consciousness, in opposition and indissoluble bondage to the atman, the self or non-ego. The Maharshi also calls the atman the "ego-ego"— significantly enough, for the self is indeed experienced as the subject of the subject, as the true source and controller of the

ego, whose (mistaken) strivings are continually directed towards appropriating the very autonomy which is intimated to it by the self.

956   This conflict is not unknown to the Westerner: for him it is the relationship of man to God. The modern Indian, as I can testify from my own experience, has largely adopted European habits of language, "self" or "atman" being essentially synonymous with "God." But, in contradistinction to the Western "man and God," the Indian posits the opposition (or correspondence) between "ego and self." "Ego," as contrasted with "man," is a distinctly psychological concept, and so is "self"—to *our* way of thinking. We might therefore be inclined to assume that in India the metaphysical problem "man and God" has been shifted on to the psychological plane. On closer inspection it is clear that this is not so, for the Indian concept of "ego" and "self" is not really psychological but—one could well say—just as metaphysical as our "man and God." The Indian lacks the epistemological standpoint just as much as our own religious language does. He is still "pre-Kantian." This complication is unknown in India and it is still largely unknown with us. In India there is no psychology in our sense of the word. India is "pre-psychological": when it speaks of the "self," it *posits* such a thing as existing. Psychology does not do this. It does not in any sense deny the existence of the dramatic conflict, but reserves the right to the poverty, or the riches, of *not* knowing about the self. Though very well acquainted with the self's peculiar and paradoxical phenomenology, we remain conscious of the fact that we are discerning, with the limited means at our disposal, something essentially unknown and expressing it in terms of psychic structures which may not be adequate to the nature of what is to be known.

957   This epistemological limitation keeps us at a remove from what we term "self" or "God." The equation self = God is shocking to the European. As Shri Ramana's statements and many others show, it is a specifically Eastern insight, to which psychology has nothing further to say except that it is not within its competence to differentiate between the two. Psychology can only establish that the empiricism of the "self" exhibits a religious symptomatology, just as does that category of assertions associated with the term "God." Although the phenomenon of

religious exaltation transcends epistemological criticism—a feature it shares with all manifestations of emotion—yet the human urge to knowledge asserts itself again and again with "ungodly" or "Luciferian" obstinacy and wilfulness, indeed with necessity, whether it be to the loss or gain of the thinking man. Sooner or later he will place his reason in opposition to the emotion that grips him and seek to withdraw from its entangling grasp in order to give an account of what has happened. If he proceeds prudently and conscientiously, he will continually discover that at least a part of his experience is a humanly limited *interpretation,* as was the case with Ignatius Loyola and his vision of the snake with multiple eyes, which he at first regarded as of divine, and later as of diabolical, origin. (Compare the exhortation in I John 4:1: "Do not believe every spirit, but test the spirits to see whether they are of God.") To the Indian it is clear that the self as the originating ground of the psyche is not different from God, and that, so far as a man is *in* the self, he is not only contained in God but actually is God. Shri Ramana is quite explicit on this point. No doubt this equation, too, is an "interpretation." Equally, it is an interpretation to regard the self as the highest good or as the goal of all desire and fulfilment, although the phenomenology of such an experience leaves no doubt that these characteristics exist *a priori* and are indispensable components of religious exaltation. But that will not prevent the critical intellect from questioning the validity of these characteristics. It is difficult to see how this question could be answered, as the intellect lacks the necessary criteria. Anything that might serve as a criterion is subject in turn to the critical question of validity. The only thing that can decide here is the preponderance of psychic facts.

958   The goal of Eastern religious practice is the same as that of Western mysticism: the shifting of the centre of gravity from the ego to the self, from man to God. This means that the ego disappears in the self, and man in God. It is evident that Shri Ramana has either really been more or less absorbed by the self, or has at least struggled earnestly all his life to extinguish his ego in it. The *Exercitia spiritualia* reveal a similar striving: they subordinate "self-possession" (possession of an ego) as much as possible to possession by Christ. Shri Ramana's elder contemporary, Ramakrishna, had the same attitude concerning

the relation to the self, only in his case the dilemma between ego and self seems to emerge more distinctly. Whereas Shri Ramana displays a "sympathetic" tolerance towards the worldly callings of his disciples, while yet exalting the extinction of the ego as the real goal of spiritual exertion, Ramakrishna shows a rather more hesitant attitude in this respect. He says: "So long as ego-seeking exists, neither knowledge (*jñāna*) nor liberation (*mukti*) is possible, and to births and deaths there is no end." [2] All the same, he has to admit the fatal tenacity of *ahamkāra* (the "I-maker"): "Very few can get rid of the sense of 'I' through *samādhi*. . . . We may discriminate a thousand times, but the sense of 'I' is bound to return again and again. You may cut down the branches of a fig-tree today, but tomorrow you will see that new twigs are sprouting." [3] He goes so far as to suggest the indestructibility of the ego with the words: "If this sense of 'I' will not leave, then let it stay on as the servant of God." [4] Compared with this concession to the ego, Shri Ramana is definitely the more radical or, in the sense of Indian tradition, the more conservative. Though the elder, Ramakrishna is the more modern of the two, and this is probably to be attributed to the fact that he was affected by the Western attitude of mind far more profoundly than was Shri Ramana.

959   If we conceive of the self as the essence of psychic wholeness, i.e., as the totality of conscious and unconscious, we do so because it does *in fact* represent something like a goal of psychic development, and this irrespective of all conscious opinions and expectations. The self is the subject-matter of a process that generally runs its course outside consciousness and makes its presence felt only by a kind of long-range effect. A critical attitude towards this natural process allows us to raise questions which are excluded at the outset by the formula self = God. This formula shows the dissolution of the ego in the atman to be the unequivocal goal of religion and ethics, as exemplified in the life and thought of Shri Ramana. The same is obviously true of Christian mysticism, which differs from Oriental philosophy only through having a different terminology. The inevitable consequence is the depreciation and abolition of the physical and psychic man (i.e., of the living body and *ahamkāra*)

2 *Worte des Ramakrishna*, ed. by Emma von Pelet, p. 77.
3 *The Gospel of Ramakrishna*, p. 56.   4 Ibid.

in favour of the pneumatic man. Shri Ramana speaks of his body as "this clod." As against this, and taking into consideration the complex nature of human experience (emotion plus interpretation), the critical standpoint admits the importance of ego-consciousness, well knowing that without *ahamkāra* there would be absolutely no one there to register what was happening. Without the Maharshi's personal ego, which, as a matter of brute experience, only exists in conjunction with the said "clod" (= body), there would be no Shri Ramana at all. Even if we agreed with him that it is no longer his ego, but the atman speaking, it is still the psychic structure of consciousness in association with the body that makes speech communication possible. Without this admittedly very troublesome physical and psychic man, the self would be entirely without substance, as Angelus Silesius has already said:

> I know that without me
> God can no moment live;
> Were I to die, then he
> No longer could survive.

960   The intrinsically goal-like quality of the self and the urge to realize this goal are, as we have said, not dependent on the participation of consciousness. They cannot be denied any more than one can deny one's ego-consciousness. It, too, puts forward its claims peremptorily, and very often in overt or covert opposition to the needs of the evolving self. In reality, i.e., with few exceptions, the entelechy of the self consists in a succession of endless compromises, ego and self laboriously keeping the scales balanced if all is to go well. Too great a swing to one side or the other is often no more than an example of how not to set about it. This certainly does not mean that extremes, when they occur in a natural way, are in themselves evil. We make the right use of them when we examine their meaning, and they give us ample opportunity to do this in a manner deserving our gratitude. Exceptional human beings, carefully hedged about and secluded, are invariably a gift of nature, enriching and widening the scope of our consciousness—but only if our capacity for reflection does not suffer shipwreck. Enthusiasm can be a veritable gift of the gods or a monster from hell. With the hybris which attends it, corruption sets in, even if the resultant clouding of

consciousness seems to put the attainment of the highest goals almost within one's grasp. The only true and lasting gain is heightened and broadened reflection.

961   Banalities apart, there is unfortunately no philosophical or psychological proposition that does not immediately have to be reversed. Thus reflection as an end in itself is nothing but a limitation if it cannot stand firm in the turmoil of chaotic extremes, just as mere dynamism for its own sake leads to inanity. Everything requires for its existence its own opposite, or else it fades into nothingness. The ego needs the self and vice versa. The changing relations between these two entities constitute a field of experience which Eastern introspection has exploited to a degree almost unattainable to Western man. The philosophy of the East, although so vastly different from ours, could be an inestimable treasure for us too; but, in order to possess it, we must first earn it. Shri Ramana's words, which Heinrich Zimmer has bequeathed to us, in excellent translation, as the last gift of his pen, bring together once again the loftiest insights that the spirit of India has garnered in the course of the ages, and the individual life and work of the Maharshi illustrate once again the passionate striving of the Indian for the liberating "Ground." I say "once again," because India is about to take the fateful step of becoming a State and entering into a community of nations whose guiding principles have anything and everything on the programme except detachment and peace of the soul.

962   The Eastern peoples are threatened with a rapid collapse of their spiritual values, and what replaces them cannot always be counted among the best that Western civilization has produced. From this point of view, one could regard Ramakrishna and Shri Ramana as modern prophets, who play the same compensatory role in relation to their people as that of the Old Testament prophets in relation to the "unfaithful" children of Israel. Not only do they exhort their compatriots to remember their thousand-year-old spiritual culture, they actually embody it and thus serve as an impressive warning, lest the demands of the soul be forgotten amid the novelties of Western civilization with its materialistic technology and commercial acquisitiveness. The breathless drive for power and aggrandizement in the political, social, and intellectual sphere, gnawing

at the soul of the Westerner with apparently insatiable greed, is spreading irresistibly in the East and threatens to have incalculable consequences. Not only in India but in China, too, much has already perished where once the soul lived and throve. The externalization of culture may do away with a great many evils whose removal seems most desirable and beneficial, yet this step forward, as experience shows, is all too dearly paid for with a loss of spiritual culture. It is undeniably much more comfortable to live in a well-planned and hygienically equipped house, but this still does not answer the question of *who* is the dweller in this house and whether his soul rejoices in the same order and cleanliness as the house which ministers to his outer life. The man whose interests are all outside is never satisfied with what is necessary, but is perpetually hankering after something more and better which, true to his bias, he always seeks outside himself. He forgets completely that, for all his outward successes, he himself remains the same inwardly, and he therefore laments his poverty if he possesses only one automobile when the majority have two. Obviously the outward lives of men could do with a lot more bettering and beautifying, but these things lose their meaning when the inner man does not keep pace with them. To be satiated with "necessities" is no doubt an inestimable source of happiness, yet the inner man continues to raise his claim, and this can be satisfied by no outward possessions. And the less this voice is heard in the chase after the brilliant things of this world, the more the inner man becomes the source of inexplicable misfortune and uncomprehended unhappiness in the midst of living conditions whose outcome was expected to be entirely different. The externalization of life turns to incurable suffering, because no one can understand why he should suffer from himself. No one wonders at his insatiability, but regards it as his lawful right, never thinking that the one-sidedness of this psychic diet leads in the end to the gravest disturbances of equilibrium. That is the sickness of Western man, and he will not rest until he has infected the whole world with his own greedy restlessness.

963   The wisdom and mysticism of the East have, therefore, very much to say to us, even when they speak their own inimitable language. They serve to remind us that we in our culture possess something similar, which we have already forgotten, and to

direct our attention to the fate of the inner man, which we set aside as trifling. The life and teaching of Shri Ramana are of significance not only for India, but for the West too. They are more than a *document humain:* they are a warning message to a humanity which threatens to lose itself in unconsciousness and anarchy. It is perhaps, in the deeper sense, no accident that Heinrich Zimmer's last book should leave us, as a testament, the life-work of a modern Indian prophet who exemplifies so impressively the problem of psychic transformation.

FOREWORD TO ABEGG:
"OSTASIEN DENKT ANDERS"[1]

1483   The author of this book, the entire text of which unfortunately I have not seen, has talked to me about her project and about her ideas with regard to the difference between Eastern and Western psychology. Thus I was able to note many points of agreement between us, and also a competence on her part to make judgments which is possible only to one who is a European and at the same time possesses the invaluable advantage of having spent more than half a lifetime in the Far East, in close contact with the mind of Asia. Without such first-hand experience it would be a hopeless task to approach the problem of Eastern psychology. One must be deeply and directly moved by the strangeness, one might almost say by the incomprehensibility, of the Eastern psyche. Decisive experiences of this kind cannot be transmitted through books; they come only from living in immediate, daily relationship with the people. Having had unusual advantages in this respect, the author is in a position to discuss what is perhaps the basic, and is in any case an extremely important, question of the difference between Eastern and Western psychology. I have often found myself in situations where I had to take account of this difference, as in the study of Chinese and East Indian literary texts and in the psychological treatment of Asiatics. Among my patients, I am sorry to say, I have never had a Chinese or a Japanese, nor have I had the privilege of visiting either China or Japan. But at least I have had the opportunity to experience with painful clarity the insufficiency of my knowledge. In this field we still have everything to learn, and whatever we learn will be to our immense advantage. Knowledge of Eastern psychology provides the indispensable basis for a

---

[1] [Zurich, 1950. ("East Asia Thinks Otherwise.") The foreword was not included in the English-language edition of the book, by Lily Abegg, *The Mind of East Asia* (London and New York, 1952). It is reproduced here, in a translation by Hildegard Nagel and Ellen Thayer, titled "The Mind of East and West," from the *Inward Light* (Washington, D.C.), no. 49, (autumn 1955), having previously appeared in the *Bulletin of the Analytical Psychology Club of New York* vol. 15, no. 3 (Mar. 1953).]

critique of Western psychology, as indeed for any objective understanding of it. And in view of the truly lamentable psychic situation of the West, the importance of a deeper understanding of our Occidental prejudices can hardly be overestimated.

1484 Long experience with the products of the unconscious has taught me that there is a very remarkable parallelism between the specific character of the Western unconscious psyche and the "manifest" psyche of the East. Since our experience shows that the biological role which the unconscious plays in the psychic economy is compensatory to consciousness, one can venture the hypothesis that the mind of the Far East is related to our Western consciousness as the unconscious is, that is, as the left hand to the right.

1485 Our unconscious has, fundamentally, a tendency toward wholeness, as I believe I have been able to prove. One would be quite justified in saying the same thing about the Eastern psyche, but with this difference: that in the East it is consciousness that is characterized by an apperception of totality, while the West has developed a differentiated and therefore necessarily one-sided attention or awareness. With it goes the Western concept of causality, a principle of cognition irreconcilably opposed to the principle of synchronicity which forms the basis and the source of Eastern "incomprehensibility," and explains as well the "strangeness" of the unconscious with which we in the West are confronted. The understanding of synchronicity is the key which unlocks the door to the Eastern apperception of totality that we find so mysterious. The author seems to have devoted particular attention to just this point. I do not hesitate to say that I look forward to the publication of her book with the greatest interest.

March 1949

FOREWORD TO THE "I CHING" [1]

64 Since I am not a Sinologue, a foreword to the Book of Changes from my hand must be a testimonial of my individual experience with this great and singular book. It also affords me a welcome opportunity to pay tribute again to the memory of my late friend, Richard Wilhelm. He himself was profoundly aware of the cultural significance of his translation of the *I Ching*, a version unrivalled in the West.

965 If the meaning of the Book of Changes were easy to grasp, the work would need no foreword. But this is far from being the case, for there is so much that is obscure about it that Western scholars have tended to dispose of it as a collection of "magic spells," either too abstruse to be intelligible or of no value whatsoever. Legge's translation of the *I Ching*, up to now the only version available in English, has done little to make the work accessible to Western minds.[2] Wilhelm, however, has made

1 [Grateful acknowledgment is made here to Cary F. Baynes for permission to use, with a few minor changes, her translation of this Foreword, which Professor Jung wrote specially for the English edition of the *I Ching or Book of Changes*, translated by Mrs. Baynes from the German translation of Richard Wilhelm (New York and London, 1950); 2nd edn. in 1 vol., 1961; 3rd edn. in small format, 1967. References are to the 3rd edn.—TRANS.]

2 Legge makes the following comment on the explanatory text for the individual lines: "According to our notions, a framer of emblems should be a good deal of a poet, but those of the *Yi* only make us think of a dryasdust. Out of more than three hundred and fifty, the greater number are only grotesque" (*The Yi King*,

189

every effort to open the way to an understanding of the symbolism of the text. He was in a position to do this because he himself was taught the philosophy and the use of the *I Ching* by the venerable sage Lao Nai-hsüan; moreover, he had over a period of many years put the peculiar technique of the oracle into practice. His grasp of the living meaning of the text gives his version of the *I Ching* a depth of perspective that an exclusively academic knowledge of Chinese philosophy could never provide.

966   I am greatly indebted to Wilhelm for the light he has thrown upon the complicated problem of the *I Ching*, and for insight into its practical application. For more than thirty years I have interested myself in this oracle technique, for it seemed to me of uncommon significance as a method of exploring the unconscious. I was already fairly familiar with the *I Ching* when I first met Wilhelm in the early nineteen twenties; he confirmed then what I already knew, and taught me many things more.

967   I do not know Chinese and have never been in China. I can assure my reader that it is not altogether easy to find the right approach to this monument of Chinese thought, which departs so completely from our ways of thinking. In order to understand what such a book is all about, it is imperative to cast off certain of our Western prejudices. It is a curious fact that such a gifted and intelligent people as the Chinese has never developed what we call science. Our science, however, is based upon the principle of causality, and causality is considered to be an axiomatic truth. But a great change in our standpoint is setting in. What Kant's *Critique of Pure Reason* failed to do is being accomplished by modern physics. The axioms of causality are being shaken to their foundations: we know now that what we term natural laws are merely statistical truths and thus must necessarily allow for exceptions. We have not sufficiently taken into account as yet that we need the laboratory with its incisive restrictions in order to demonstrate the invariable validity of natural law. If we leave things to nature, we see a very different

---

p. 22). Of the "lessons" of the hexagrams, the same author says: "But why, it may be asked, why should they be conveyed to us by such an array of lineal figures, and in such a farrago of emblematic representations" (p. 25). However, we are nowhere told that Legge ever bothered to put the method to a practical test.

picture: every process is partially or totally interfered with by chance, so much so that under natural circumstances a course of events absolutely conforming to specific laws is almost an exception.

968　　The Chinese mind, as I see it at work in the *I Ching*, seems to be exclusively preoccupied with the chance aspect of events. What we call coincidence seems to be the chief concern of this peculiar mind, and what we worship as causality passes almost unnoticed. We must admit that there is something to be said for the immense importance of chance. An incalculable amount of human effort is directed to combatting and restricting the nuisance or danger that chance represents. Theoretical considerations of cause and effect often look pale and dusty in comparison with the practical results of chance. It is all very well to say that the crystal of quartz is a hexagonal prism. The statement is quite true in so far as an ideal crystal is envisaged. But in nature one finds no two crystals exactly alike, although all are unmistakably hexagonal. The actual form, however, seems to appeal more to the Chinese sage than the ideal one. The jumble of natural laws constituting empirical reality holds more significance for him than a causal explanation of events that, in addition, must usually be separated from one another in order to be properly dealt with.

969　　The manner in which the *I Ching* tends to look upon reality seems to disfavour our causal procedures. The moment under actual observation appears to the ancient Chinese view more of a chance hit than a clearly defined result of concurrent causal chains. The matter of interest seems to be the configuration formed by chance events at the moment of observation, and not at all the hypothetical reasons that seemingly account for the coincidence. While the Western mind carefully sifts, weighs, selects, classifies, isolates, the Chinese picture of the moment encompasses everything down to the minutest nonsensical detail, because all of the ingredients make up the observed moment.

970　　Thus it happens that when one throws the three coins, or counts through the forty-nine yarrow-stalks, these chance details enter into the picture of the moment of observation and form a part of it—a part that is insignificant to us, yet most meaningful to the Chinese mind. With us it would be a banal and almost meaningless statement (at least on the face of it) to say that whatever happens in a given moment has inevitably the quality peculiar to that moment. This is not an abstract argument but a very practical one. There are certain connoisseurs who can tell you merely from the appearance, taste, and behaviour of a wine the site of its vineyard and the year of its origin. There are antiquarians who with almost uncanny accuracy will name the time and place of origin and the maker of an *objet d'art* or piece of furniture on merely looking at it. And there are even astrologers who can tell you, without any previous knowledge of your nativity, what the position of sun and moon was and what zodiacal sign rose above the horizon at the moment of your birth. In the face of such facts, it must be admitted that moments can leave long-lasting traces.

971 In other words, whoever invented the *I Ching* was convinced that the hexagram worked out in a certain moment coincided with the latter in quality no less than in time. To him the hexagram was the exponent of the moment in which it was cast —even more so than the hours of the clock or the divisions of the calendar could be—inasmuch as the hexagram was understood to be an indicator of the essential situation prevailing at the moment of its origin.

972 This assumption involves a certain curious principle which I have termed synchronicity,[3] a concept that formulates a point of view diametrically opposed to that of causality. Since the latter is a merely statistical truth and not absolute, it is a sort of working hypothesis of how events evolve one out of another, whereas synchronicity takes the coincidence of events in space and time as meaning something more than mere chance, namely, a peculiar interdependence of objective events among themselves as well as with the subjective (psychic) states of the observer or observers.

973 The ancient Chinese mind contemplates the cosmos in a way comparable to that of the modern physicist, who cannot deny that his model of the world is a decidedly psychophysical structure. The microphysical event includes the observer just as much as the reality underlying the *I Ching* comprises subjective, i.e., psychic conditions in the totality of the momentary

[3] [Cf. Jung's "Synchronicity: An Acausal Connecting Principle." In that work (pp. 450–53) he is concerned with the synchronistic aspects of the *I Ching*.— EDITORS.]

situation. Just as causality describes the sequence of events, so synchronicity to the Chinese mind deals with the coincidence of events. The causal point of view tells us a dramatic story about how *D* came into existence: it took its origin from *C*, which existed before *D*, and *C* in its turn had a father, *B*, etc. The synchronistic view on the other hand tries to produce an equally meaningful picture of coincidence. How does it happen that *A'*, *B'*, *C'*, *D'*, etc., appear all at the same moment and in the same place? It happens in the first place because the physical events *A'* and *B'* are of the same quality as the psychic events *C'* and *D'*, and further because all are the exponents of one and the same momentary situation. The situation is assumed to represent a legible or understandable picture.

974   Now the sixty-four hexagrams of the *I Ching* are the instrument by which the meaning of sixty-four different yet typical situations can be determined. These interpretations are equivalent to causal explanations. Causal connection can be determined statistically and can be subjected to experiment. Inasmuch as situations are unique and cannot be repeated, experimenting with synchronicity seems to be impossible under ordinary conditions.[4] In the *I Ching*, the only criterion of the validity of synchronicity is the observer's opinion that the text of the hexagram amounts to a true rendering of his psychic condition. It is assumed that the fall of the coins or the result of the division of the bundle of yarrow-stalks is what it necessarily must be in a given "situation," inasmuch as anything happening at that moment belongs to it as an indispensable part of the picture. If a handful of matches is thrown to the floor, they form the pattern characteristic of that moment. But such an obvious truth as this reveals its meaningful nature only if it is possible to read the pattern and to verify its interpretation, partly by the observer's knowledge of the subjective and objective situation, partly by the character of subsequent events. It is obviously not a procedure that appeals to a critical mind used to experimental verification of facts or to factual evidence. But for someone who likes to look at the world at the angle from which ancient China saw it, the *I Ching* may have some attraction.

975   My argument as outlined above has of course never entered

4 Cf. J. B. Rhine, *The Reach of the Mind.*

a Chinese mind. On the contrary, according to the old tradition, it is "spiritual agencies," acting in a mysterious way, that make the yarrow-stalks give a meaningful answer.[5] These powers form, as it were, the living soul of the book. As the latter is thus a sort of animated being, the tradition assumes that one can put questions to the *I Ching* and expect to receive intelligent answers. Thus it occurred to me that it might interest the uninitiated reader to see the *I Ching* at work. For this purpose I made an experiment strictly in accordance with the Chinese conception: I personified the book in a sense, asking its judgment about its present situation, i.e., my intention to introduce it to the English-speaking public.

976   Although this procedure is well within the premises of Taoist philosophy, it appears exceedingly odd to us. However, not even the strangeness of insane delusions or of primitive superstition has ever shocked me. I have always tried to remain unbiased and curious—*rerum novarum cupidus*. Why not venture a dialogue with an ancient book that purports to be animated? There can be no harm in it, and the reader may watch a psychological procedure that has been carried out time and again throughout the millennia of Chinese civilization, representing to a Confucius or a Lao-tzu both a supreme expression of spiritual authority and a philosophical enigma. I made use of the coin method, and the answer obtained was hexagram 50, Ting, THE CAULDRON.[6]

977   In accordance with the way my question was phrased, the text of the hexagram must be regarded as though the *I Ching* itself were the speaking person. Thus it describes itself as a cauldron, that is, as a ritual vessel containing cooked food. Here the food is to be understood as spiritual nourishment. Wilhelm says about this:

The *ting*, as a utensil pertaining to a refined civilization, suggests the fostering and nourishing of able men, which redounded to the benefit of the state. . . . Here we see civilization as it reaches its culmination in religion. The *ting* serves in offering sacrifice to God. . . . The supreme revelation of God appears in prophets and holy men. To venerate them is true veneration of God. The will of God, as revealed through them, should be accepted in humility.

[5] They are *shên*, that is, 'spirit-like.' "Heaven produced the 'spirit-like things'" (Legge, p. 41).   [6] [Cf. the *I Ching*, pp. 193ff.—EDITORS.]

978   Keeping to our hypothesis, we must conclude that the *I Ching* is here testifying concerning itself.

979   When any of the lines of a given hexagram have the value of six or nine, it means that they are specially emphasized and hence important in the interpretation.[7] In my hexagram the "spiritual agencies" have given the emphasis of a nine to the lines in the second and in the third place. The text says:

> Nine in the second place means:
>
> There is food in the *ting*.
> My comrades are envious,
> But they cannot harm me.
> Good fortune.

980   Thus the *I Ching* says of itself: "I contain (spiritual) nourishment." Since a share in something great always arouses envy, the chorus of the envious [8] is part of the picture. The envious want to rob the *I Ching* of its great possession, that is, they seek to rob it of meaning, or to destroy its meaning. But their enmity is in vain. Its richness of meaning is assured; that is, it is convinced of its positive achievements, which no one can take away. The text continues:

> Nine in the third place means:
>
> The handle of the *ting* is altered.
> One is impeded in his way of life.
> The fat of the pheasant is not eaten.
> Once rain falls, remorse is spent.
> Good fortune comes in the end.

981   The handle [German *Griff*] is the part by which the *ting* can be grasped [*gegriffen*]. Thus it signifies the concept [9] [*Begriff*] one has of the *I Ching* (the *ting*). In the course of time this concept has apparently changed, so that today we can no longer grasp [*begreifen*] the *I Ching*. Thus "one is impeded in

7 See the explanation of the method, ibid., pp. 721ff.
8 For example, the *invidi* ('the envious') are a constantly recurring image in the old Latin books on alchemy, especially in the *Turba philosophorum* (11th or 12th cent.).
9 From the Latin *concipere*, 'to take together,' e.g., in a vessel: *concipere* derives from *capere*, 'to take,' 'to grasp.'

his way of life." We are no longer supported by the wise counsel and deep insight of the oracle; therefore we no longer find our way through the mazes of fate and the obscurities of our own natures. The fat of the pheasant, that is, the best and richest part of a good dish, is no longer eaten. But when the thirsty earth finally receives rain again, that is, when this state of want has been overcome, "remorse," that is, sorrow over the loss of wisdom, is ended, and then comes the longed-for opportunity. Wilhelm comments: "This describes a man who, in a highly evolved civilization, finds himself in a place where no one notices or recognizes him. This is a severe block to his effectiveness." The *I Ching* is complaining, as it were, that its excellent qualities go unrecognized and hence lie fallow. It comforts itself with the hope that it is about to regain recognition.

982   The answer given in these two salient lines to the question I put to the *I Ching* requires no particular subtlety for its interpretation, no artifices, and no unusual knowledge. Anyone with a little common sense can understand the meaning of the answer; it is the answer of one who has a good opinion of himself, but whose value is neither generally recognized nor even widely known. The answering subject has an interesting notion of itself: it looks upon itself as a vessel in which sacrificial offerings are brought to the gods, ritual food for their nourishment. It conceives of itself as a cult utensil serving to provide spiritual nourishment for the unconscious elements or forces ("spiritual agencies") that have been projected as gods—in other words, to give these forces the attention they need in order to play their part in the life of the individual. Indeed, this is the original meaning of the word *religio*—a careful observation and taking account of (from *relegere* [10]) the numinous.

983   The method of the *I Ching* does indeed take into account the hidden individual quality in things and men, and in one's own unconscious self as well. I questioned the *I Ching* as one questions a person whom one is about to introduce to friends: one asks whether or not it will be agreeable to him. In answer the *I Ching* tells me of its religious significance, of the fact that at present it is unknown and misjudged, of its hope of

---

[10] This is the classical etymology. The derivation of *religio* from *religare*, 'reconnect,' 'link back,' originated with the Church Fathers.

being restored to a place of honour—this last obviously with a sidelong glance at my as yet unwritten foreword,[11] and above all at the English translation. This seems a perfectly understandable reaction, such as one could expect also from a person in a similar situation.

984   But how has this reaction come about? Simply because I threw three small coins into the air and let them fall, roll, and come to rest, heads up or tails up as the case might be. This peculiar fact—that a reaction that makes sense arises out of a technique which at the outset seemingly excludes all sense—is the great achievement of the *I Ching*. The instance I have just given is not unique; meaningful answers are the rule. Western sinologues and distinguished Chinese scholars have been at pains to inform me that the *I Ching* is a collection of obsolete "magic spells." In the course of these conversations my informant has sometimes admitted having consulted the oracle through a fortune teller, usually a Taoist priest. This could be "only nonsense" of course. But oddly enough, the answer received apparently coincided with the questioner's psychological blind spot remarkably well.

985   I agree with Western thinking that any number of answers to my question were possible, and I certainly cannot assert that another answer would not have been equally significant. However, the answer received was the first and only one; we know nothing of other possible answers. It pleased and satisfied me. To ask the same question a second time would have been tactless and so I did not do it: "the master speaks but once." The heavy-handed pedagogic approach that attempts to fit irrational phenomena into a preconceived rational pattern is anathema to me. Indeed, such things as this answer should remain as they were when they first emerged to view, for only then do we know what nature does when left to herself undisturbed by the meddlesomeness of man. One ought not to go to dead bodies to study life. Moreover, a repetition of the experiment is impossible, for the simple reason that the original situation cannot be reconstructed. Therefore in each instance there is only a first and single answer.

986   To return to the hexagram itself. There is nothing strange in the fact that all of Ting, THE CAULDRON, amplifies the themes

11 I made this experiment before I actually wrote the foreword.

announced by the two salient lines.[12] The first line of the hexagram says:

> A *ting* with legs upturned
> Furthers removal of stagnating stuff.
> One takes a concubine for the sake of her son.
> No blame.

987 A *ting* that is turned upside down is not in use. Hence the *I Ching* is like an unused cauldron. Turning it over serves to remove stagnating matter, as the line says. Just as a man takes a concubine when his wife has no son, so the *I Ching* is called upon when one sees no other way out. Despite the quasi-legal status of the concubine in China, she is in reality only a somewhat awkward makeshift; so likewise the magic procedure of the oracle is an expedient that may be utilized for a higher purpose. There is no blame, although it is an exceptional recourse.

988 The second and third lines have already been discussed. The fourth line says:

> The legs of the *ting* are broken.
> The prince's meal is spilled
> And his person is soiled.
> Misfortune.

989 Here the *ting* has been put to use, but evidently in a very clumsy manner, that is, the oracle has been abused or misinterpreted. In this way the divine food is lost, and one puts oneself to shame. Legge translates as follows: "Its subject will be made to blush for shame." Abuse of a cult utensil such as the *ting* (i.e., the *I Ching*) is a gross profanation. The *I Ching* is evidently insisting here on its dignity as a ritual vessel and protesting against being profanely used.

990 The fifth line says:

> The *ting* has yellow handles, golden carrying rings.
> Perseverance furthers.

[12] The Chinese interpret only the changing lines in the hexagram obtained by use of the oracle. I have found all the lines of the hexagram to be relevant in most cases.

991 The *I Ching* has, it seems, met with a new, correct (yellow) understanding, that is, a new concept [*Begriff*] by which it can be grasped. This concept is valuable (golden). There is indeed a new edition in English, making the book more accessible to the Western world than before.

992 The sixth line says:

> The *ting* has rings of jade.
> Great good fortune.
> Nothing that would not act to further.

993 Jade is distinguished for its beauty and soft sheen. If the carrying rings are of jade, the whole vessel is enhanced in beauty, honour, and value. The *I Ching* expresses itself here as being not only well satisfied but indeed very optimistic. One can only await further events and in the meantime remain content with the pleasant conclusion that the *I Ching* approves of the new edition.

994 I have shown in this example as objectively as I can how the oracle proceeds in a given case. Of course the procedure varies somewhat according to the way the question is put. If for instance a person finds himself in a confusing situation, he may himself appear in the oracle as the speaker. Or, if the question concerns a relationship with another person, that person may appear as the speaker. However, the identity of the speaker does not depend entirely on the manner in which the question is phrased, inasmuch as our relations with our fellow beings are not always determined by the latter. Very often our relations depend almost exclusively on our own attitudes, though we may be quite unaware of this fact. Hence, if an individual is unconscious of his role in a relationship, there may be a surprise in store for him; contrary to expectation, he himself may appear as the chief agent, as is sometimes unmistakably indicated by the text. It may also happen that we take a situation too seriously and consider it extremely important, whereas the answer we get on consulting the *I Ching* draws attention to some unsuspected other aspect implicit in the question.

995 Such instances might at first lead one to think that the oracle is fallacious. Confucius is said to have received only one inappropriate answer, i.e., hexagram 22, GRACE—a thoroughly aesthetic hexagram. This is reminiscent of the advice given to

Socrates by his daemon—"You ought to make more music"—whereupon Socrates took to playing the flute. Confucius and Socrates compete for first place as far as rationality and a pedagogic attitude to life are concerned; but it is unlikely that either of them occupied himself with "lending grace to the beard on his chin," as the second line of this hexagram advises. Unfortunately, reason and pedagogy often lack charm and grace, and so the oracle may not have been wrong after all.

996   To come back once more to our hexagram. Though the *I Ching* not only seems to be satisfied with its new edition, but even expresses emphatic optimism, this still does not foretell anything about the effect it will have on the public it is intended to reach. Since we have in our hexagram two *yang* lines stressed by the numerical value nine, we are in a position to find out what sort of prognosis the *I Ching* makes for itself. Lines designated by a six or a nine have, according to the ancient conception, an inner tension so great as to cause them to change into their opposites, that is, *yang* into *yin*, and vice versa. Through this change we obtain in the present instance hexagram 35, Chin, PROGRESS.

997   The subject of this hexagram is someone who meets with all sorts of vicissitudes of fortune in his climb upward, and the text describes how he should behave. The *I Ching* is in this same situation: it rises like the sun and declares itself, but it is rebuffed and finds no confidence—it is "progressing, but in sorrow." However, "one obtains great happiness from one's ancestress." Psychology can help us to elucidate this obscure passage. In dreams and fairy tales the grandmother, or ancestress, often represents the unconscious, because the latter in a man contains the feminine component of the psyche. If the *I Ching* is not accepted by the conscious, at least the unconscious meets it halfway, for the *I Ching* is more closely connected with the unconscious than with the rational attitude of consciousness. Since the unconscious is often represented in dreams by a feminine figure, this may be the explanation here. The feminine person might be the translator, who has given the book her maternal care, and this might easily appear to the *I Ching* a "great happiness." It anticipates general understanding, but is afraid of misuse—"Progress like a hamster." But it is mindful of the admonition, "Take not gain and loss to heart." It remains

free of "partisan motives." It does not thrust itself on anyone.

998   The *I Ching* therefore faces its future on the American book market calmly and expresses itself here just about as any reasonable person would in regard to the fate of so controversial a work. This prediction is so very reasonable and full of common sense that it would be hard to think of a more fitting answer.

999   All this happened before I had written the foregoing paragraphs. When I reached this point, I wished to know the attitude of the *I Ching* to the new situation. The state of things had been altered by what I had written, inasmuch as I myself had now entered upon the scene, and I therefore expected to hear something referring to my own action. I must confess that I had not been feeling too happy in the course of writing this foreword, for, as a person with a sense of responsibility toward science, I am not in the habit of asserting something I cannot prove or at least present as acceptable to reason. It is a dubious task indeed to try to introduce a collection of archaic "magic spells" to a critical modern public with the idea of making them more or less acceptable. I have undertaken it because I myself think that there is more to the ancient Chinese way of thinking than meets the eye. But it is embarrassing to me that I must appeal to the good will and imagination of the reader, instead of giving him conclusive proofs and scientifically watertight explanations. Unfortunately I am only too well aware of the arguments that can be brought against this age-old oracle technique. We are not even certain that the ship that is to carry us over the unknown seas has not sprung a leak somewhere. May not the old text be corrupt? Is Wilhelm's translation accurate? Are we not self-deluded in our explanations?

1000   The *I Ching* insists upon self-knowledge throughout. The method by which this is to be achieved is open to every kind of misuse, and is therefore not for the frivolous-minded and immature; nor is it for intellectualists and rationalists. It is appropriate only for thoughtful and reflective people who like to think about what they do and what happens to them—a predilection not to be confused with the morbid brooding of the hypochondriac. As I have indicated above, I have no answer to the multitude of problems that arise when we seek to harmonize the oracle of the *I Ching* with our accepted scientific canons. But needless to say, nothing "occult" is to be inferred. My position

201

in these matters is pragmatic, and the great disciplines that have taught me the practical usefulness of this viewpoint are psychotherapy and medical psychology. Probably in no other field do we have to reckon with so many unknown quantities, and nowhere else do we become more accustomed to adopting methods that work even though for a long time we may not know why they work. Unexpected cures may arise from questionable therapies and unexpected failures from allegedly reliable methods. In the exploration of the unconscious we come upon very strange things, from which a rationalist turns away with horror, claiming afterward that he did not see anything. The irrational fulness of life has taught me never to discard anything, even when it goes against all our theories (so short-lived at best) or otherwise admits of no immediate explanation. It is of course disquieting, and one is not certain whether the compass is pointing true or not; but security, certitude, and peace do not lead to discoveries. It is the same with this Chinese mode of divination. Clearly the method aims at self-knowledge, though at all times it has also been put to superstitious use.

1001   I of course am thoroughly convinced of the value of self-knowledge, but is there any use in recommending such insight, when the wisest of men throughout the ages have preached the need of it without success? Even to the most biased eye it is obvious that this book represents one long admonition to careful scrutiny of one's own character, attitude, and motives. This attitude appeals to me and has induced me to undertake the foreword. Only once before have I expressed myself in regard to the problem of the *I Ching:* this was in a memorial address in tribute to Richard Wilhelm.[13] For the rest I have maintained a discreet silence. It is by no means easy to feel one's way into such a remote and mysterious mentality as that underlying the *I Ching*. One cannot easily disregard such great minds as Confucius and Lao-tzu, if one is at all able to appreciate the quality of the thoughts they represent; much less can one overlook the fact that the *I Ching* was their main source of inspiration. I know that previously I would not have dared to express myself

[13] [Cf. Wilhelm and Jung, *The Secret of the Golden Flower* (1931), in which this address appears as an appendix. The book did not appear in English until a year after Wilhelm's death.—C. F. B.]

[For the address, see vol. 15 of the *Coll. Works.*—EDITORS.]

so explicitly about so uncertain a matter. I can take this risk because I am now in my eighth decade, and the changing opinions of men scarcely impress me any more; the thoughts of the old masters are of greater value to me than the philosophical prejudices of the Western mind.

1002   I do not like to burden my reader with these personal considerations; but, as already indicated, one's own personality is very often implicated in the answer of the oracle. Indeed, in formulating my question I even invited the oracle to comment directly on my action. The answer was hexagram 29, K'an, THE ABYSMAL. Special emphasis is given to the third place by the fact that the line is designated by a six. This line says:

> Forward and backward, abyss on abyss.
> In danger like this, pause at first and wait,
> Otherwise you will fall into a pit in the abyss.
> Do not act in this way.

1003   Formerly I would have accepted unconditionally the advice, "Do not act in this way," and would have refused to give my opinion of the *I Ching,* for the sole reason that I had none. But now the counsel may serve as an example of the way in which the *I Ching* functions. It is a fact that if one begins to think about it, the problems of the *I Ching* do represent "abyss on abyss," and unavoidably one must "pause at first and wait" in the midst of the dangers of limitless and uncritical speculation; otherwise one really will lose one's way in the darkness. Could there be a more uncomfortable position intellectually than that of floating in the thin air of unproven possibilities, not knowing whether what one sees is truth or illusion? This is the dreamlike atmosphere of the *I Ching,* and in it one has nothing to rely upon except one's own so fallible subjective judgment. I cannot but admit that this line represents very appropriately the feelings with which I wrote the foregoing passages. Equally fitting is the comforting beginning of this hexagram—"If you are sincere, you have success in your heart"—for it indicates that the decisive thing here is not the outer danger but the subjective condition, that is, whether one believes oneself to be "sincere" or not.

1004   The hexagram compares the dynamic action in this situation to the behaviour of flowing water, which is not afraid of any dangerous place but plunges over cliffs and fills up the pits that lie in its course (K'an also stands for water). This is the way in which the "superior man" acts and "carries on the business of teaching."

1005   K'an is definitely one of the less agreeable hexagrams. It describes a situation in which the subject seems in grave danger of being caught in all sorts of pitfalls. I have found that K'an often turned up with patients who were too much under the sway of the unconscious (water) and hence threatened with the possible occurrence of psychotic phenomena. If one were superstitious, one would be inclined to assume that some such meaning attaches intrinsically to this hexagram. But just as, in interpreting a dream, one must follow the dream-text with the utmost exactitude, so in consulting the oracle one must keep in mind the form of the question put, for this sets a definite limit to the interpretation of the answer. When I consulted the oracle the first time, I was thinking above all of the meaning for the *I Ching* of the foreword I had still to write. I thus put the book in the foreground and made it, so to speak, the acting subject. But in my second question, it is I who am the acting subject. So it would be illogical to take the *I Ching* as the subject in this case too, and, in addition, the interpretation would become unintelligible. But if I am the subject, the interpretation is meaningful to me, because it expresses the undeniable feeling of uncertainty and risk present in my mind. If one ventures upon such uncertain ground, it is easy to come dangerously under the influence of the unconscious without knowing it.

1006   The first line of the hexagram notes the presence of the danger: "In the abyss one falls into a pit." The second line does the same, then adds the counsel: "One should strive to attain small things only." I apparently anticipated this advice by limiting myself in this foreword to a demonstration of how the *I Ching* functions in the Chinese mind, and by renouncing the more ambitious project of writing a psychological commentary on the whole book.

1007   The simplification of my task is expressed in the fourth line, which says:

> A jug of wine, a bowl of rice with it;
> Earthen vessels
> Simply handed in through the window.
> There is certainly no blame in this.

1008   Wilhelm makes the following comment here:

> Although as a rule it is customary for an official to present certain introductory gifts and recommendations before he is appointed, here everything is simplified to the utmost. The gifts are insignificant, there is no one to sponsor him, he introduces himself; yet all this need not be humiliating if only there is the honest intention of mutual help in danger.

1009   The fifth line continues the theme of limitation. If one studies the nature of water, one sees that it fills a pit only to the rim and then flows on. It does not stay caught there:

> The abyss is not filled to overflowing,
> It is filled only to the rim.

1010   But if, tempted by the danger, and just because of the uncertainty, one were to insist on forcing conviction by special efforts, such as elaborate commentaries and the like, one would only be bogged down in the difficulty, which the top line describes very accurately as a tied-up and caged-in condition. Indeed, the last line often shows the consequences that result when one does not take the meaning of the hexagram to heart.

1011   In our hexagram we have a six in the third place. This *yin* line of mounting tension changes into a *yang* line and thus produces a new hexagram showing a new possibility or tendency. We now have hexagram 48, Ching, THE WELL. The water hole no longer means danger, however, but rather something beneficial, a well:

> Thus the superior man encourages the people at
>   their work,
> And exhorts them to help one another.

1012   The image of people helping one another would seem to refer to the reconstruction of the well, for it is broken down and full of mud. Not even animals drink from it. There are fishes living in it, and one can catch these, but the well is not used for drinking, that is, for human needs. This description is reminiscent of the overturned and unused *ting* that is to receive a new handle. Moreover, like the *ting*, "the well is cleaned, but no one drinks from it":

> This is my heart's sorrow,
> For one might draw from it.

1013   The dangerous water-hole or abyss pointed to the *I Ching*, and so does the well, but the latter has a positive meaning: it contains the waters of life. It should be restored to use. But one has no concept [*Begriff*] of it, no utensil with which to carry the water; the jug is broken and leaks. The *ting* needs new handles and carrying rings by which to grasp it, and so also the well must be newly lined, for it contains "a clear, cold spring from which one can drink." One may draw water from it, because "it is dependable."

1014   It is clear that in this prognosis the speaking subject is once more the *I Ching*, representing itself as a spring of living water. The previous hexagram described in detail the danger confronting the person who accidentally falls into the pit within the abyss. He must work his way out of it, in order to discover that it is an old, ruined well, buried in mud, but capable of being restored to use again.

1015   I submitted two questions to the method of chance represented by the coin oracle, the second question being put after I had written my analysis of the answer to the first. The first question was directed, as it were, to the *I Ching*: what had it to say about my intention to write a foreword? The second question concerned my own action, or rather the situation in which I was the acting subject who had discussed the first hexagram. To the first question the *I Ching* replied by comparing itself to a cauldron, a ritual vessel in need of renovation, a vessel that was finding only doubtful favour with the public. To the second question the reply was that I had fallen into a difficulty, for the *I Ching* represented a deep and dangerous water-hole in which one might easily be bogged down. However, the water-hole proved to be an old well that needed only to be renovated in order to be put to useful purposes once more.

1016   These four hexagrams are in the main consistent as regards theme (vessel, pit, well); and as regards intellectual content, they seem to be meaningful. Had a human being made such replies, I should, as a psychiatrist, have had to pronounce him of sound mind, at least on the basis of the material presented.

Indeed, I should not have been able to discover anything delirious, idiotic, or schizophrenic in the four answers. In view of the *I Ching's* extreme age and its Chinese origin, I cannot consider its archaic, symbolic, and flowery language abnormal. On the contrary, I should have had to congratulate this hypothetical person on the extent of his insight into my unexpressed state of doubt. On the other hand, any person of clever and versatile mind can turn the whole thing around and show how I have projected my subjective contents into the symbolism of the hexagrams. Such a critique, though catastrophic from the standpoint of Western rationality, does no harm to the function of the *I Ching*. On the contrary, the Chinese sage would smilingly tell me: "Don't you see how useful the *I Ching* is in making you project your hitherto unrealized thoughts into its abstruse symbolism? You could have written your foreword without ever realizing what an avalanche of misunderstanding might be released by it."

1017   The Chinese standpoint does not concern itself with the attitude one takes toward the performance of the oracle. It is only we who are puzzled, because we trip time and again over our prejudice, viz., the notion of causality. The ancient wisdom of the East lays stress upon the fact that the intelligent individual realizes his own thoughts, but not in the least upon the way in which he does it. The less one thinks about the theory of the *I Ching*, the more soundly one sleeps.

1018   It would seem to me that on the basis of this example an unprejudiced reader should now be in a position to form at least a tentative judgment on the operation of the *I Ching*.[14] More cannot be expected from a simple introduction. If by means of this demonstration I have succeeded in elucidating the psychological phenomenology of the *I Ching*, I shall have carried out my purpose. As to the thousands of questions, doubts, and criticisms that this singular book stirs up—I cannot answer these. The *I Ching* does not offer itself with proofs and results; it does not vaunt itself, nor is it easy to approach. Like a part of nature, it waits until it is discovered. It offers neither facts nor power, but for lovers of self-knowledge, of wisdom—if there be such—it

14 The reader will find it helpful to look up all four of these hexagrams in the [Baynes-Wilhelm] text and to read them together with the relevant commentaries.

seems to be the right book. To one person its spirit appears as clear as day; to another, shadowy as twilight; to a third, dark as night. He who is not pleased by it does not have to use it, and he who is against it is not obliged to find it true. Let it go forth into the world for the benefit of those who can discern its meaning.

ON THE DISCOURSES OF THE BUDDHA[1]

1575   It was neither the history of religion nor the study of philosophy that first drew me to the world of Buddhist thought, but my professional interests as a doctor. My task was the treatment of psychic suffering, and it was this that impelled me to become acquainted with the views and methods of that great teacher of humanity whose principal theme was the "chain of suffering, old age, sickness, and death." For although the healing of the sick naturally lies closest to the doctor's heart, he is bound to recognize that there are many diseases and states of suffering which, not being susceptible of a direct cure, demand from both patient and doctor some kind of attitude to their irremediable nature. Even though it may not amount to actual incurability, in all such cases there are inevitably phases of stagnation and hopelessness which seem unendurable and require treatment just as much as a direct symptom of illness. They call for a kind of moral attitude such as is provided by religious faith or a philosophical belief. In this respect the study of Buddhist literature was of great help to me, since it trains one to observe suffering objectively and to take a universal view of its causes. According to tradition, it was by objectively observing the chain of causes that the Buddha was able to extricate his consciousness from the snares of the ten thousand things, and to rescue his feelings from the entanglements of emotion and illusion. So also in our sphere of culture the suffering and the sick can derive considerable benefit from this prototype of the Buddhist mentality, however strange it may appear.

1576   The discourses of the Buddha, here presented in K. E. Neumann's new translation, have an importance that should not be

[1] [Statement in the publisher's prospectus for *Die Reden Gotamo Buddhos*, translated from the Pali Canon by Karl Eugen Neumann, 3 vols. Zurich, Stuttgart, Vienna, 1956). Statements were also contributed to the prospectus by Thomas Mann and Albert Schweitzer. Neumann (1865–1915) had published an earlier version of his translation in 1911, which Jung cited in *Wandlungen und Symbole der Libido* (1911–12); cf. *Psychology of the Unconscious* (New York, 1916), p. 538, n. 25. The present statement was published as "Zu *Die Reden Gotamo Buddhos*" in *Gesam. Werke*, XI, Anhang.]

underestimated. Quite apart from their profound meaning, their solemn, almost ritual form emits a penetrating radiance which has an exhilarating and exalting effect and cannot fail to work directly upon one's feelings. Against this use of the spiritual treasures of the East it might be—and indeed, often has been—objected from the Christian point of view that the faith of the West offers consolations that are at least as significant, and that there is no need to invoke the spirit of Buddhism with its markedly rational attitude. Aside from the fact that in most cases the Christian faith of which people speak simply isn't there, and no one can tell how it might be obtained (except by the special providence of God), it is a truism that anything known becomes so familiar and hackneyed by frequent use that it gradually loses its meaning and hence its effect; whereas anything strange and unknown, and so completely different in its nature, can open doors hitherto locked and new possibilities of understanding. If a Christian insists so much on his faith when it does not even help him to ward off a neurosis, then his faith is vain, and it is better to accept humbly what he needs no matter where he finds it, if only it helps. There is no need for him to deny his religion convictions if he acknowledges his debt to Buddhism, for he is only following the Pauline injunction: "Prove all things; hold fast that which is good" (I Thess. 5:21).

1577　To this good which should be held fast one must reckon the discourses of the Buddha, which have much to offer even to those who cannot boast of any Christian convictions. They offer Western man ways and means of disciplining his inner psychic life, thus remedying an often regrettable defect in the various brands of Christianity. The teachings of the Buddha can give him a helpful training when either the Christian ritual has lost its meaning or the authority of religious ideas has collapsed, as all too frequently happens in psychogenic disorders.

1578　People have often accused me of regarding religion as "mental hygiene." Perhaps one may pardon a doctor his professional humility in not undertaking to prove the truth of metaphysical assertions and in shunning confessions of faith. I am content to emphasize the importance of having a *Weltanschauung* and the therapeutic necessity of adopting some kind of attitude to the problem of psychic suffering. Suffering that is not understood is hard to bear, while on the other hand it is often astounding to see how much a person can endure when he understands the why and the wherefore. A philosophical or religious view of the world enables him to do this, and such views prove to be, at the very least, psychic methods of healing if not of salvation. Even Christ and his disciples did not scorn to heal the sick, thereby demonstrating the therapeutic power of their mission. The doctor has to cope with actual suffering for better or worse, and ultimately has nothing to rely on except the mystery of divine Providence. It is no wonder, then, that he values religious ideas and attitudes, so far as they prove helpful, as therapeutic systems, and singles out the Buddha in particular, the essence of whose teaching is deliverance from suffering through the maximum development of consciousness, as one of the supreme helpers on the road to salvation. From ancient times physicians have sought a panacea, a *medicina catholica,* and their persistent efforts have unconsciously brought them nearer to the central ideas of the religion and philosophy of the East.

1579   Anyone who is familiar with methods of suggestion under hypnosis knows that plausible suggestions work better than those which run counter to the patient's own nature. Consequently, whether he liked it or not, the doctor was obliged to develop conceptions which corresponded as closely as possible with the actual psychological conditions. Thus, there grew up a realm of theory which not only drew upon traditional thought but took account of the unconscious products that compensated its inevitable one-sidedness—that is to say, all those psychic factors which Christian philosophy left unsatisfied. Among these were not a few aspects which, unknown to the West, had been developed in Eastern philosophy from very early times.

1580   So if, as a doctor, I acknowledge the immense help and stimulation I have received from the Buddhist teachings, I am following a line which can be traced back some two thousand years in the history of human thought.

THE COLLECTED WORKS OF
C. G. JUNG

EDITORS: SIR HERBERT READ, MICHAEL FORDHAM, AND GERHARD ADLER; *EXECUTIVE EDITOR*, WILLIAM McGUIRE. *TRANSLATED BY* R.F.C. HULL, EXCEPT WHERE NOTED.

IN THE FOLLOWING LIST, dates of original publication are given in parentheses (of original composition, in brackets). Multiple dates indicate revisions.

(*continued*)

(continued)

(continued)

(continued)

16. (*continued*)

The Psychology of the Transference (1946)
Appendix: The Realities of Practical Psychotherapy ([1937] added 1966)

17. THE DEVELOPMENT OF PERSONALITY (1954)
Psychic Conflicts in a Child (1910/1946)
Introduction to Wickes's "Analyses der Kinderseele" (1927/1931)
Child Development and Education (1928)
Analytical Psychology and Education: Three Lectures (1926/1946)
The Gifted Child (1943)
The Significance of the Unconscious in Individual Education (1928)
The Development of Personality (1934)
Marriage as a Psychological Relationship (1925)

18. THE SYMBOLIC LIFE (1954)
Translated by R.F.C. Hull and others

Miscellaneous writings

19. COMPLETE BIBLIOGRAPHY OF C. G. JUNG'S WRITINGS (1976; 2nd edn., 1992)

20. GENERAL INDEX TO THE COLLECTED WORKS (1979)

THE ZOFINGIA LECTURES (1983)
Supplementary Volume A to The Collected Works. Edited by William McGuire, translated by Jan van Heurck, introduction by Marie-Louise von Franz

PSYCHOLOGY OF THE UNCONSCIOUS ([1912] 1992)

A STUDY OF THE TRANSFORMATIONS AND SYMBOLISMS OF THE LIBIDO.
A CONTRIBUTION TO THE HISTORY OF THE EVOLUTION OF THOUGHT

Supplementary Volume B to the Collected Works. Translated by Beatrice M. Hinkle, introduction by William McGuire

Related publications:

THE BASIC WRITINGS OF C. G. JUNG
Selected and introduced by Violet S. de Laszlo

C. G. JUNG: LETTERS
Selected and edited by Gerhard Adler, in collaboration with Aniela Jaffé. Translations from the German by R.F.C. Hull.

VOL. 1: 1906–1950
VOL. 2: 1951–1961

C. G. JUNG SPEAKING: Interviews and Encounters
Edited by William McGuire and R.F.C. Hull

C. G. JUNG: Word and Image
Edited by Aniela Jaffé

THE ESSENTIAL JUNG
Selected and introduced by Anthony Storr

THE GNOSTIC JUNG
Selected and introduced by Robert A. Segal

PSYCHE AND SYMBOL
Selected and introduced by Violet S. de Laszlo

Notes of C. G. Jung's Seminars:

DREAM ANALYSIS ([1928–30] 1984)
Edited by William McGuire

NIETZSCHE'S *ZARATHUSTRA* ([1934–39] 1988)
Edited by James L. Jarrett (2 vols.)

ANALYTICAL PSYCHOLOGY ([1925] 1989)
Edited by William McGuire

PRINCETON / BOLLINGEN PAPERBACK EDITIONS
FROM THE COLLECTED WORKS OF C. G. JUNG

Aion (CW 9,ii)
Alchemical Studies (CW 13)
Analytical Psychology
Answer to Job
Archetypes and the Collective Unconscious (CW 9,i)
Aspects of the Feminine
Aspects of the Masculine
Basic Writings of C. G. Jung
The Development of Personality (CW 17)
Dreams
Essay on Contemporary Events
Essays on a Science of Mythology
The Essential Jung
Experimental Researches (CW 2)
Flying Saucers
Four Archetypes
Freud and Psychoanalysis (CW 4)
The Gnostic Jung
Mandala Symbolism
Mysterium Coniunctionis (CW 14)
On the Nature of the Psyche
The Practice of Psychotherapy (CW 16)
Psyche and Symbol
Psychiatric Studies (CW 1)
Psychogenesis of Mental Disease (CW 3)
Psychological Types (CW 6)
Psychology and Alchemy (CW 12)
Psychology and the East
Psychology and the Occult
Psychology and Western Religion
The Psychology of the Transference
The Spirit in Man, Art, and Literature (CW 15)
Symbols of Transformation (CW 5)
Synchronicity
Two Essays on Analytical Psychology (CW 7)
The Undiscovered Self

OTHER BOLLINGEN PAPERBACKS DEVOTED TO C. G. JUNG

C. G. Jung Speaking
Complex/Archetype/Symbol in the Psychology of C. G. Jung
Psychological Reflections
Selected Letters
C. G. Jung: Word & Image